THE
FLEET STREET
GIRLS

THE FLEET STREET GIRLS

The Women Who Broke Down the Doors of the Gentlemen's Club

Julie Welch

First published in Great Britain in 2020 by Trapeze,
an imprint of The Orion Publishing Group Ltd
Carmelite House, 50 Victoria Embankment,
London EC4Y 0DZ

An Hachette UK company

1 3 5 7 9 10 8 6 4 2

A CIP catalogue record for this book is
available from the British Library.

ISBN (Hardback): 978 1 4091 8782 0
ISBN (eBook) 978 1 4091 8784 4

Typeset by Born Group
Printed and bound in Great Britain by Clays Ltd, Elcograf S.p.A.

MIX
Paper from
responsible sources
FSC   FSC® C104740
www.fsc.org

www.orionbooks.co.uk

Contents

Prologue

The Gentlemen of the Press

Coventry City Football Club, August 1973

What if they won't let me in?

My heart lurches and I pause as the crowd rushes past me; as cars crawl along the congested road, scarves flapping from windows, engines revving; as horns sound amid the men's singing and chanting, like everyone's on some sort of holy pilgrimage. I take a deep breath, thus filling my lungs with gusts of exhaust and the scent of onions from the burger van.

What if I've got it all wrong?

And I think for a moment that this is some sort of psychotic episode in which I hallucinate that I have been sent to report a football match, when in reality I am still the sports desk secretary, scuttling round the *Observer* newsroom fetching the chief sub's expenses and asking who wants bacon sandwiches and who wants sausage.

That's stupid. For reassurance I feel in my pocket for my press pass, a small rectangle of bendy cardboard inked with a seat number. Suddenly, from being frozen with panic, my mood switches to gloating. This budget item of cardboard is something precious, something covetable, a ticket that not only gets me into the stadium for free but authorises me to tell thousands of readers about what I am here to see. Coventry

City v Tottenham Hotspur. For this I will earn a fee of twelve guineas. I am being paid to watch football.

It therefore makes me the envy of every man in the country. Well, that's an exaggeration – some, inexplicably, prefer rugby or cricket – but a large proportion anyway, because, to quote *Charlie Buchan's Football Monthly*, this is Our National Pastime.

Except how can it be national if 50 per cent of the public don't get the chance to play it, write about it or voice their opinion? That is what I am hoping to change. And I am prepared to stand up for my rights if the man guarding the door marked 'Press Entrance' cuts up rough.

I have worked myself up into such a state of indignation that I am almost disappointed when he barely gives it a glance.

'Ah yes, the girl from the *Observer*,' he says jovially.

Eh? It's as if he was expecting me. Halfway up the steps, I stop for the second time in five minutes.

They've been warned in advance. Isn't that a bit . . . weird? My thoughts follow a sequence:

1. It's thoughtful of the *Observer* to smooth my path in this way.
2. Why do they need to? Is it to forestall a mass outbreak of the vapours among the gentlemen of the press?
3. Is all this an even bigger deal than I thought?

Nervous again, I climb the rest of the stairs to a long, carpeted corridor. This is not what I am used to. My football watching usually involves the clang of turnstiles followed by scuffling and battling through the massed ranks of the White Hart Lane faithful to a seat so high up (and therefore cheap) it practically has cloud cover.

In contrast, this is the VIPs' floor, where all the directors and bigwigs hang out. I can almost smell the Henri Wintermans cigars and sheepskin coats and pre-match whiskies. Windows give a view of the pitch. The stands are packed tight with males, as though a giant with a huge dustpan and brush has swept up every single one for miles around and emptied them into the stadium. It's so normal I've never really thought about it before, the way I never really think about the *Observer* newsroom being full of men. It's just the way things are, like a forest being full of trees.

Here goes.

I push open the door to the press lounge. The jabber stops just for a millisecond, owing to two dozen men sucking in their breath in unison at the sight of this alien being with bobbed hair, bosoms and lipstick. Then, as if someone has said, 'Nothing to see here, move along please,' the hubbub begins again. Men resume yakking to each other and bashing away at portable typewriters. The room is redolent of aftershave and cigarette smoke and Bri-Nylon shirts. Even the tea lady is a man. He pours me something magnolia-coloured from a giant metal teapot and I examine the biscuits and choose a scuffed pink wafer. I am not at all hungry but it seems the right thing to do.

The press box is across the corridor from the lounge and consists of three rows of seats. In front of each is a pull-down flap to make a work surface. It's all a bit school desky and rather a squash, except that the *Observer*'s is between those of two middle-aged men rather than little girls. I hope they don't mind having to sit next to The Woman. I scan them quickly to see if I can spot terror in their eyes, then sit down, squeezing my legs together to avoid any accidental side-swipe of thighs. 'Hello,' says one. 'Come to do the woman's angle, have you?'

'Ha ha ha,' I trill politely. Twat. Then comes a loudly penetrating voice from the row behind me.

'Women in the press box. So it's come to that.'

'Appalling,' murmured his companion.

Bloody hell, is Victoria still on the throne? Now what do I do? Turn round and offer them the smelling salts? They obviously mean me to hear, so the best thing is to play deaf. Actually, I feel a bit shaky.

The men on the *Observer* sports desk have been great. I couldn't wish for better, more supportive colleagues. It's lulled me into a false sense of security. I start cursing myself for being naive. So I think I'm going to be able to change things? What an ass.

Then I feel a spark of anger. I remember how I wanted to howl with frustration all through my growing up, at how limited the options were for girls; at how all life seemed to consist of was people telling you what you couldn't do, not what you could do; at how if you wanted to be something new or different then you'd be called overambitious or unfeminine or, worst of all, *odd*. Well, even if I am, so what? It isn't *his* press box. What gives men like him the right to say who's allowed in and who isn't? Why shouldn't a woman be a sports-writer? Sport is for everyone. It's playing, it's belonging, it's great deeds and huge emotions, it's a natural expression of being human, part of life. I've been given the chance to show what women are capable of, and I am not going to let a dinosaur like him get in my way.

I won't bore you with the details of what turns out to be a rather dreary game. One goal decides it, and it isn't scored by the team of my heart, Spurs. Back in the press room after the final whistle, I find myself a sliver of work surface, then get out my notebook.

I have to file by six o'clock. Suddenly my brain feels as if it's about to crack open. The pressure starts to build, as much in my head as in my chest, which only makes it worse.

This must be what walking the tightrope is like. Don't look down. Don't think about how far you'll fall. But I have never had to file a live report before. Why did I blithely think that I didn't need to do the proper training that all real journalists have to go through; why had I been so cocky as to think I could get by on talent alone? Suddenly, writing 500 words to a deadline seems a massive undertaking, like journeying solo overland from Mongolia by yak.

Oh, get a grip. This is my chance to stand alongside my heroines. All those women who have had to fight, to put themselves in the firing line, to break the rules to prove themselves. Think of Billie Jean King, the first woman athlete to win more than $100,000 in prize money, using her primacy to fight on behalf of other women for equal pay, confronting the chauvinists, not prepared to accept being devalued for the crime of being female.

Think of Kathrine Switzer, running the Boston Marathon in 1967, when females were barred from competing in long-distance races, out of fake concern for our health. Informed by her coach that the marathon was too much for 'a fragile woman', Switzer entered using her initials K.V. Switzer, so the powers that be mistook her for a man when she was actually a goddess-come-down. She was given the race number 261, pinned it on her vest and ran alongside her boyfriend Tom. On the way round a race official tried to rip it off, shouting, 'Get the hell out of my race and give me that number!' Tom shoved him aside, and sent him flying. By the time the official got up off the pavement Switzer was away, unassailable within a protective ring of good men and true who surrounded her all the way to the finish.

Remember what the race director said: 'Women can't run in the marathon because the rules forbid it. Unless we have rules, society will be in chaos. If that girl were my daughter, I would spank her.'

Remember what Switzer said: 'I knew if I quit, nobody would ever believe that women have the capability to run twenty-six-plus miles. It would set women's sports back, way back, instead of forwards. If I'd quit, that race official and all the others like him would win.'

And I am not going to let the chauvinists win, either. Compared to running a marathon and winning the US Tennis Open, coming up with 500 words on Coventry v Spurs isn't a lot to ask.

I can actually pinpoint the moment when life floods back into me: when I think of what I've been through to get here today. I am twenty-four years old. I have dreamed of being a Fleet Street reporter since I was twelve. I have got myself onto the first rung of the ladder before, only to have it break in half. There must be a lot of young women out there who would love to be doing what I am today, but I'm the one who has been given the golden chance. Well, I'm not going to be world number one at any sport, but I am going to be the first to do this.

What do I say to the god of failure? Not today, thank you.

Pfft, crisis over. What is my intro going to be? I rack my brains for an opening line. This is the *Observer* I'm writing for, the pre-eminent house journal of the intellectual centre-left. I feel a slightly hysterical urge to giggle. Long words are a must, the more obscure and polysyllabic the better. How would the celebrated football writer and TV dramatist Arthur Hopcraft, my role model, put it?

'Coventry,' my Biro rumbles sonorously, 'have the gift of ebullience. Their play, though unprofound, exudes a collective fervour that proved all too much for listless Tottenham.' Yes! Excellent Arthur-ese, that.

Suddenly all is well with the world. I have the first sentence sorted out. I am on my way. It's just something I seem automatically to know how to do, like breathing. This is what I am born to do, and it's a joy. Half a pack of Benson & Hedges later, I reach the magic 500 and pick up the phone.

'Copy,' says a disembodied voice, wearily. Oh God, I've got the Bored Copytaker, the one who is famous for asking, 'Is there much more of this?' when the writer has delivered two paragraphs of his or her finest prose. He is never a springboard for the spirits.

A hiatus ensues during which I listen to him rolling paper into his Remington and adjusting his headphones. I am so tense, so alert to everything that I can even, I am certain, hear him polishing his glasses. My heart starts to thump, not only because my bloodstream is by now almost entirely nicotine, but because suddenly I am fully aware that this is make-or-break time. I have taken a gamble. If it comes off, it will be glorious. I will have made my mark. I will be a trailblazer. If I fail to get it right, I will not be given a second chance.

More to the point, it will screw it up for other women. I sneak a glance at the men all around me, tapping away on their typewriters or standing up and spouting their copy over the phones. Do they have any idea what it's like to be me? Of course they don't. They've never had to worry about representing a whole gender.

'Begin,' says the copytaker in a yawny voice.

'Coventry City – one. Tottenham Hotspur – nil.' I adopt the deepest tone I can muster so it will not stand out among the stentorian chorus around me. 'Coventry have the gift of ebullience,' I rasp.

'You'll have to speak up.'

'Coventry have the gift of EBULLIENCE!' I roar, and then I shrug off all the self-consciousness and doubt and just get on with it, reeling off words that might mean everything or nothing to the flat rattle of typewriter keys, and intoning,

'Full point. New par' at intervals till there are no more left. And then the satisfying clunk of the receiver going back on the hook and it's all over.

And then the silence. In this press room there is not a single sound. All the men around me *have been listening.*

I swallow. My mouth is so dry I'm sure they must have heard that too. And the *thump-thump-thump* of my heart. The man sitting next to me does a kind thing. 'That was very good,' he says. Actually, he sounds a bit relieved. I am, too, if truth be told. Men do feel very uncomfortable if a woman embarrasses herself, and I've already sent two of the press pack into maidenly hand-wringing.

I try to mutter a manly, 'Cheers' – and have to take such a deep breath to speak I realise I've been holding it in.

And now I face another ordeal. I have to ring the sports desk to find out if they think it's very good, too.

'Hello, any queries?'

Ron, the sports editor, puts his hand over the mouthpiece. All I can hear is offstage barking.

His voice comes back on the line. 'Only just arrived. Ring again later.'

Nooooo! I want praise! I want applause! 'When? How much later?'

But he's put the phone down. I stuff my notebook and pen into my handbag and hurry out. I will have to ring before I get on the train. My head swivels to and fro as I search unsuccessfully for a taxi. So then I half-walk, half-jog to the station, where the London train is just about to rumble up to the platform. The call will have to wait.

I find a seat and light another cigarette. Phew. Anyway, I've done it. I've reported a football match. I can't believe how easy it was in the end.

Too easy?

I start going back over the report, sentence by sentence, hundreds of words stampeding past my eyes. I feel a dart of apprehension, hear a little whispering internal voice of doubt – *It isn't as good as you think it is, is it?*

Oh, stop it. Think of something else. The political situation in Northern Ireland. Mike Oldfield's *Tubular Bells*. Football hooliganism – should the government bring back the birch?

Ebullience . . . unprofound . . . exudes a collective fervour . . .

I suppress a groan. What a load of hoity-toity, pontificatory crap. It's awful. I never talk like that. It doesn't sound like me at all.

I try to concentrate on the scenery, but night is falling, and now all I can see from the window are muzzy trees and dark mounds, with occasional blurts of illumination and blurred platforms as the train whooshes past stations.

They'll leave it out of the paper. I can see my report now, flapping dismally on the spike, that dreaded item of paraphernalia on the news desk on which all pieces of unwanted copy are stabbed to death. I wish I hadn't told all my friends. I imagine them opening the *Observer* the next morning and looking for my by-line and not finding it, and I'll have to live it down.

By now, I have reached a state of profound, debilitating anxiety and, as the train draws into Euston and I stand up to leave the carriage, my leg muscles seem to have turned to wool. I can hardly walk.

Somehow I make it down the platform on wibble-wobble, newborn-foal legs. I stagger around the forecourt looking for a phone booth, but am so suffused with anxiety that I can't remember what a phone booth looks like. I am looking at porters' trolleys and confectionery kiosks and thinking, *Is that one?* When I do identify one, I realise I have no small change but a 50p piece, which my shaky fingers drop before I can put it in the slot.

9

I am put through to the sports desk.

'Was it okay?'

'Yes, fine.'

This means nothing. I have listened to sports editors telling people their report is 'fine' just to get them out of their hair. Ron could mean anything from 'I haven't read it yet' to 'It's been spiked'.

'Will it get in the paper?'

'*Yes*. Well done.' Then he starts banging on about the *wonderful* report filed by the other new young writer he'd commissioned. Who is a man, of course.

I get the message. Don't get above yourself. You're a woman. Pretend you've done nothing special.

But I have, I know I have. I perform a little celebration to myself right there. I don't mean I stretch out my arms and thrust out my tits and glory in it, but all the way back to my car I am murmuring, *I did it, I did it. I am the first woman in Fleet Street to report a football match*. So what if people think I'm mad? It's so fabulous I won't believe it's happened till I've said it out loud. I'm so happy I don't even go into my usual catastrophe mode, imagining some awful event like the IRA blowing up the *Observer* before they've got the second edition out. Because I've done it, I've done it. I haven't let Womanhood down.

My car is still there where I parked it this morning, in a sordid side street a few blocks behind the station. To add to my joy, no one has broken into it. I drive down Woburn Place, through Bloomsbury and Holborn and Clerkenwell, down Farringdon Road, past deserted pavements, shop fronts in darkness and broodingly tall and empty office blocks because this is the weekend and everywhere is silent and dead. Then I draw up at the lights at Ludgate Circus and look to my right. Fleet Street. What a beautiful sight. The whole place is glowing with light and life, pubs roaring, presses rumbling, walls shaking, as though a treasure chest has burst open and all the jewels and coins are pouring out. The sheer, miraculous, ruthless, glamorous, sexy, wicked energy of it all. And now I am part of it.

PART 1

The Decision

Chapter 1

The Big Dream

Fleet Street, London EC4. Look at that name. Just breathe the air. Smell the ink.

These lovely, evocative words aren't mine. They were spoken by the late, very loved *Daily Mirror* columnist Sue Carroll, and in no time at all they'll be half a century old. The place she was talking about was Fleet Street in the second half of the twentieth century, not now when it's just a boring London through-road, but when it was a small industrial town in itself: when a single edition of one of the papers churned out by its news factories could sell millions of copies; where the world was intensified and brightened, so that when you went home (which many of its inhabitants avoided as much as possible) everything seemed dull and plain in comparison.

It was populated by characters who infused everything with charm and cynicism and wit: men – they were invariably men – who made you feel interesting and sexy and brilliant. It stood for glamour, fame and opportunity, and the magical excitement that came with the adrenaline rush of hunting down your story and returning with it in triumph to this centre of the universe. A place where you bashed out your words through clouds of cigarette smoke, among overflowing ashtrays, on a beaten-up Remington, to a soundtrack of chittering Telex machines and subs bawling, 'Copy, please!' at lurking messengers. Where you learned to talk on the phone and type at the same time and, as the presses started rolling, the whole building shook, and your body along with it. Actually, that was quite erotic.

The street was dominated by the Art Deco edifices of Express Newspapers – all gleaming black glass and steel – and the tastefully colonnaded home of the *Daily* and *Sunday Telegraph*. It was cluttered with news vans, taxis and giant trucks piled with rolls of newsprint, and bracketed (as it still is, of course) by the law and the Almighty. At one end, just where it turns into the Strand, sat the Royal Courts of Justice. At the other, on top of the hill-rise from Ludgate Circus, you could see St Paul's Cathedral – sometimes two of them, late at night, if you'd just staggered out of the pub. And there were so many, many pubs. I can still reel them off like a catechism: The Albion, the Old Bell, the Punch Tavern, the Printer's Pie . . . that just took care of a mere twenty-five yards on one side of the road. Roy Greenslade, a former editor of the *Daily Mirror*, once described it as 'a 24-hour village permanently *en fête*'. 'You would never mistake it for an insurance company,' observes Sue Peart, who joined Fleet Street from the fragrant, civilised world of *Cosmopolitan* magazine.

'I had the time of my life there, though half of it I don't remember,' says Angie Mulligan. Angie, who worked as a secretary at the racy *News of the World*, was a fount of the kind of stories that have to be told in lowered tones. It was she who recalled the time Sue Carroll lay down in front of the Old Bell as some kind of obeisance. 'Sue was in love with a chief sub called Bell. She didn't lie down on the pavement. It was in the middle of the road.'

Mary Kenny's *Something of Myself and Others* is a delicious memoir in which she recounts, among other stories, some gems from a career that began in the mid-1960s on the *Evening Standard*. 'Journalism was not, in those days, an entirely respectable profession,' she writes.

'It was seedy in Fleet Street,' echoes Wendy Holden, and when she worked on the *Evening Standard* another twenty years had passed. Of course, Fleet Street's merry disreputability might have been part of the appeal for girls whose schools had corralled them with rules and whose mothers had been consigned, however serenely, to domestic roles, living lives that were like letters that never got opened. I know that was true of me. But whatever the reason, it was the ultimate goal for many of us from childhood onwards. In the words of Valerie Grove, who arrived on the scene via the *Evening Standard*'s Londoner's Diary, moved to *The Times*, and is the author of acclaimed biographies of the poet and author Laurie Lee and Sir John Mortimer of *Rumpole of the Bailey* fame, 'I was never going to go anywhere else. Never.' Scarth Flett, who did the big interviews for the *Sunday Express* in the 1970s and 80s, is another. She travelled from Australia, the other side of the world, to get there. 'England was where we wanted to go,' she told me. 'Work in Fleet Street. That was the big dream.'

Do you really need to ask why? 'It was a really glamorous thing to do,' says Tina Moran, who, from *Bristol Evening Post* trainee, worked her way up to the role of number three at the *Daily Express*. 'Those glorious broadsheets, selling four and a half million a day – I thought, I want to get my name in there. I want to get my name doing something.'

'It was romantic,' says Sue Peart, who from the *Daily Express* in 1983 went on to high-level roles at *The Times* and the *Mail on Sunday*, where she was editor of *You* magazine for eighteen years. 'The characters were so vivid. Often very flawed, but interesting and volatile and clever, and I can't think of a colleague I didn't like. It was a really rewarding job, where every day was different. You needed stamina; you would put in a full day and be ready to leave and then something would happen – a death, or disaster – and it would be jackets off again.'

Emma Lee-Potter, now an author as well as a freelance contributor to multiple papers, started as a staff news reporter on the *Evening Standard*. 'I lived in a tiny flat off Lavender Hill in Clapham,' she says. 'The News Desk would often call in the middle of the night, because the deadline for the first edition was at 9 a.m. It was just the house phone – there were no mobiles. You had to be contactable at all times. You had to add your phone number to a long list on the news desk. If you went out at lunch, you would leave the name and phone number of the place you were going to. When you went on holiday, you had to make sure you told them the location and the name of the hotel. I thought, You must be joking! But if a story broke, they'd want to know where you were.'

The phone in her living room would ring. She would answer it in her nightie. 'Oh my God,' she would think. 'This can only be one thing. I'm being sent somewhere.' She would snap into reporter mode. 'What the job is. Where to go. Go now.'

Those were two of the essential characteristics of life as a Fleet Street reporter – all-hands-to-the-deck urgency and unpredictability. When planning ahead, whether a social arrangement or even your own wedding, it was customary to utter the traditional incantation: 'If the Queen Mother dies, all bets are off.' Hilary Bonner, later *Mail on Sunday* showbiz editor and now the award-winning author of crime thrillers, landed her first Fleet Street job on the *Sun*. After writing about road closures and council meetings on parochial West Country papers, the brinkmanship was exhilarating. 'The news editor slapped a bit of Press Association copy down in front of me,' she remembers. '"Give us a page six comment piece on the chances of World War Three breaking out this year, old girl. You've got till lunchtime." I can't do anything unless I'm chasing a deadline. If we've got people coming to dinner

I only start cooking when I see the whites of their eyes. I couldn't grumble. It was all that I loved about it.'

'It was a riot,' says Lynn Barber, of her years on the *Sunday Express*, which launched her as one of the most formidable interviewers of her generation. 'We just used to sit around, flick through magazines all morning and discuss where we were going for lunch. If someone had a contact who could be entertained on expenses, we'd all pile in with them. The deputy editor would complain if I was claiming too little. "Six pounds?" he would say. "Where can you get lunch for six pounds?" If I was going to New York, I'd get a chit for £500. Now you have to go on the cheapest available flight, landing at 3 a.m.'

And how exciting it was to arrive at work in the morning with no idea what you'd be doing or where you'd end up that day, or that week. For me it might be a 90mph drive north for lunch at a local diner with the entire Liverpool first team (all very decorous, but just fancy), or hurtling up the M1 to Watford to interview Elton John at the football club he'd just bought. This was an era when a young woman could charm her way out of receiving speeding tickets. I danced the night away with the London Broncos rugby league team in Huyton Labour Club. I once left it so late to get back to Fleet Street after the Grand National that the cabbie had to drive onto the platform at Lime Street so I could fling myself onto the London train. I have been carried out of the press lounge at Aston Villa and decanted into a taxi by the half-time crowd entertainment (Birmingham's answer to the Rockney duo Chas & Dave) after extended revels.

My press ticket would admit me to Wimbledon's Centre Court every day of The Fortnight. Brian Clough, then the most famous football manager in Britain, became godfather (and a wonderful one at that) to one of my sons. I could telephone a football club and summon the player of my choice for an interview, once making the mistake of ringing the amiable England international Mick Channon after a very jolly lunch. The next day, having forgotten all about it, I phoned to arrange the interview again. He was amused. To quote Valerie Grove, 'What larks, eh?'

Added to that was the cachet that came from having access to the rich and celebrated (however fleetingly so) and their haunts. A list of Scarth Flett's interview subjects in the 1970s and 80s is a cross between a newsreel and a *Who's Who*: Kirk Douglas, Sylvester Stallone, Liza Minnelli, Eric Morecambe. In Monte Carlo, she had lunch with the 'dashing bachelor' Prince Albert, son of Prince Rainier and Grace Kelly, and heir to the principality's throne. In her article, her expert reporter's eye roves over the scene:

'On a fresh spring day the sun trickled lightly across the harbour to the pinky-beige royal palace on the cliff where a white flag fluttered in the breeze . . .'

I can see Scarth there right now, with that dark brown hair the colour of strong coffee, confident and gorgeous, a journalist at the very top of her profession. 'I ordered oysters so I could eat them with one hand and write down what he said with the other,' she says.

'We were all in our early twenties and we had such fun,' says Valerie Grove. She arrived hotfoot from Cambridge in 1968, dressed in red, raven-haired, a kind of bluestocking Cathy McGowan: 'June 22 was Degree Day and on June 24 I started at the *Standard*.' She worked on Londoner's Diary with a team of posh boys, 'in an office full of laughter and jokes and finding everything hilarious. One big noisy room in sooty Shoe Lane just off Fleet Street.' It was a world, she says, of 'speaking looks and little notes across the typewriter, and swarming out at lunchtime to El Vino's. The boys talking in their special Etonian jargon, and an old man called Philip to keep a steady rein on everything. Every night we went to publishing parties. Any interesting person visiting London would be interviewed – Edward Albee, Arthur Miller, the most amazing people. It was priceless. Copy on pulleys. The stone underneath. The noise of typewriters, the noise of telephones. Gigantic Fleet Street names.'

It's a sad fact of life that a Fleet Street by-line is an ephemeral thing. Look at those names now and unless you lived through those times you could well think, Who? But these were great journalists: Vincent Mulchrone of the *Daily Mail* (not only one of the biggest names but one of the nicest – and the most versatile; he covered everything from the withdrawal of US troops from Vietnam to the decline of the English sausage). The wit and eloquence of the *Observer* sportswriter Hugh McIlvanney ensured he transcended his genre. There were celebrated columnists like the *Times*'s Bernard Levin, one of the most famous and controversial writers of his day. There were renowned editors such as Charles Wintour (whose austere demeanour had him christened 'Chilly Charlie' long before the famous *froideur* of his daughter Anna). Bernard Shrimsley, who edited Rupert Murdoch's *Sun* in the 1970s, once scrawled disapprovingly across a photograph of a page-three girl, 'Nipples too fantastic.' In a later interview, he said they 'looked like a couple of plastic coat pegs'. Hugh Cudlipp was an editor-superstar – he turned the *Daily Mirror* into the biggest-selling paper of the 1950s and 60s – who had the distinction of being banned from El Vino's for bad behaviour, and was ultimately sacked for plotting to overthrow Harold Wilson's Labour government.

But even if you have never heard of any of them, you will notice a pattern. All these gigantic names belonged to men.

When Valerie applied to the *Standard* for a job Charles Wintour wrote back, 'It is not our practice to have more than one woman on the Diary, and we already have Mary Kenny, but we are prepared to make an exception for you.' Valerie notched up many achievements as a journalist but one that is overlooked is that she was the first woman to be the second woman on Londoner's Diary.

When Sue Peart joined the *Daily Express*, its editor was Larry Lamb. 'A big man with a scar on his forehead from where he'd fallen on the spike one day,' she said. 'He'd employed me at a time when there weren't many women journalists; he had recognised that women were part of an important cohort in terms of markets and he was quite proud of me.' Lamb would take her in his Jaguar to the American Bar to drink champagne, and then drive her back to take her down to the presses, which by then were rolling away full pelt. In that hot, cacophonous, subterranean, stinky, man-stuffed environment, he would pull off a flong, the mould from which a printing stereotype is made, to show her.

It is lovely to picture this scene, which seems like some chivalric ritual of a medieval knight towards his lady. 'The men would all stand to attention,' says Sue. 'This Sloane Ranger in pearls and a pink dress, wearing perfume – I don't think they'd seen anything like it.'

Not many of them had. Whenever I told people what I did for a living, they always responded the same way. 'That's a very unusual job for a woman, isn't it?' I was Girl In The Press Box – the first woman on Fleet Street to be a general sportswriter, the only one who reported football, a pioneer. But as Hilary Bonner says, 'We were all pioneers in our way.' At the start of the 1970s, as the only girl in the newsroom among a band of drunken men, she fielded with a sweet smile comments such as, 'Good afternoon, Hilary. You're looking particularly radiant today. You must have had a very good fuck last night.'

And here's Maureen Paton who, also in the early 1970s, was told by the chief sub on *Melody Maker*, with a certain amount of cynical amusement, that he knew exactly why she had got the job – because the editor had just been to a conference about bringing more women into journalism.

Another ten years, and things still hadn't changed much. 'You needed an incredibly thick skin because it was so male-dominated,' says Wendy Holden. 'The business of the day was done in the pub, not the office. A sense of humour was essential. The sexism was rampant. I wish I'd had a million pounds for every slap on the bum. We just lived with it.'

'I've nothing against women, but why must they always infiltrate?' bleated dear old Brian Chapman, the distinguished deputy sports editor of the *Observer,* when, in 1973, a group of female journalists campaigned unsuccessfully to be admitted to the men-only Press Club. All sorts of clubs and institutions were no-go places for us, sometimes not officially, either. You could be kept out with the excuse that, 'We don't have the facilities.' At least El Vino's was open in its disdain. Women were forbidden to enter via the front. A side door in an alleyway was where we were admitted, and then only if we were accompanied by a male. There we'd sit in a dim back room (women were banned from going up to the bar and ordering a drink), listening to the distant roars and trumpetings of the Gigantic Fleet Street Names at the front. It was a bit like standing against the outer wall of Regent's Park Zoo.

Jennifer Selway, of the *Observer* and the *Daily Express*, was fifteen when she went to the Stones in the Park concert in 1969, the one when Mick Jagger released the butterflies, after Brian Jones had died. 'Marianne Faithfull sitting by the side of the stage. Policed by Hell's Angels. People sitting in trees.

I was wearing a pink minidress and no shoes and I had ink on my fingers because I'd been doing exams. I sat with my friend Vicky and her brother Pete, who was at Essex University, which was hardcore, and he smoked dope, and I thought, This is the new world and I am part of this.'

The news hadn't penetrated as far as Fleet Street, though. We might have felt it was the best time in British history to be a young woman. We might have shops full of cheap clothes designed by other young women because we didn't have to dress like our mothers any more. We might no longer have to read magazines aimed at our mothers, either, because instead of knitting patterns, recipes and tantalising hints of debauchery from agony aunts ('What you describe is perfectly normal and nothing to worry about') we had *Honey*, the first magazine for young women, with its talk about premarital sex and all the other things we couldn't ask our parents about. We might, after years of having it dinned into us that Nice Girls Didn't Till They Got Married, have the Pill, so important it became a proper noun. We might have believed the world was at our feet at last. But in Fleet Street women were almost a separate species, pigeonholed as fashion mavens, agony aunts, bitchy columnists or experts on childcare and domestic life. Half the human race and its thoughts and insights were cordoned off in an area called The Women's Pages. Our sphere of interest was deemed to be fashion, home and children. Anything 'serious' was written by men: politics, business, finance, sport, news itself.

Because this 'women's sphere' was not considered important, neither were the vast majority of women journalists. The expression 'glass ceiling' only sprang into popular use in 1978, but we knew all about it well before; we'd hit our heads on that insidious, invisible barrier beyond which it was deemed tough or impossible for women to rise above a certain level in the hierarchy. According to David Robson, who in the mid-1970s edited the *Sunday Times* Look! section – basically its women's pages – 'Men were the ruling classes.' Two decades later, when he was features editor of the *Independent*, they were still running everything. At neither paper were any women at the mid-morning editorial conference where the decisions were made as to what went in the paper. 'At the *Indie*, once a week up until 1993, there would be a lunch for "assistant editors",' David recalled. 'Out of eight or ten attendees, there would be no women.' Moreover, any female who did manage to break the mould had to battle with the popular assumption that she hadn't got her job through hard work and talent. No, it was obviously because she was sleeping with a powerful man. That, of course, only fuelled our resolve to hang on in there and prove our worth.

It's easy to forget how beta-class women were for the first three-fifths of the twentieth century. This secondary status was enshrined in law, and perpetuated by it. To give examples, we might have earned fabulous salaries but they were – as they still are in many cases – disproportionately lower than men's. We might have been household names, but as late as the mid-1970s we still needed our husband's or father's signature if we wanted a bank loan, or to buy something on hire purchase. Until 1982, it was still legal for a pub landlord to refuse to serve us a drink. Married women were not taxed independently; their income was treated as an addition to the earnings of their husbands. During that period, I sought a mortgage. Eventually I succeeded, but the process was so drawn-out, so seemingly unprecedented – a woman? wanting a *mortgage*? so she could *buy her own house*? – that I might have been asking to have the moon thrown into my arms.

Because our lives as journalists have spanned more than fifty years and a corresponding age gap exists between youngest and oldest, I decided not to tell our stories chronologically. Instead, I've concentrated on topics that have been common to all of us. What made us want to be journalists? How did we find a way in; and was it a struggle? Who helped us? What were the obstacles we faced? Did others find it as difficult and lonely as I sometimes did? If they had children, how did they manage the long hours and the social life that was an extension of working life? As David Robson says, 'One of the nostrums and glories and tragedies of old-style journalism was that work–life balance played no part in it.'

Some of the issues that affected us – sexism, the gender pay gap, sexual harassment, maternity rights, childcare – were not peculiar to us as journalists, and it's a sorry thought that these are still with us in the workplace now and that various rights – for instance, to women's safe spaces – are newly endangered. But I don't want to get all worthy and dreary because that is the last way to describe our Fleet Street lives. Of course there were pains. There was the stress of having to get your story, the imperative to file whatever the circumstances, the sexism and the groping, the pressure of having to be twice as good as our male peers to get anywhere. These were secondary, though, to the joys. Love, fame, laughter, money, excitement were all there for the taking and we knew that once we left Fleet Street nothing would ever be so naughty, thrilling, so ground-breaking again.

Newspaper headlines informed us that Woman Does This, or Woman Does That (followed by an article marvelling that a female person had run a marathon or become a neurosurgeon). Though it would be 1979 before Woman Becomes Prime Minister, we walked into Fleet Street with one intention. With what Angie Mulligan calls A&D – Ambition and Determination – we were going to achieve things we hadn't been allowed to do in the past. The world was changing. We weren't just part of that change; we were the journalists who were going to propel it forward. We were not going to settle for eulogising kitchen utensils or telling mothers how to bath baby. We were the new generation. We would go anywhere the men did, report anything, but we would allow ourselves to write as women, to *be* women, not just imitation men. We would go for some of those 'ruling class' jobs, so that we too could make decisions about what went into our papers. We would take what had been sidelined as 'women's interests', prove they were relevant to everyone, and make sure our voices were heard.

We were going to break down the doors of the gentlemen's club.

Chapter 2

Adorable Dads and Ambivalent Mothers

I did not grow up in a family that could be described as 'bookish'. My mother's taste was intellectually undemanding, with Georgette Heyer at the apogee and Mills & Boon the nadir. At least she read something. I never saw my father open a book, though I always had to pass my *Beano* on to him once I'd finished with it. In mitigation, though, I shall point to the amount of newsprint that cascaded through our letterbox: *Telegraphs*, *Mails*, *Standards*, the *Evening News*, the *Sunday Express*, the *Sunday Dispatch* and, after that closed in 1961, the *Sunday Telegraph*. We had four papers every weekday, two on Sundays, and six on Fridays when the local papers arrived. My father featured regularly in the latter – he was a great sitter on council committees – so my mother examined these minutely.

Scrolling through yards of microfilm at the British Library, I was astounded at how dismal and scrappy these newspapers from the 1950s and 60s look now. I'd remembered them in my mind's eye as vivid and dramatic. I loved the dusting of ink they would leave on my fingers; I loved their *smell* and what accompanied their arrival, that feeling of joy and anticipation: Ooh, it's a new day! New news!

'I loved newspapers,' said Valerie Grove – it was almost the first thing she said to me. 'I collected cuttings from the 1950s and edited everything I could, like school magazines.

My sister Alison had a friend, Rozzie, who had a horse called Will Sommers, after the court jester to Henry VIII, and we started *Horse & Pony Times* (price one penny).'

Tina Moran remembers much the same thing: 'We had papers every day. *Daily* and *Sunday Express, Bristol Evening Post*. There were always newspapers in the house. A lot of journalists say that.'

Sue Peart and I share a memory. Albeit eight years apart, we were pupils at the same boarding school, a rather grand one in Suffolk that was a popular choice of MPs from the shires to educate their daughters. The right tone had to be set and only one paper passed muster. Both can still picture it – the copy of *The Times* placed every morning on a lectern in the school library. 'It was kind of rationed,' Sue reminded me, 'which made it even more exciting and desirable. It was the highlight of my day. No competition – none of the other papers were allowed over the threshold. Beautifully edited. It was wonderful.'

Sue recalled the column by Mel Calman that ran across the bottom of the front page – The Best Place to Have Tea in Britain. In my day, that front page bore nothing so exciting; it was, in fact, deadly dull, just pile after pile of classified ads that put a barrier between the reader and the stories within, like a tinted window to a sex shop. I liked my news out there and vulgar. Between 1959 and 1961, when I attended the City of London School for Girls, I travelled on the Central line every morning in rush hour, beguiling the journey with a *Daily Mirror* bought covertly at the newsagent's in the forecourt of Loughton station once my mother's Ford Anglia had disappeared up the road. The *Mirror* was forbidden at home because, said my mother, it was working class but, between the end of the Second World War and the Beatles' first LP, it outsold every other national paper.

I seized on it for the football coverage, which was jauntier and much more knowledgeable than in the stuffy *Telegraph*, but it was a long journey to Blackfriars so I read everything else as well. The paper contained everything an inquisitive pre-teen with a sheltered upbringing could want to know about this naughty world: jewellery heists, hangings, sex scandals, with much added spice in the form of which film star had been photographed 'in a clinch' with whom. You would not have learned a lot about the clinches if you read *The Times*. Nor would the eight-year-old Hilary Bonner from reading the *Daily Mirror* belonging to her grandad, which by the time he handed it over to her had holes in it where once had been its more prurient revelations.

'We were a real newspaper family,' she said. 'The *Western Morning News* was delivered to us every day. Our neighbours took the *Daily Express*, and at one o'clock, when Dad hung the "Closed" sign on the door of his butcher's shop and came home for his dinner, he and the neighbours would swap papers. Then in the evening the *Express & Echo* would be delivered.

'But when I was eight, my grandparents came to live with us, and they brought the *Daily Mirror* into our home. Grandad reckoned it was the best racing paper. He thought there was a lot in the *Mirror* I shouldn't see, so he used to cut out the salacious bits, and I would read it through ragged holes. I'd never seen anything like it. I could understand in the *Daily Mirror* things I couldn't understand in other papers. In *The Times* you might see a story about the price of grain having gone up so many rupees in Calcutta. The *Mirror*'s angle would be, because the price of grain has gone up, the housewife will have to pay fivepence more for her bread. The stories were about other people's lives. It's the basis of tabloid journalism. I picked it up one day and I was just knocked out. I pointed to it and said, "I want to work for them one day."'

*

The *Daily Express*'s Tina Moran grew up in Bristol; her father, Johnny, was a staff photographer with the *Daily* and *Sunday Express*, covering sport for the whole of the West Country. An unfeasible number of miles in his little Mini was clocked up. 'But he had London wages,' said Tina, 'so we had a nice lifestyle.'

It was the era when the newspaper industry was flying, when papers had district offices countrywide and Bristol was a media hub. The BBC and HTV had studios; the *Bristol Evening Post*, South West News Agency and *Western Daily Press* were based there; all the nationals had reps in the city. Tina was the eldest of four children; her mother had her work cut out – she was a press widow. Johnny Moran was happy to take Tina off her hands. 'I adored my dad,' she said. 'He would say, "I'm popping down to the Badminton Horse Trials," and take me for the day. I accompanied him on news stories.' She recalled 'the magic of him wiring his photos back', and the posse of company cars that headed afterwards to the pub: 'It was a massive drinking culture. My mum told me some of the things that went on – how the phone would ring at the back of the bar – "Is Johnny Moran here?" "No, no," the barmaid would say, lying through her teeth. It was something a lot of the wives had to put up with!'

Because of the way her dad operated, she never experienced office life. 'It was always the camaraderie, the buzz of being out on assignment, setting off down the M5 at 5 a.m. with my dad to do a story. The excitement of being the only people on the road. From the time I was eight years old I got to meet a lot of his colleagues. They all knew me; they'd all pat me on the head. The only woman was a lady called Liz. They'd all regularly rock up wherever we were. These were people who spent all their time on the road. They'd have a few pints at lunch. It would get a bit jollier. It just seemed a really nice culture.

'I spent many afternoons in the darkroom at the *Express*'s Bristol office, breathing in the smell of developing fluid and fixer in the pitch-dark. I loved it. He was a lovely dad. To be honest, I wasn't much trouble. I sat quietly in the corner and watched him hang up his negatives. Apart from at five wanting to be an air hostess I can't remember anything else but wanting to be a reporter.'

It's a story that has echoes in Valerie Grove's account of growing up the daughter of a newspaperman in the Northeast. Doug Smith was a cartoonist, first on the *Shields Gazette* and then the *Newcastle Chronicle* before joining the *London Evening News*. 'My father was simply adorable and his being a cartoonist made him different from everyone else's father,' she said. 'All the things he loved, I followed him in. I loved everything about being his daughter.' In her contribution to a Virago book, *On the Death of a Parent*, she reflected on his unstinting support, and how, unlike other fathers, he never complained about spending money on a daughter's education because, so the mantra went, she would only get married.

Both Scarth Flett and Wendy Holden had benefited from their fathers' support, too. 'My father was just the most wonderful person,' said Scarth. 'He was an ally growing up. Whenever I was in trouble, he was my back-up.'

'My father was extraordinary,' recalled Wendy. 'He was born in India; his father died when he was eleven and, from living a very nice, British colonial life, he lost everything. His education was halted. He was completely self-taught, but he ended up a major in the army, fought the Japanese in Burma, and went on to have a good career in business. Both my parents were very resilient – my mother's fiancé had been killed in the war – and resilience was key in Fleet Street. They taught me that you can't whimper because it's unfair. If you can't change a situation then you find a way to rise above it.' Her writing, in consequence, has a distinguishing theme. 'Always people who refused to be cowed or bowed.'

Monty Court, father of *Daily Express* journalist and *Cosmopolitan* editor Louise, was a strict but loving father, not conventionally adorable but someone who set very high standards. 'There was a lot of swearing in our house,' she said. 'We used to say, "He thinks he's running a newsroom."' This was, in fact, what he did as investigations editor and then news editor of the *Sunday Mirror*. He was also its father of the chapel – the person who represented its NUJ members. One day he took Louise and her older brother, Nick, on a tour of the Mirror Group's Holborn Circus skyscraper. They visited the machine room. 'DON'T TOUCH ANYTHING! YOU'LL CAUSE A STRIKE!' he roared.

What was it like, being the daughter of a Fleet Street legend? I asked.

'I think it was similar to being the children of policemen,' she said. 'He saw human nature's dark side every week. He was very aware of what could happen, and protective. I was growing up in the punk era. He once accused me of coming back from a concert with fleas! We'd have massive rows. "It's not really like that, Dad," I'd say, and he'd say, "Yes it is," and get out a copy of the *Sunday Mirror* to prove his point.

'He was brought up in a matriarchy, because his father was very ill after being gassed in the First World War. Nanny had to bring up six children. My dad was strict because he'd grown up in an army family. His three sisters were all incredibly strong women, and I was brought up to believe I was totally equal to boys and men; I never thought of myself as a girly girl. When I was younger, I was always late, and he'd always bollock me: "It's most selfish to be late because you're using someone else's time." When I was fifteen I was meant to be going out on a date with a boy. The boy phoned up to say he didn't have any money, so we couldn't go. Dad was mad at me: "How old is he?"

'"Eighteen."

'"He's a schoolboy!" Dad admonished. "Why should he pay for you?"'

He could never, Louise told me, let his professional standards slip. When she started getting her first by-lines, whereas other people's parents would coo, 'Darling, that's amazing!', he'd go, 'Never start an intro with "when".' Or if he thought it was clichéd, he'd tell her. She recalls being told by a woman journalist who Monty had trained, and who was still incredibly fond of him despite his tough exterior, that his reaction to her first pieces of copy was, 'What's this? It's not bloody *Noddy*.' But she sums him up positively: 'He could be challenging as a father, but he was fair and I always knew I was loved, which is the most important thing. I also knew he thought I was smart.'

Adorable. An ally. Extraordinary. Knowing you were loved. Suddenly I was seized with something close to a sense of injustice. It was easy for fathers to be heroes. Where did our mothers come into the picture? The spring of 1970 saw the first ever National Women's Liberation Conference in the UK. That year also saw the publication of Kate Millett's *Sexual Politics* and Germaine Greer's *The Female Eunuch*. The women's rights movement had begun in the US in the 1960s; it seemed utterly reasonable to ask for equal rights and opportunities, and greater personal freedom, so of course it was the cue for male outrage, jokes about bra-burning, dungarees and Doc Martens, and minatory statements from prominent patriarchs on either side of the political divide.

During my early years at the *Observer*, its editor-proprietor was David Astor. He was a decent, idealistic man who used his abundant wealth to do good, but he had some cranky views about women, once feeling able to inform Katharine Whitehorn, whose weekly columns in the *Observer* were the first to close the gap between 'women's writing' and 'serious' – i.e. men's – journalism, that she had 'penis envy'. He was a proponent of Freud and believed that mothers should be at home with their children. 'The libbers are misery makers,' he said of this first ever conference, because as an immensely rich Old Etonian he knew at first hand what it was like to be stuck at home with two under-threes and an overflowing nappy bucket.

Our mothers really did know. They were from the genera-tion that was expected to give up work – if indeed they ever had jobs – once they married and had children, at which point they would retreat into domesticity and that was the last the world out there ever saw of them. If you were lucky, they were happy with their role. 'Mum didn't work after having children,' said Louise. 'She was our rock, the stability. She had to be, because of all the long hours my dad worked during those years in Fleet Street.'

Some mothers might have encouraged their daughter but others tended to be the jug of cold water poured over burning ambition. High hopes – what was the point? Clare Arron, who worked for the *Telegraph* and *Mail*, grew up with jour-nalism in the same way as did Tina Moran. Her father was a photographer based in Manchester, working for the *News of the World*, the *Mirror*, the *Telegraph*, the *Financial Times* – 'A proper freelance,' Clare said. 'I couldn't think of anything else to do – I wasn't great at school, being a photographer was the only thing that was open to me, and I was good at it.' Not that she had any encouragement from her mum. Clare remembered her crying. 'She was mortified. She was a stay-at-home mum, and it wasn't necessarily her choice. She didn't like the fact that she was at the beck and call of newspapers. If it's not actually you it's happening to, it's no fun.'

Then there's Scarth Flett. When she announced she might like to be a journalist, her mother was horrified. 'But women journalists are all lesbians!' exclaimed Isabelle Flett. 'They all smoke and drink such a lot and they have to be so tough.'

Scarth was born during the war in Melbourne, Australia, where her father, Harald Flett, was an officer with the Royal Australian Air Force. Later, the family returned to Sydney, where her father's company had based him in 1935, and, when she was nine and her sister Rhana two, he took over their Brisbane office. Her mother was from a well-to-do New Zealand family. 'In those days, if you could afford it, you did the Grand Tour, and in England she was presented at court, wearing a ballgown and ostrich feather fan and all that malarkey. She met my Scottish-born father on the ship back. He worked for the shipping line that later became P&O in London and was on his way home after a short stint in the Port Said office. They actually met on deck sailing through the Bay of Naples. Very romantic. She was very young – nineteen – and very beautiful. I think they were happy at first. She had a very sharp wit and all the men used to adore her. She'd have been a wonderful interior decorator. She was good with colour and she liked doing up my father's offices. But as time went on she wasn't so happy.

'I had a tricky relationship with her. My father travelled a lot. She had a privileged life but was discontented. She was sort of jealous of my youth and didn't like getting old. She didn't like me. I don't look like her at all. She was always on about my big nose and said my C-cup boobs were so big, I would never be able to breast-feed. She was wrong there

– years later I successfully breastfed my son. I think she just wanted me to get married.'

Maureen Paton's mother was negative out of loving concern, not wanting her daughter to be hurt or disappointed. 'I was a working-class girl,' Maureen explained. 'She was forty when she had me. I was born in an unmarried mothers' home; my father had done a runner. I grew up with my mother's foster sister and husband – they gave Mum and me a home. I thought about being a journalist at university, but my mother said, "You're aiming above your station." Mum loved me and wanted the best for me, but to her that was being a hairdresser or at the very most a secretary.'

The only exception was Emma Lee-Potter's mother Lynda, who was something of a trailblazer, being, for more than three decades, one of the best-known journalists in Britain, the *Daily Mail*'s Voice of Middle England. Her column appeared every Wednesday. It was witty and knowing, and delivered blisteringly rude comments about people that others might concur with but were too polite to say. In person she was a nice woman, a bit shy; the subs loved her. 'She'd come over and chat to us,' said a friend who worked on the *Mail* at the time, 'and say self-deprecating things like, "Here's some very ordinary copy for you to make the best of."'

Her story is a vivid example of what can be achieved with A&D – Ambition and Determination. The daughter of a Lancastrian miner and shoe shop assistant, her first ambition was to act, and at eighteen she left for London and the Guildhall School of Music and Drama. 'I got on the train at Warrington with a Lancashire accent and got off at Euston without it,' she said. She changed her name too – it was one Lynda Berrison who played in a Brian Rix farce at the Whitehall Theatre. And again when she married a medical student, Jeremy Lee-Potter, who ended up chairman of the British Medical Association.

She started off in features – she was a wonderful interviewer – and became a columnist in the early 1970s when Jean Rook, that other Voice of Middle England, jumped ship for the *Express*. Along the way she had three children. How, I asked Emma, did she manage? 'She just did,' said Emma. And had some good fortune. 'When I was eight, my great-aunt moved in with us, so she had twenty-four-hour help. She was devoted to my mother.'

All three children, Emma, the eldest, sister Charlie and brother Adam, went into the media. For Emma, it was a foregone conclusion. 'We talked so much about newspapers. It was endlessly fascinating to learn about how she worked. I went with her on some interviews. At the theatre, she'd go backstage. I saw how she worked. But it was an instinct. I always wanted to do it. It just seemed an exciting and glamorous world.'

Parental example could be less direct. Jennifer Selway spent her first three years in a village on the west coast of Ireland, where her father was in charge of a factory that made widgets. The family occupied a beautiful colonial bungalow in a remote, idyllic village called Portumna, and Lionel Selway, an engineer, installed an aerial in the garden, so they were the first people in the area to have TV. Jennifer's first Fleet Street job was writing the TV guide on the *Observer*.

It was the mid-1950s, when the IRA were very active in Eire. Jennifer's father had to negotiate with them so he could run the factory. One day they came round to the bungalow mob-handed to sort him out. 'My mother was terrified and, grabbing me, fled, expecting to come back and find him beaten to a bloody pulp. But when we crept inside, we found them all pissed, all laughing, slapping each other's back, saying, "He's a fine fellow and we'll get on famously." He had out-Irished the Irish.'

Another night there was a knock on the door and, when they opened it, a man forced his way in, armed with a boulder. He shouted, 'I've come to find Ruby Keeler. I know you've got her here.' Ruby Keeler was a film star, at one point the wife of Al Jolson. What she might be doing in a bungalow in County Galway, who knows? 'Mummy locked herself and me into a room,' said Jennifer. 'My father sat there with this lunatic holding a boulder all night. Finally, the *gardaí* came to take him away.'

In the later years of her career Jennifer was assistant editor at the *Daily Express*, which at the time suffered an astonishing turnover of editors, including Peter Hill. 'Everybody was nervous when Peter Hill took over – [he'd been editing the *Star*] and was reputed not to suffer fools gladly,' said Jennifer. 'I sat there in his first editorial conference thinking, Oh God what's going to happen?'

When I asked her what constituted the essential quality to succeed in journalism, she replied, 'Reptilian calm.'

'I am the child of very old parents,' Mary Kenny said. 'My father was born in 1877, my mother in 1902. They were married in 1925, had three children between 1928 and 1933, thought their family was complete, and then, to Ma's horror, she found herself pregnant with me ten years later. Poor Pa was delighted, although he died five years later.

'Ma was the daughter of teachers, and rather otherworldly, with lofty ideas and a notion that it was vulgar to talk about money. I grew up in Dublin in a rambling old Victorian house that was always desperately cold because we couldn't afford to heat it. I was the *enfant terrible* from the start.'

Widowed and impoverished, with an unruly child and three teenagers to cope with, her mother was at her wits' end. Then one day Mary's aunt and uncle, who lived nearby, came to lunch, during the course of which Aunt Dorothy, who was childless, observed how lucky her sister-in-law was to have been blessed with four.

'Take one of mine!' cried Ita Kenny. 'Take Mary, for goodness' sake!'

So, for a while Mary went to live with Aunt Dorothy. The contrast was dramatic. She went from a ramshackle Victorian household with an ethos of 'Liberty Hall', a place where occupants could do as they liked, to a three-bedroomed suburban semi where Aunt Dorothy, an experienced dog trainer, organised everything from meals on the dot to which day of the week she had her hair done.

'My mother was adorable but in some ways head-in-the-clouds,' said Mary. 'Quite vague. She was mad about Byron and Oscar Wilde, all that Romantic stuff. "All that tosh," my aunt would say. She was a very different kind of person, much tougher, conscientious. My uncle was a civil servant, and she came from a well-to-do farming background, and had a pretty good dowry, which was still a thing in Ireland. "Remember, Mary," she told me, "when you get married, it's 'What's thine is mine, and what's mine is mine.' Always have your own money."'

This, of course, is an excellent message to pass on to a girl, as is that passed on by Sue Peart's mother – that it's important for a woman to have a separate identity outside the home. 'I was brought up in Sheffield,' she said, 'and had a lovely, very stable background. My mother's name (Lord love her) was Hylda – she never forgave her parents! She had a Scottish, artistic, dramatic lineage and trained as a fashion designer with Norman Hartnell. When my sister and I were in our teens and my brother was going off to boarding school she went back to work as an occupational therapist. She was happy to be back. It made an impression on me.'

So, in a different way, did my mother make an impression on me. I was born in 1948. We lived in a house in Essex, on the edge of Epping Forest. My father owned several engineering companies and was on the local and county councils, so our family was prominent locally. Born in 1913, my mother, like most women of her generation, had missed out on further education because as a girl she was just expected to find a husband. She was energetic and intelligent, and domestic life was frustrating for her. Having been deprived herself, she was determined that my sister and I would have careers.

My mother was in charge of passing on our family history, and told wonderful stories about my male ancestors: the one who was the last to be hanged for sheep-stealing; the one who went into the military and was court-martialled for insubordination; the one who invented the vital component that made the pneumatic tyre work and who also built the first tandem. I was strangely proud of being descended from such a lawless, bloody-minded and eccentrically creative line. What about the women? Didn't they do anything thrilling or interesting? But my mother regularly disparaged the aunties and grannies; they were dotty, they were religious nutters, they couldn't hook husbands, they were generally just hopeless pains in the neck. That decided me. I wasn't going to be restrained by Girl Rules. I would go out into the world and show her what women could do.

When did people start talking about role models for girls? The concept was certainly never articulated during my childhood, although my prep school clearly had something exemplary in mind when it named its houses Brontë, Nightingale and Fry. Nowadays, there are some – if not enough – successful women in every field who can lead and inspire, but we Fleet Street girls were not alone in having to discover for ourselves who we would like to be when we grew up.

Wendy Holden, the bookworm, always wanted to be Jo in *Little Women*. Later on, in the manner of those making pilgrimages to Elvis's pad in Graceland, she visited Louisa May Alcott's house. 'Turned to mush, I did.' A teenage Scarth Flett, growing up in Australia and casting around for someone to emulate, was impressed by a girl called Shirley Gott, who had gone on to be the London correspondent of the *Melbourne Herald*. 'When she came back to Melbourne, she was treated like royalty. I thought being an Australian journalist and having a column for an Australian paper would be fun.'

'Maureen Cleave of the *Evening Standard* was the interviewer I admired most,' said Valerie Grove. 'She always brought out the best in people and made them seem interesting and amusing. She was absolutely the funniest, most witty person. It was to her that John Lennon said the Beatles were bigger than Jesus Christ. This didn't go down well in the United States, where they were about to tour; there were Ku Klux Klan marches and death threats. "Say I made it all up," Cleave suggested to John, "that'll get you off the hook." But he refused. The Beatles loved her. John holed up in her flat when he left Cynthia. I imitated her hair.'

I suppose it's predictable that my influences were drawn from the sports pages and from BBC's *Sportsview* and *Grandstand*. I must have watched something else on television as a child but sometimes it seems like a straight leap from Mr Pastry and Muffin the Mule to international Puissance jumping at the Horse of the Year Show and the FA Charity Shield (highlights of Bolton Wanderers v Wolverhampton Wanderers). I wasn't picky. I thrilled to broadcasts of everything from Fred Winter winning the 1957 Grand National on the chestnut 20–1 shot Sundew (all in black and white, of course, but I painted in his gorgeous goldenness in my mind's eye) to the World

Amateur Team Golf Championship, played on the old course at St Andrews. Wimbledon meant a whole fortnight lying on the floor of the living room with the curtains closed gawping up at the small screen. As an eleven-year-old I was transfixed by Abebe Bikila winning marathon gold in the 1960 Olympics, running barefoot through Rome. It was entrancing, spirit-freeing, life-affirming.

But why was there no women's marathon? Because it wasn't allowed. What about the 10,000 metres? Same. The 5,000 metres? Same, same. Suddenly I couldn't stop myself asking questions. Why weren't there any women jockeys? Why weren't we allowed to play football? Why did everyone stop women *doing* things? And even if a woman did achieve something in sport, why was she only worth a mimsy little paragraph or two on the sports pages when even quite mediocre showings by men merited blazing headlines? I didn't think anything of it at the time, but when you're young you absorb these messages subliminally. The Wimbledon men's singles final was on Saturday, in that era the closing day of the championships – it was the showpiece. The ladies' singles final was dispensed with on the Friday. It was less important. Subconsciously I took it on board; whatever we achieved, it didn't matter so much.

I had a female sporting hero in real life. Well, sort of. My riding instructor, Miss De Berry, was the most glorious and terrifying creature I had ever encountered; for the first time I realised it was possible simultaneously to entertain adoration and dread. Once I got her to sign my autograph book and was astonished to discover her Christian name was Odette, like the good swan in *Swan Lake*. Anyone less swan-like would be hard to imagine – she had a red leathery face, and her hair was a burning bush. (You could see it at all times because she never wore a hard hat.) She smoked, sometimes even when she was riding along. The other thing about her was that she wore tinted glasses. Always, even in the middle of winter. It made her look slightly sinister. My older sister, who had a quite separate and far more interesting life than mine (she went to pubs), used to see her serving behind the bar at the Roebuck. Still wearing the dark glasses. Heather said she must have something wrong with her eyesight, but I reckoned it was to shield herself from her own glare.

Those after-school hours at the Buckhurst Hill Riding School were some of the most harrowing of my life. I was petrified of her, even more petrified than of my form mistress Mouldy Warp, who was almost bald and had a voice like a coffin lid creaking open. Miss De Berry hollered: if you bounced all over the place instead of rising to the trot, for instance, or if you let your pony bolt with you, or fell off when he refused to jump a log. What a relief when the riding lesson was all over.

On one occasion, I thought I'd killed one of the ponies. Tony was all saddled up and ready when I went to lead him out of his stall for my lesson, but he refused to budge. What was wrong with him? Was he ill? Just being naughty? He stared doggedly ahead at the manger. I tugged at his reins and suddenly, with a great scraping and sliding of hooves, he collapsed onto his bedding. I was horrified. He was cast in his box (a phrase I had learned from *Horse and Hound* and liked to insert into conversation whenever I could; it meant that if he couldn't get up, he would have to be shot).

Miss De Berry raced in and bellowed, 'Tony! Tony, get up!' I was stunned – her voice was actually cracking with emotion . . . what was it? Fear? Finally, he stuck out one foreleg and then the other, and got to his feet. The reason he hadn't moved before was that he was still tethered by his halter. I hadn't noticed. How could I have been so unobservant, so stupid? The shame, the smirks of the other children on the ride – it was humiliating. But the next time I arrived for a lesson, Miss De Berry let me fetch Tony from his stall and ride him as usual, as if to say, 'I've still got confidence in you.' So she was kind as well as frightening. And when, not long after the Tony episode, I fell off and got left behind by the others, I thought: I can't just stand around and wait for her to help me, I've got to do this on my own – and flung myself back in the saddle. That afternoon, my mother arrived to collect me as usual, and Miss De Berry positively cooed at her, repeating, 'She's a natural rider,' like a jammed tape.

She had praised me! It's easy to fall in love a bit with someone who praises you. Well, I do. It struck me in later life that Miss De B was probably terrified I'd complain to my mother and was further terrified that my mother would remove me from the stables and switch me to lah-di-dah Van der Gucht's, which was creaming off a lot of little girls around that time because they had an indoor school where you could learn dressage. She couldn't afford to lose any more pupils, just as she could not have afforded to lose Tony. That would explain why she worked as a barmaid, to make ends meet.

Looking back, I realise how much I learned from her. Life was a struggle; she had poor eyesight, she had to work all hours to keep her business going, but she wasn't going to give up doing what she loved. Above all, I'm grateful that she turned me into someone who wouldn't just stand there crying and wait to be rescued. The message was: always get back on your horse. I would need that kind of resilience and persistence to make it as a journalist.

I never thought falling off was anything very life-threatening but you could say it was the reason I became a sportswriter, because when the jockey Manny Mercer fell off Priddy Fair at Ascot he was in fact killed. My whole obsession with sport really started because I was determined to find a way to get my father's attention. Most of the time I might as well have been talking to the hatstand. Every morning, though, he would spread out the *Daily Mail* and *Daily Telegraph* on the breakfast table and mark his fancies on the race card, so I developed a strategic interest in horse racing.

Every minute of my spare time, therefore, was devoted to it. My bedside reading was the *Register of Thoroughbred Stallions*, a tenth-birthday present, with the help of which I memorised every bloodline from the Godolphin Arab, one of the three horses who founded the modern thoroughbred along with the Darley Arabian and the Byerley Turk. (Another Horse Fact I liked to insert into my conversation wherever possible.) I spent an enormous amount of effort building up my racing stable, an idea I stole from *National Velvet*, cutting out photos from *Horse and Hound*, pasting them on cardboard and taking them for gallops in the garden. I also received my first literary rejection, from *Pony* magazine, to whom I had sent a short story about the reincarnation of a grey sprinter, The Tetrarch (by Roi Herode out of Vahren – I can tell you that now without accessing Google). He was undefeated in seven starts and sired Mumtaz Mahal, one of the century's most important broodmares. A kind handwritten letter from the editor accompanied my returned manuscript: 'Your story is a little too fanciful for us.'

So it was the last week of the summer holidays, and I was killing time hanging upside down from a tree in our garden when I spotted my father walking towards me with a folded copy of the *Evening Standard* under his arm. 'Poor old Manny Mercer,' he called out, and I made out the big black letters under the masthead: MANNY MERCER KILLED.

Manny Mercer had been cantering Priddy Fair to the start of the Red Deer Stakes when she threw him into the railings and kicked him in the head. It was the front-page splash, and my father had sought me out to break the bad news. I was sad for Manny Mercer, of course, but in a thrilled kind of way because it was *me* my father had rushed to share it with. As we talked about what had happened, I could tell that he too found the news shocking but in an exciting kind of way. He could not possibly have had that conversation with anyone else in his acquaintance – they wouldn't have understood. It was the connection with my father that I had craved, something that shaped my attitude to sport and the newspapers and put a marker down for the course my life would take.

Chapter 3

Jobs for the Girls

'I remember those days as being a time of great optimism,' said Sue Peart in an email about her first years in Fleet Street. 'The royal wedding had just happened, everyone loved Princess Di (and she was newspaper gold), Madonna had just burst onto the scene, we lived through the Wham! era, the ill-fated marriage of Madonna and Sean Penn, Bill Wyman and Mandy Smith, Barry Manilow . . . Lots of fun to be had, and women could have not just jobs but CAREERS.'

That Sue used capslock for emphasis shows that before the 1980s the idea that a girl might join the paid labour force with a purpose in mind beyond filling in time till she married and had children was still worthy of comment. Here are some statistics. In 1971, the seasonally adjusted figures for female employment aged sixteen to sixty-four were 52.8 per cent. There was something of a spike in 1979 when it reached nearly 59 per cent, coinciding with Margaret Thatcher becoming prime minister. By 2019, the figure for the same age range was 72 per cent. Employment for men was 97.1 per cent during the same age range. You see the picture. Expectations differed from those laid on boys.

On page one of the prospectus for Felixstowe College, the boarding school I attended in the 1960s, is the following paragraph:

The aim of the College is to give girls between the ages of 11 and 18 a sound education on a religious basis and on modern lines, to stimulate wide interests and to develop individuality . . . Girls are encouraged amid their beautiful surroundings to cultivate a taste for the natural and unaffected rather than for the artificial and luxurious and to equip themselves to play a useful part in life.

'A useful part in life' sounds like the title of a Barbara Pym novel, possibly the sequel to *Excellent Women*. Under its breath it murmurs 'years of genteel unpaid work' on parish councils and Women's Institute committees. We were taught how to walk downstairs in a ballgown, hold a plate, glass and umbrella at the same time (conjuring up images of rain-sodden church fetes and garden parties). We had weekly lessons in public speaking, because it was taken as read that we would grow up to be the kind of women who gave votes of thanks (assuredly after we had put our plates, glasses and umbrellas carefully to one side).

I cherish my old school magazines, which remind me of five years of darling friends, hilariously weird spinster teachers and jolly Malory Towers-type japes but – though I'm not a great one for clichés – it really was a different world. An annual feature, 'News of Old Girls', lists what everyone was up to once they had sung 'Lord, Dismiss Us with Thy Blessing', thrown aside their boaters (our school was too posh for mere panamas) and left Felixstowe behind to embark on the next stage of their lives. Here's a summary of what they were doing in 1964. Seven girls out of a sixth form of some thirty were at university, four at teacher training college, two studying nursing. Others were at finishing school (Lucie Clayton and Switzerland featured strongly), domestic science college, art school or doing upmarket secretarial courses. One was At

Home (I imagined her sitting around waiting for Mr Right). The trouble with having ambitions, if you were a girl in the 1950s, 60s and even 70s, was the paucity of options.

We've already touched briefly on Scarth's difficult relationship with her mother, who just wanted her to get married. When Scarth was thirteen, she was sent away with the words, 'You're so vile I'm sending you to boarding school.' But a happy turn of events meant she was rescued after eighteen months. In 1958 her father's head office required him to return to London for four months of briefings before taking over their Melbourne branch, and the family went with him, all expenses paid. 'I was taken out of boarding school in June 1958,' she said, 'and we left Australia a month later.' She celebrated her sixteenth birthday with a family party at Quaglino's.

When they returned to Melbourne, her parents didn't seem to know what to do with her. 'Why didn't they send me back to school?' she asked rhetorically. 'I think it was because I was a girl. A boy would have been sent back. But we never had that conversation.' She was sent to do a six-week course at the Bambi Smith Modelling School instead.

Jennifer Selway was much luckier. She attended Francis Holland, an academic London day school with an inspiring headmistress, Heather Brigstocke. 'She was extraordinary and very beautiful. The other person who was important to me was Antony Bridge, the school chaplain, who afterwards became the Dean of Guildford. He was a friend of Mrs Brigstocke. He was a late convert – he had been in the army, in military intelligence. So romantic. I just admired him so much. He was very appealing to young women – big, good-looking, and would talk about art and music and poetry in a way that was devastatingly lovely. He wasn't flirtatious, he didn't do anything awful, you just wanted to be with him.'

At a recent school reunion, she noticed almost every single one of her contemporaries had done *something*. 'There was always someone popping in to talk about careers,' she said. 'They were inspiring women like the *Observer* columnist Katharine Whitehorn and the journalist and author Marghanita Laski. Going to a school like that in London in the 1960s was as good as it was going to get in terms of the possibilities, the people. Andrew Loog Oldham, the manager of the Rolling Stones, had a flat up the road. The Stones were always hanging around, and the big girls used to hang around too.'

The subjects Jennifer loved best were English, drama and art. 'I did a lot of drama – played Hamlet once. I usually got to play boys, which I didn't mind. I liked directing, too. I designed and directed a weird version of *Alice Through the Looking Glass* for the drama competition. It was judged by the actor Edward Woodward and we won a prize.' In summer 1972, before she went to university, she took a gap-year job. 'It was for a giveaway magazine called *This Is London*, and it was my first proper job. It was distributed around hotels and edited by a formidable woman called Ella Glazer,' she said. 'I worked in a little office in the eaves in Bruton Street, just off Berkeley Square. There was me and a cockney secretary called Maxine, who was great and smoked all the time. Dave was the sub/production editor. He came in on press day. Simon sold advertising. I was sent off to write about terrible Soho cabaret shows. They were more genteel than Raymond Revuebar but tacky – girls with feathery headdresses and sparkly costumes, fan dances, some ghastly *duck à l'orange* and black cherry gateau dinner. I'd never been to anything like that in my life and I had to write about it. I had to say nice things because they advertised with us.'

Was it dire? I asked.

'No. It was so exciting. You're seventeen, going to all these nightclubs. You could name-drop L'Hirondelle in Swallow

Street and The Talk of The Town. I'd already thought about writing about the stage or films.' She worked there for eight months and thought, Well, yes, this is probably what I'll end up doing.

As I was to discover for myself, if you realise early that you're going to write for a living, no consideration need be given to alternative careers. This happened to Wendy Holden, growing up in the affluent London suburb of Pinner. 'I absolutely knew. I didn't have a choice. I have written something almost every day since I was able. Diaries. Poems. My first play when I was six.' This was *The Queen's Birthday Cake*, which won a competition to be staged at her school.

Wendy's family were encouraging: 'Whatever we wanted to do was fine as long as we were happy.' This was, of course, disadvantageous when she left journalism for books. 'As a novelist, I was cursed with a happy childhood.'

She read in a continuum. When any family photograph was taken, it was preceded by the mantra, 'Wendy, get your nose out of that book.' There's a small gap between that and her decision to become a journalist. She planned to be an author, but when she was eleven her school careers advisor said, 'You have to be something else first. Why don't you be a journalist?' Wendy wanted to know exactly what a journalist did and that teacher asked what paper her parents read. The *Daily Telegraph*, Wendy told her.

'Well, there's your example,' said the teacher. And, of course, all those years later when Wendy actually got a job on the *Daily Telegraph* her parents were thrilled because it was their newspaper for life.

This is a great case of someone at school pointing you in the right direction. That didn't always happen. As a child growing up in Devon, Hilary Bonner experienced several mortifications.

When you are a child, you long to be the same as everyone else and at her private junior school, where everyone else's father was a doctor or a lawyer, she was the butcher's daughter. Something else that marked her out was her height.

'I'm five foot eleven. I grew to be that height when I was thirteen. It was horrible, absolutely horrible. Particularly in north Devon, where people were shorter. There was one girl in my school taller than me – six foot one. She was considered to be a real freak. I was grateful she was there.'

Hilary's English teacher at Bideford's strictly Methodist Edgehill College was Miss Edwardes, known as Ted. She was diminutive to the point of being microscopic, whereas Hilary was not only nearly six foot but already showing signs of a worrying originality.

'She was the only English teacher I had,' said Hilary. 'She was always correcting everything I wrote. It seemed to me she had no time for my ability whatsoever.' Hilary, it appeared, needed cutting down to size. 'When I told her I wanted to be a journalist, she said, "Well, at least you're a tall girl. You'll be able to look over other people's heads."'

Hilary was later to find out that for a journalist being very tall was useful, as it meant she could see over the heads of everyone else in a media scrum.

So this is how it started for me. The City of London School for Girls, which I went to between 1959 and 1961, was situated back then in Carmelite Street. As was the *Daily Mail*. The classroom walls seemed to shake when the presses started rolling. My three best friends were Jewish, all Spurs fans because Spurs was 'the Jewish club'.

I had by then reached the Age of the Crush, and was obsessed with Lester Piggott, as well as enjoying various subcrushes on other jockeys. However, once Spurs entered my life,

Lester Piggott and company were upstaged, because jockeys were teeny-tiny and bow-legged whereas footballers were huge and manly and their legs absolutely stupendous.

Danny Blanchflower was the captain of Spurs, and a hugely glamorous and exciting figure. His Irish eyes smiled, his dark blond hair tumbled in an attractive forelock in the heat of battle, and he *wrote books*. Above all, he was leading Spurs to the Double, a feat never before achieved in the history of the universe: winning the League Championship and the FA Cup in a single season. He was my hero.

One Friday in May 1961, shortly after Spurs had beaten Leicester City 2–0 at Wembley, I was wandering along Tudor Street after school when I happened on a funny sort of building that seemed like a row of old houses joined together. On the wall beside one of its front doors was a glass-fronted case displaying a photo of Danny Blanchflower lifting the FA Cup. Copies of this photo could be bought for ten shillings if I applied within. I looked up to see what Within might be, and found I was outside the *Observer*. I had never heard of the *Observer* but from that moment on its masthead might have been printed in gold as far as I was concerned.

I had to have that photo. It was treasure. I had twelve shillings and threepence-halfpenny in my Post Office savings account, thanks mainly to my godmother Auntie Bessie, who had come good with a postal order at Christmas instead of the usual bath cubes. On Saturday morning, I appropriated my savings book and executed a secret mission to Loughton Post Office to withdraw a ten-shilling note. Sunday and most of Monday were, in consequence, agony. I did not know if the photo would still be available. I sat through lessons knowing that while I was clamped to my desk every Spurs fan in London would be applying Within and making away with their photos, hundreds and hundreds of them till there wasn't a single one left.

The final bell rang and off to Tudor Street I sprinted. The photo was still there in the glass case, and I tiptoed Within. It was dim in there, a sort of warren of little offices with a narrow staircase at the back, and very quiet. Were they all dead? By the door was a cubbyhole with a hatch, the sort at which you would buy your train ticket, but not a soul behind it. I waited, shuffling my feet and making 'ahem' noises. Eventually, a garden gnome-ish sort of person appeared. He took my money, and I had my photo of Danny Blanchflower.

I took the tube home with it in my satchel, peeking at it now and then and thinking that Fleet Street must be some kind of magic place. It was then that the idea was planted in my mind. One day I was going to work there myself.

Now came the obvious issue – that of finding a way in.

Chapter 4

First Rung on the Ladder

In December 1964, Valerie Grove got a lovely telegram. AWARDED EXHIBITION GIRTON COLLEGE CAMBRIDGE. 'A feeling that would be hard to beat, ever,' she wrote in the Virago book, *On the Death of a Parent*. The exhibition scholarship was worth £40 a year, which meant £10 off her termly bill. It was no surprise, really. She'd worked hard and was brilliant anyway. In O-level year at her grammar school, she had edited a magazine called *The Fifth Former* and wrote in it a little something about the Latin text of *De Bello Gallico*, Julius Caesar's account of the Gallic Wars – and it had found its way into the *Evening Standard*'s Londoner's Diary as 'The Last Word'.

She wouldn't be going up to Cambridge till the following October so she went to work on the *Shields Gazette*, her father's old paper. 'I got to know the whole business, including Pitman's shorthand,' she said. 'I just loved it. The Women's Page needed an editor so they handed it to me at eighteen. The pay was seven guineas a week including five shillings per A-level.' The editor was Bill Wood, 'a lovely old school gentleman editor'. Doug Smith, her father, wrote to him, asking how she was getting on. Mr Wood wrote back:

'Valerie has taken to journalism like a duck to water. I only have to tell her something once and she does it.'

She was glowing. 'Lovely, lovely times,' she said. 'Cambridge seemed like, "Oh, god." Something I didn't want to do.'

She got a stern talking-to by Mr Wood and her dad. 'You'll always regret it if you don't go,' they said, so off she went to Cambridge.

Valerie's father had always wanted to get to Fleet Street. In particular he wanted to work for the *Evening Standard* where his best friend Angus McGill, another alumnus of the *Shields Gazette*, had a page called 'Mainly For Men'. 'In 1960 my Pa went to the *Standard* and an idiot editor called Percy Something turned him down,' said Valerie. 'The *Evening News* took him on instead. In 1967, when I was on the student paper, *Varsity*, everyone was thinking of summer vac jobs, so I was vaguely thinking of the *News*. Two of my Varsity colleagues, Peter Cole and Simon Hoggart, who'd both worked on newspapers before coming up, had similar ideas. Peter moved first, and he immediately got taken on by the *Evening News* – which made me rather cross and galvanised me into trying for the *Standard*. As I sat there in his office, Charles Wintour carefully read the *Varsity* interview I'd brought along, about Gerald Scarfe [the cartoonist and illustrator], and said coolly: "Very good". That got me a summer job on the "Londoner's Diary". I absolutely adored life on the Diary. At the end of summer, Charles said I could come back the following year – which I did. And I stayed for eighteen years.'

It's impossible not to feel a batsqueak of regret that I never did any formal training before entering Fleet Street – the official way in, as Valerie took, via local and regional papers. I've missed out, I realise, on that part of your career when you made lifelong friends, perfected your shorthand in a Plymouth Portakabin (like Emma Lee-Potter), and wrote wedding reports ('Ghastly,' said Tina Moran. 'I thought, is this actually what I signed up for? But at least it taught me how to spell fuchsia'). You might find love. Valerie met her first husband,

David Jenkins, on the *Shields Gazette*, and Wendy Holden was nineteen and on the *Middlesex Chronicle* in Hounslow when she found her forever husband, Chris Taylor. You became initiated into the horrors of doorstepping – of which more later – and the mysteries of Monday morning phone calls to the fire brigade (arson), the police (break-ins and flashers), the undertakers in the towns and villages ('Hi! Who's died this week?'). This was it – your foot on the first rung of the ladder.

You also lived away from home for the first time. Having always enjoyed writing, Louise Court decided she wanted to follow her father Monty into journalism. 'He really wanted me to be a journalist too, because it was one of the few professions, in the late 1970s, where you could get equal pay,' she remembered. 'But as soon as he said he wanted me to, being a typical teenager, I rebelled and thought, What do I want to do that for?, and decided I wanted to be a teacher instead. Which would mean going to university, whereas in those days you didn't need a degree to be a journalist. My brother, Nick, who was four years older than me, left school after A-levels to do the National Council for the Training of Journalists course at Harlow, and was already working on the *Surrey Comet* at Kingston.

'So we reached a compromise: I would do the same pre-entry course as Nick's, and if I liked it I'd carry on, and if I didn't I'd go to university. My dad knew what he was doing! I loved it!'

Part of the joy was Mrs Poole. 'I got very lucky, living with the best landlady in Harlow,' she recalled. 'I had friends who had really horrible landladies, really horrible digs with families who only did it because they had to, to make ends meet, whereas Mrs Poole had a very nice detached five-bedroomed house and I was totally spoiled.

'Normally she only took people for a term, but we got on so well she let me stay for a year. I could ask my friends round, and she'd cook for them – and she was a great cook; it was French cuisine. One night someone came to dinner with her, an old lady who at one point rolled her sleeve up. Her arm had numbers tattooed on it. I didn't know what it was. Mrs Poole said to her friend, "Tell Louise about it." I was gobsmacked, because I suppose I hadn't thought there were any survivors. I didn't know what to say. I wish I'd asked her more. As a wannabe journalist, I should have composed myself and come out with something sensible.'

Whenever she watches programmes on the Holocaust, she always thinks of that old lady with the numbers tattooed on her arm: 'Very petite, very well-groomed.'

All this happened towards the end of the 1970s, by which time the NCTJ courses were well established; Emma Lee-Potter, Wendy Holden and Tina Moran also graduated that way. But how, in the middle of the 1960s, did you get into journalism if your school was no help and your family hadn't a clue? An obvious solution was to ask a local paper if they would take you on. This was something tried by Hilary Bonner, who started sending letters in her O-level year. 'All over the country. Hundreds of letters. I would come home from school and Mum would say, "There's two more letters for you. Don't go getting in a bad mood, now."

'They all said the same thing: "Unfortunately, our complement is to the full." Why not just say, "Unfortunately, we have a full complement?"

'There was no internet to help you back then. My parents were wonderful, but they didn't know how. My school was hopeless. Miss Richards, known as Dick – we were very innocent – was in charge of careers. She wore a gown. When the time came for the careers talk, she went through all the options then said, "If any of you girls is interested in anything else, come up and see me afterwards and I'll do what I can to find out."'

Up Hilary trotted. 'Please, Miss Richards, I want to be a journalist.'

Miss Richards looked at her in horror. 'Don't be ridiculous, girl. You know perfectly well you can go to university if you try.'

It's worth noting here that, for a girl in that era, going to university was a big thing. Some ten years later, Tina Moran, then a day girl at the Bristol-based school Redmaids, was offered much the same advice. 'We had career days. Teaching, nursing, the police, the forces, shop management – that was pretty much it. I was useless at maths and good at English – I enjoyed writing stories. But my real education was on the road with my father. The school wanted me to go to university. I told them I didn't see the point of learning Shakespeare when all I wanted to do was report for newspapers.'

Even then, Tina had much the same problem as had Hilary – how to find a way in. 'It was only because Mum happened to be listening to the radio one day when it mentioned the National Council for the Training of Journalists scheme,' Tina said. 'Mum took down the details. Sorted.'

Late in 1960, in Australia, her birthplace, a similar element of chance provided Scarth Flett with an opening. After she had finished her six-week course at the Bambi Smith Modelling School, she studied for a Certificate of Art covering advertising, fashion and fabric printing at the Caulfield Technical School. 'I was quite good but not exceptional. But I'd been good at English at school. Well, my father said I was good at composition. I thought of being a journalist. But I couldn't see a way in.'

She took a Christmas job at Myers, a sort of Australian John Lewis, fibbing her way to a post selling skirts and blouses in American Separates by claiming she wanted to be a trainee buyer. Otherwise she would have been made to languish in Kitchen Utensils. 'One day, my mother had a row with my father and wouldn't go to a party with him. She was so horrible to him. So my dad took me instead.'

At the party, Scarth was introduced to Norma Ferris, women's editor of a Melbourne-based weekly paper called *Truth*, and told her she wanted to be a journalist.

'Oh, I need some help,' said Norma Ferris. 'Why don't you come and work for me?'

But what was Hilary going to do? Having learned that she could not take a degree in English because entry requirements included O-level Latin, which she did not have, she had applied to study fine arts. When the course turned out to be history of art-based rather than practical, she had begun to feel very unenthusiastic and cancelled her UCCA form.

Here, again, luck played a part. The Mirror Group had just bought up six West Country papers in order to bring on trainees. It was a serious venture, for graduates and school leavers. Graduates trained for two years on a local paper, school leavers for three. The scheme, based in Plymouth, included the *Sunday Independent*, one of the local papers to which Hilary had written. One day a letter from its editor arrived for her, enclosing an application form.

'I decided that no one was taking any notice of me so I had written back this embarrassing letter, Monty Pythonesque, trying to be funny,' said Hilary. 'It clearly caught someone's eye. I got a holding letter and then, out of the blue, I got a letter telling me I'd been selected for interview. I couldn't believe it. I'd had nothing but noes, and now, all of a sudden, I'd been invited to go for an interview in London.'

The day arrived. They all went – Mum, Dad, Hilary and her boyfriend. 'Being a control freak, I'd booked us into some dire hotel in Paddington,' she said. 'I was up at five. I got everybody to the *Mirror* building at 8.30 for a ten o'clock interview. We sat in a café. I couldn't stand it. I couldn't wait. I managed to hold off long enough to get to the *Mirror* building at 9.30.'

It was daunting. Everybody else there seemed to be Oxbridge, or Old Etonian, or came from families connected with journalism. She was the butcher's daughter. She went up to the ninth-floor boardroom and stood there gulping at the long mahogany table and leather-bound blotters. There she was greeted by a man wearing the Mirror Group executive uniform of black suit, white shirt and red braces. This was A. Norman Walker, Director of Training. He was smoking a large cigar. What followed was eight minutes of conversation remembered as if it were yesterday.

'You're early,' A. Norman Walker observed.

'I'm ever so sorry,' said Hilary. 'I couldn't wait.'

'Which one are you? Ah yeee-s. You're the Bideford girl. I go there on holiday.'

He named the hotel at which he had stayed, and asked if Hilary knew it. 'Oh yes,' said Hilary. 'My dad sends them their meat.'

'Didn't it burn down a year ago?'

'Yes. People in Bideford don't think it was quite what it seemed.'

'Really? Yes, I'd heard something like that.'

'Oh yes,' she said. 'They say locally it was an insurance job.'

Which was, Hilary realised later, a classic journalist's ploy – prise open the interviewee with a question and wait for the beans to spill out. Next, the candidates were shown two newsreel clips, one of a shipwreck, the other of the model Jean Shrimpton being turned away from Melbourne racecourse for being improperly dressed. These had to be written up in *Mirror* style. Hilary sat next to a mature-looking man who made immaculate shorthand notes. 'I took against him,' she recalled. 'He looked so together.' The afternoon proved to be even more daunting: an interview panel, consisting of Michael Christiansen, editor of the *Sunday Mirror*, Lee Howard, editor of the *Daily Mirror*, a psychiatrist and the head of HR. And so back to the awful hotel for a second, nerve-racking night before what might turn out to be the most significant, or disappointing, day of her life. Had she passed her English A-level? Had she been accepted?

The family set off back to Bideford in the morning. When they arrived, the envelope containing her A-level results was on the doormat. She had taken English, history and art and passed all three, but who cared about history and art? English was the one that mattered. But what if she'd got this far only for the *Mirror* to turn her down?

Then the phone rang.

'It's for you,' called her mother.

It was a telegram, which back then would be read out to you by the operator.

```
FROM A NORMAN WALKER STOP DELIGHTED OFFER YOU
PLACE DAILY MIRROR TRAINING SCHEME STOP SUBJECT
TO A LEVEL ENGLISH STOP CONGRATULATIONS STOP
```

Hilary and her boyfriend jumped up and down in the hall. She was ecstatic. It was a dream come true, it was the miracle!

She made a point of telling Miss Edwardes, the English teacher who had mocked her for being tall. 'I think she was slightly dumbfounded,' said Hilary. 'She didn't allow herself to be impressed. Maybe she might have been if it was the *Guardian* that had offered me a training place, but not the *Mirror*.'

Scarth Flett started her job on *Truth* on 9 January 1961. She was a cadet, Australia's version of the trainee journalist. *Truth* specialised in crime and sport. It was like the *News of the World.* 'Only common people read it!' said her mother. That, said Scarth, wasn't quite the case. Everybody read it. They just pretended they never bought it. 'They'd say, "Oh, I just happened to see it when my cleaning lady left it in the laundry."'

The *Truth* newsroom was pretty much a female-free zone. 'I was nineteen. There were no women news reporters, no women there except Norma, and secretaries of course – all older than me,' said Scarth. 'Norma was a lovely woman, in her forties, very attractive. But I hadn't been there very long when she got chicken pox. For a few weeks, I had four pages of Women's Truth to do on my own. It was a bit tough. But all the blokes there were lovely, from the head of the composing room to the editor. They all helped me. I was in my element.'

Not for long. Fairfax Ltd, owner of *Truth*, were bought out by Rupert Murdoch's News Limited. There was a change of management. Scarth was just told, 'The management doesn't want any cadets,' and she was sacked.

'A very nice PR agency offered me a job and I was there for four months. Four miserable months. It wasn't the agency's fault. I just couldn't bear being a PR. That middle person! Neither fish nor fowl. I wasn't the journalist and I wasn't the client. I was just the mug who'd arranged everything. Oh, I hated it.'

Another fortuitous meeting at a party resulted in her being rescued again. Freda Irvine edited the Melbourne edition of Australian *Woman's Weekly*. 'I'd often met her at events when I was on *Truth*. She was a much older woman, and turned out to be a great supporter. She asked me how I was getting on, and I told her about being let go by *Truth* and having to work in PR. Freda offered me a job, and I joined *Woman's Weekly* in May 1962.'

The shock of one knockback suffered by Louise Court remains with her now. While she was at Harlow, she was given a week's work experience at the *Surrey Mirror*, 'where I got the impression that there could be a job if I did okay. I was nervous but the paper came out at the end of the week, and I had lots of by-lines. On the Friday afternoon, I had my assessment.'

'I'm sorry, Louise,' she was told. 'We only take high-flyers.'

'What a terrible, mean thing to say to a nineteen-year-old,' said Louise. 'There's plenty of ways of saying that I wasn't right which could be helpful without being cruel. They could have suggested ways I could improve.

'I try to be a positive person because if you live with my father you aren't allowed to sit and feel sorry for yourself, but I was really upset. I sat there trying not to cry. I was in shock. I had to come out and speak to other people asking, "Oh, what happened?"'

After Louise went home, her father,who was by then racing editor of the *Sunday Mirror*, interrupted his coverage of a race meeting in Goodwood to call from a phone box. 'How did it go?' he asked, and when she poured her heart out to him, he punched the glass of the phone box because he was so angry.

There is a satisfying pay-off to this because many years later, when Louise was Editor of *Cosmopolitan*, she found herself at a Buckingham Palace reception and part of a small group selected to meet the Queen. I wonder if this counts as being a high-flyer now? she thought.

Bouncing back from mini-crises and setbacks was, of course, an essential part of learning to become a journalist. This was a lesson Hilary was taught early on. When she arrived in Plymouth to start training, she found a grim contrast with life at home. There was no Mrs Poole. She had to share a house with three other girls. There were various boyfriends coming and going, and not leaving, and sitting in front of the fire, spitting at their boots to polish them. She was overcome with homesickness. She rang in sick, fled to Bideford and told her parents she wasn't going back.

Her dad was sympathetic: 'Okay, just stay here with us,' he said. Her mum was no-nonsense: 'Oh no you don't. All your life you've wanted to do this.'

As for A. Norman Walker, he was furious. 'What are you doing?' he bawled. 'You don't just go home because you've got a cold.'

Given her second chance, Hilary went on to her first posting as a proper reporter. Her impression of the *Torquay Times* was that it was considerably overstaffed. 'In those days at the *Mirror*, nobody was sacked, nobody changed jobs,' she said. 'The *Torquay Times* kept all the senior staff – editor, deputy editor, two subs, two or three senior reporters, three or four photographers – but was shipping in all these trainees. And this was a weekly paper. They were mainly chaps and they all wore dark suits, and they'd been there for ever and would tell you how they were king of the castle and had turned down jobs on Fleet Street etc. Yeah, yeah, course you did. We were all these bright young things bouncing about. We were known as the Plymouth Brethren.'

Hilary was given one of the lowliest jobs, that of the children's column, which she had to write under the name of Uncle Bob. Children would enrol – or their mothers would do it for them – in Uncle Bob's Club, giving details such as the date of their birthday, their hobbies and where they went to school. Each week a child would be picked out to be interviewed. 'We had this huge ledger, handwritten and full of mistakes, in the reporters' room, which got filled in every week with what was going on. You phoned up Child of the Week to tell them they'd been chosen, then knocked on their door. "I'm Uncle Bob's assistant." (Well, I couldn't pass as Uncle Bob, could I?) It was one of the most stressful jobs I've ever done. All those handwritten entries. Is that an "a"? Is that an "e"? It's amazing what you can say about people and get away with it, but get their names wrong and you're dead.'

Another thing you learned on a local paper was that just because a huge national event happened right before your eyes, it didn't mean that you had a scoop.

The Plymouth Brethren had to live in the town, and Hilary had a bedsit in Braddons Hill West. 'It was kind of like the Earls Court of Torquay. One day there was quite a kerfuffle in the area. Helicopters overhead, emergency vehicles, police vans racing through town. Bruce Reynolds, one of the Great Train Robbers, had been found to be living incognito in Torquay. Not just in Torquay, but in Braddons Hill West. We knew him because he was always washing his car. He looked ordinary. Like everybody else.'

Hilary would not be getting a front-page splash, though. It wasn't local news, and the next edition of the *Torquay Times* didn't mention it at all.

The disappointment at the *Surrey Mirror* left Louise Court hunting around for a first job. 'I didn't want to move from being close to London because my whole social life was there. I had been offered one on the *South London Press*, but for some reason best known to myself I turned it down. It was a great paper. I was a wimp. At that point, I couldn't drive and I didn't like the thought of traipsing back from council meetings at midnight all across South London, struggling to get home. So I went to the *East Grinstead Courier* in Sussex. Which was *delightful*. Just wonderful. You had your patch of villages. You had to go and have tea with the vicars. Everyone was just so lovely. I sat next to a girl called Catherine Utley, whose father was T.E. Utley, deputy editor and leader writer of the *Telegraph*. He used to write some of Margaret Thatcher's speeches.

'She was on holiday when I joined, and while she was away all I heard was Catherine this, Catherine that. Everybody loved her. I was quite left-wing, and I thought, Ooh, I'm going to hate her. Meanwhile, she thought she was going to hate me because I'd be some sort of punk rocker type. We were totally different but we became really, really good friends.

'By this time I'd learnt to drive, invaluable for a local news-paper reporter, and there were old, dark green newspaper vans you had to use to cover meetings and interviews, with a row of keys in the office, and you'd say which car park in town you were taking it from, or where you'd left it: "I'm taking it from the cattle market car park," or, "I parked it in the high street." Every Thursday, Cath and I had to drive into Tunbridge Wells for shorthand lessons, and because we were so different but got on like a house on fire we *never* discussed politics. One thing we shared was a love of musicals and we'd career around in this van singing songs from *My Fair Lady*, and hymns.

'I started off by doing the wedding write-ups. They were easy because you had a photo, and someone would have filled in a form. The forms had a space for everything, such as "Bride wore . . . (a white organza frock with a lily of the valley bouquet)"; "She was the daughter of . . . (blah blah blah)"; "Bridesmaids wore . . . (it was the 1980s, so there was a lot of apricot going on)".'

Next came the Monday morning calls to the police, fire brigade and the undertakers. 'Sometimes you'd have tragic stories such as the death of a child. Sometimes the undertaker would say, "This could be of interest," if it was a local coun-cillor, for instance. Then you'd have to phone up relatives, and that taught me you could ask anybody anything as long as you did it politely, sensitively and with respect. Phoning from a local paper, you would say to the grieving widow or the bereaved parent, "I'm sorry for your loss – is there anything you'd like to tell me about, pay tribute?"

'Some people would be really cross. "How dare you phone at a time like this!" Other people would welcome the call. Their nearest and dearest would keep off the subject for fear of upsetting them, and they just wanted to talk.'

Then came the excitement of your first by-line. Released from the travails of Uncle Bob, Hilary Bonner went into general reporting and hit the front page of the *Torquay Times* with 'Road Chaos on the Outskirts of Torquay. SHIPHAY RESIDENTS UP IN ARMS'. Louise, meanwhile, was given a Village Page that she had to fill every week.

'First it was the Felbridge page and then I got promoted to Copthorne, Crawley Down and Turners Hill. We had Father Fred, the priest at Crawley Down, a very large, colourful, avuncular man. He had an organ in his front room that he used to play. Alex, the Turners Hill vicar, was really nice. Cup of tea, give you some eggs, you'd be shown the top of the bell tower. It was such fun. Then at the weekend I'd be in London, living a very urban life, going to gigs like Joy Division, The Cure, Siouxsie and the Banshees, The Fall, it was really exciting.

'There was an office dog owned by the chief photographer (known as Chiefie), called Bung. Bung would come and lie under your desk and you'd end up stroking him, and he'd howl, *awooooo!* You weren't meant to pay any attention to him – the editor disapproved – but he'd grass you up by caterwauling when you were trying to type copy at the same time.

'The paper was near Saint Hill, UK headquarters of the Scientologists. They'd come in with stories and look at you really intensely. They were behind lots of community initiatives but were very controversial in the town and the paper was cautious about covering them.

'I just had the best time there. Made friends, had fun. It was just so different from my life in London. You'd go to a country pub, see people on farms. But I knew it wasn't going to be for life. You find yourself thinking, It's the third time I've done the flower show, and that's when you realise you've been there too long.

'I passed my exams in 1981, so then I became a senior reporter. It was inspiring because you're looking at your next step, what you're going to do, and because my social life was so much about London I didn't want to work on a provincial/ evening paper. The *Croydon Advertiser* was a bigger paper, which meant more money. I went on to become chief reporter on the *Coulsdon & Purley Advertiser*.'

Along the way, she broke into Fleet Street through proving her worth on trial shifts at the *Sunday Express*. To get these, she had to endure an interview with its editor John Junor, a famous Fleet Street ogre.

'I probably dressed really inappropriately for the interview,' she said. 'I had a summer dress on. I was very into vintage – spent all my Saturdays combing jumble sales etc. – so it was very 1950s-style. White with pink flowers, and a full skirt. It wasn't what anyone was wearing into the office. And I had this basket, not a briefcase. There was a logic to it. It was for my cuttings book – a scrapbook with examples of work I'd had published.'

'Louise, are you going for a picnic?' he said.

'No,' she replied. 'I'm coming to see you about a job.' But he was very nice.

Was a little bit of nepotism involved? I asked.

'Well – my dad knew him.'

It was a well-known maxim in journalism that you used what you'd got. On the other hand, you might not only have lacked formal training and useful connections, but been so hopelessly failed by your education that you had left with no idea what to do at all. How on earth did you get to Fleet Street if you were chucked out of school?

The photographer's daughter Clare Arron grew up in middle-class Hale, near Altrincham in Cheshire, and went to an all-girls grammar school which, at sixteen, she was invited to stop gracing with her presence. It was, she said, the best thing that could have happened.

'My brother was encouraged at home but I was ignored,' she said. 'I passed two O-levels, and I was told I could either stay down a year or leave. I couldn't stay in that building any longer. I just sat there wanting to leave, waiting for it to end. So then I went to the local college for thick people. It opened my eyes to people who didn't read the *Daily Telegraph*. I met nice, interesting people who were often in the same boat, written off. It was a place where they asked, "What are you interested in?"'

In her first year she did communications studies, which would now be media studies. It was set up by a lecturer called Kevin Cahill, who 'really had ideas' and went on to be CEO of Red Nose Day. She sat her A-levels, and was taught photography. 'It was a revelation. I loved it. They encouraged me like mad, helped me think about what to do next.'

This was to enrol at the Polytechnic of Central London. 'It was an amazing place to be, quite a cultural shock for someone from Hale. It was the late 1970s and Sloane Square was full of all those punks. My course was Film and Photographic Arts. It was a bit shambolic. I thought I was going to do documentary films, but in a funny way I probably made the decision to become a photographer in my last year. It wasn't a course for supporting people to go into the media, but after two years I was desperate to get to work. I'm not a loner but I'm quite single-minded. That work appealed.'

She got a job at the *South London Press* in Streatham. It was the early 1980s by then, and an obscure football club in SW19 called Wimbledon had recently begun its rise from the oubliette of non-League to the sunlit uplands of the First Division. Wimbledon FC was not a bit like its genteel namesake, the All England Lawn Tennis Club. Its stadium was a dump called Plough Lane, its offices were two Portakabins in a mud-caked yard, and its players were known as the Crazy Gang; they revelled in being the naughtiest boys in the game, playing up to their reputation for on-pitch thuggery and sometimes life-threatening practical jokes. They had a charming, very bright manager, Dave Bassett, who, when I went to interview him at the club's training ground – a couple of unkempt playing fields out in the sticks – would steer me away from the changing room and into a copse so I wouldn't get flashed at. They were also responsible for the moment Clare knew she would not stay in newspaper photography for ever.

'I went to photograph a couple of their new players. I was wearing pale blue trousers with a denim shirt. When I bent down, one of them made a comment about being able to see down my shirt – a disgusting comment about tits. I said nothing. But I thought, Oh, fuck this, I'm not going to do this all my life, and told the editor I was going to go freelance.'

The first paper she sold a picture to was the *Guardian*. 'It was of the most tattooed man in Britain. Head to foot. He had pants on and I had no idea what was under there but everywhere else was completely tattooed.'

Mary Kenny was the same age as Clare when, to cap her childhood as the *enfant terrible*, the Loreto Convent, Dublin, washed its hands of her. 'You must now sink or swim by your own efforts,' declared Mother Annunciata. 'It will be your choice.'

'Irish education in the 1950s was very conformist,' Mary told me, 'and I was disruptive. I sometimes wonder if I had ADHD. If I'd gone to an imaginative school it might have been different. But I think I was bold and difficult . . . at the same time, I do regret not having a formal education. Now that I'm old and decrepit I'm kind of chippy about it. But then again – if you know about Adler's Theory of the inferiority complex – it's because we feel inferior that we strive.'

She got a job as a waitress, and then as a typist-secretary. Then, at nineteen, she applied to be an au pair in Paris. Looking back, she suspected a streak of masochism had gone into her choice. Why else pick a family with seven children (admittedly this was from an advert she put in *La Croix*, the Catholic paper, and many of the families were large)? She had no idea about managing a household. Her predecessor had been a German girl. 'I never heard the end of how wonderful Gisela had been,' she said. 'The mistress followed me around as I hoovered saying, "*Mademoiselle, il faut tout déplacer!*"' She can still hear the voice. She learned that it was considered decadent to read novels in the afternoon. If she had finished the housework, she was given some sewing to do.

What astonished her was the formality of French life, even at the most domestic level. Ireland, she said, would be seen, at this time, as repressive and authoritarian, but paradoxically, in actual lifestyle, it was quite laid-back. 'At fifteen or sixteen, I wandered around Dublin alone at all hours of the day and night. Life was safe. In France, for the first time, I learned the word (and concept, which I'd never heard before) of rape: "*Mademoiselle, vous serez violée!*" I kept being told.'

Eventually, the French family decided they wanted another Gisela and kicked her out. They didn't just cast her into the street, but absolved their guilt by delivering her to a convent in Paris near the Pont d'Alma. French convents, then, doubled up as digs for young girls, to protect them from the snares of wicked city life. In spite of the restrictions, Mary recalled, it seemed to be all great larks – there was a heavenly garden and the food was good because even French nuns shared the national love of gastronomy.

What followed was a series of non-jobs. One was as companion to an eccentric old lady, a retired diplomat. 'She took me around a bit to her soirees, and tried to impart worldly wisdom to me, such as what the correct procedure is when the wife meets the mistress on a social occasion.' Next came a summer in the Pyrenees, teaching English to nuns, followed by a job with the Quinns, 'an adorable American couple living in Montparnasse, babysitting and taking their children to school and back. I had a maid's room, in a separate annexe where the toilet was unspeakable.'

In *Something of Myself and Others*, Mary writes of absorbing the lesson that journalism is often about opportunity and timing. In the 1960s, people often got into journalism by haunting the bars and pubs where newspapermen drank, in the hope of getting a bit of freelance work, and after returning to Paris Mary hung out in The Falstaff and Le Montparnasse with two Irish journalists, Joe Carroll and Peter Lennon; Lennon later directed the documentary film about Ireland's Easter Rising, *Rocky Road to Dublin*. By now, she had observed a lot about French life, and sent an article about their obsession with food to the *Dublin Evening Press* on spec. They published it and paid her three guineas. She had got her break. Drifting on to London, she kept up the supply of freelance pieces while doing a series of non-jobs that included secretarial work for the novelist Edna O'Brien. She was supposed to deal with her letters, but mainly they talked about men over cakes and burgundy, 'which I thought was terribly sophisticated'. Finally, she arrived at the *Guardian*, where she worked as secretary to its London editor, Gerard Fay. Discovering her ambition to be a full-time journalist, he advised her to apply to Charles Wintour, editor of the *Evening Standard*.

'I wormed my way into Fleet Street through a mixture of chutzpah, luck and timing,' said Mary. 'I had accrued quite a lot of cuttings by then and wrote a very bold letter to Charles Wintour and he offered me an interview. I actually turned down the first job he offered as I didn't think it was grand enough for me . . . but having done all sorts of temping office jobs and a stint in a cuttings agency from which I was fired for not being much good, I went back to Wintour.'

'Why should I hire you, Miss Kenny?' he asked.

'You'll never know what you've missed if you don't,' said Mary. He took her on immediately.

Chapter 5

Making Mayonnaise with Kingsley Amis

The *Daily Telegraph* was not quite as posh as *The Times*, but much more interesting. The front page was full of little one-paragraph items of news jammed in any old place around the main stories, so you'd be reading about the Duke and Duchess of Kent's tour of Papua New Guinea and suddenly in would bounce MAN STRUCK BY PROPELLER. I skipped the women's page (How to make a New Year's Nightie from a sales remnant), pored over Forthcoming Marriages because it often featured people I'd been at school with, then went on to the sex page. This was where all the juiciest divorce cases were reported. You could locate it straight away because the headlines contained words such as 'Don Juan playboy', 'Actress' and 'Yacht', with all sorts of delicious subheadings: 'Did not like pink pants'; 'Home used as base for bachelor ways'; 'Continental mentality'.

But, most of all, the *Daily Telegraph* had been the cement in my relationship with my father, the paper over which he and I had bent our heads together in the mornings, because we both loved sport, and the *Telegraph* reported it in wads, from soccer to squash rackets to ladies' cricket (England Women Bat Briskly). When I was ten, on my first trip to France and dreadfully homesick, he sent copies by air mail to soothe my aching soul. At fourteen and at boarding school, convinced the Cuban Crisis signalled the imminent end of the world, I wrote home forlornly and received by return of post the *Telegraph* to comfort me.

Then later I only read it when I was home for the vacation. I was a bit reluctant to be seen with it at university, because it was 1968, the year of sit-ins, acid trips and protest songs, and we all went round brandishing our worthy *Guardians*. But the *Telegraph* was my secret favourite and that Christmas, 1968, newly returned from Bristol, almost the first thing I did was to plonk myself on the sofa and spread it out for a good, long session in *Daily Telegraph*-land.

Our living room was furnished with a three-piece suite in turquoise Dralon, a grand piano that no one played but was a useful repository for the drinks tray, the wingback chair that my father fell asleep in, and a squat upholstered box in which my mother stored her copies of *Woman's Journal* and *The Lady*. It was known as the pouffe. I loved being home, in small doses, and the *Telegraph* magazine was stuffed with advertisements that were my family's comfy, suburban way of life writ large: swanky televisions, giant fridges, big cars, Benson & Hedges Pure Gold cigarettes (with Special Filter). On our coffee table was a Ronson cigarette lighter similar to the one pictured in the magazine, set in a sort of knobbly kneecap-shaped lump of onyx. And page after page featured bottles. Sherry and gin, Pimm's No. 1 Cup, brandy and red burgundy (Full of Honest Everyday Good Living), just like the ones in our family dining room that crowded on the sideboard like a public lined up on the quay to wave the troops off to war. I flipped through this montage of middle-class consumption and was about to place it in the pouffe when a large box paragraph caught my eye:

WHO WILL BE THE YOUNG WRITER OF THE YEAR?
A bronze specially designed by the eminent sculptor Eduardo Paolozzi will be the leading award in a major competition for young writers launched by the *Daily Telegraph* Magazine in co-operation with Pergamon Press. Anyone living in Britain, under

the age of 24, is eligible for the Young Writer of the Year competition, which is designed to encourage new talent to add to the lustre of British writing in the year ahead.

The object of the exercise was to write an essay 'under a loose heading of Britain Today' and no end of prizes would be showered on the winner – a huge cheque, the Paolozzi sculpture, a free trip to Canada and, the ultimate, a job on the *Telegraph* magazine.

At that point my career plan was very defined in one way, but on the airy-fairy side in almost every other. The defined part was a negative; my mother wanted me to join the family business empire, in lieu of the son of which fate had deprived her. My father's group of companies specialised in the manufacture and hire of mining equipment, a commodity about which I knew nothing and cared less, so I was not going to do that under any circumstances. I was going to be a major novelist. Obviously, though, I would have to support myself on my way to being the new Evelyn Waugh and the best way to do this would be with journalism. In Fleet Street, where I had wanted to work since practically for ever. Winning this competition would be my way in.

The closing date for entries was near – I had to be quick. This was probably fortuitous because it usually comes out better if you write as though your life depends on it and don't have time to agonise. As the theme was Britain Today, I just described student life. Well, that was my Today; aged twenty, soon to take my finals, living with my boyfriend in the stereotypical student flat heated by a paraffin stove and furnished with unspeakable sanitary ware.

A friend was faced with the decision whether or not to have an abortion; I wrote about that, and about a gay friend, and the usual bed-hopping, and lectures, and thwarted pursuits

78

of love. Thinking the judges would be looking for something edgy, I sprinkled the story with mentions of acid and morning glory seeds. I had no idea what morning glory seeds were but a slightly mad and rackety friend called Dottie told me they were hallucinogenic. I'd also tried LSD once. Jack, my boyfriend, obtained two lysergic acid-impregnated sugar lumps from someone called Jesus Graham, so-called because of his Son-of-God hairdo. I crunched on mine, wondering if this was a big mistake and horrible creatures would swirl up from the depths of my subconscious. Then I waited, but nothing happened. This was a great relief, and I went to bed. Jack didn't come back till midday the next day. He'd had a proper trip but a very nice one. The highlight was gazing in the window of the baker's in Princess Victoria Street, where he laughed at some cakes.

I posted off my entry, and then forgot about it. The only prize I had ever won was a five-shilling postal order for a drawing of a pony in *Riding* magazine at thirteen. When, in April, the *Daily Telegraph* called to say, hey presto, my entry was the winner, it didn't seem real. A lot of that was due to my father's reaction – or, rather, non-reaction. The days when he and I had bonded over the *Telegraph* were long gone. He was wrapped up in his own life as local bigwig and owner of several companies, and I was twenty, an adult woman, off his hands. Writing and books just weren't part of his world and it didn't occur to him to make a big fuss of me. It never occurred to me, either, that he might have done. I suspect, though, that somewhere deep down I desperately wanted his approval, and not receiving it has left me with the feeling that nothing I achieve is very important.

My mother was thrilled, of course. Like most mothers – myself included – she loved having a child's achievement to boast about to her friends, and not only was I about to be showered with all those wonderful prizes, there was going to be an article about me in the magazine. To which end, I would be interviewed by Kingsley Amis. I was nearly as excited about this as I was about the job offer. Kingsley Amis would be the first famous person I'd met, if I discounted Wilfred Pickles. In 1965, Wilfred Pickles had visited our home town to record an episode of *Have a Go*. This was a BBC radio game show that gave away money prizes, and Mr Pickles was its genial, Yorkshire-born-and-bred host. After the recording, he was to be entertained in The Roebuck, Buckhurst Hill, by my father in his role as chairman of the local council. My mother and I were introduced to Mr Pickles and Mummy babbled, 'Have a go! Have a go!' at him, complete with peals of nervous laughter. Mr Pickles definitely gritted his teeth at us. He was probably tired, because he was old, but I did wish he'd smiled at us because it would have made my mother happy. I prayed I wouldn't be such a flop with Kingsley Amis.

Come the day of the interview, I travelled from Bristol. The *Telegraph*'s photographer met me at Paddington, handily placed for the short drive to Maida Vale, where we would collect Kingsley Amis and be whisked off to lunch at the French Horn in Sonning.

The photographer was tall with untidy curls and a slightly harassed expression, and skinny except for enormous shoulders which he must have developed heaving around all those camera bags full of valuable equipment. His car was a Citroën saloon, the one with slanted headlights, a long bonnet and a curved front bumper that made it look as though it was grimacing. I sat in the back, which was scattered with children's toys. We reached Maida Vale. The photographer left me in the car while he walked up the road and knocked on Kingsley Amis's front door.

The photographer spent ages yakking to the person who answered it, and when he came back gestured to me to wind down the window. He rested one hand on the car roof and poked his head in.

'He isn't there.'

It turned out Kingsley Amis had moved to Barnet. I sat in the car watching the world turn while the photographer sloped off to find a telephone box to phone the *Telegraph* to explain to them about this disaster and then there was all the waiting around while the *Telegraph* tracked down Kingsley Amis's new address and phone number, and rang him.

And so to Barnet. Kingsley Amis's new house was very grand. It stood in grounds. The front door was painted white, and over it was a Georgian fanlight like a raised eyebrow. I couldn't see much of the interior, but just knew it would be the height of style and desirability. This was not the kind of household that contained a pouffe.

Kingsley Amis joined me in the Citroën, studiedly unruffled of demeanour. What a challenge. I was trapped in the back of a car with one of the pre-eminent novelists of post-war Britain, and faced with having to make insouciant conversation from Hertfordshire to Berkshire. At first, I was reluctant to open my mouth, in case I turned into my mother and shrieked, 'Lucky Jim! Lucky Jim!' at him. What on earth were we going to talk about? Obviously he hadn't read my winning essay because it had been sent to Maida Vale. Also, I suspected, he'd forgotten completely that he had agreed to do this.

'So, what are you interested in?' he asked.

Spurs . . . clothes . . . dissolute behaviour at parties . . . I searched my mind for something that would sound intelligent and mature. All that came into it was an image of the wonderful kitchen that I imagined his grand house would contain, in which his wife Elizabeth Jane Howard would produce sophisticated meals in between writing acclaimed novels.

'My hobby is cooking,' I proclaimed. 'I enjoy making mayonnaise.' This was a high-grade fib. The truth was that I enjoyed reading about making mayonnaise. I had recently bought a paperback copy of Elizabeth David's *French Provincial Cooking*, which was a revelation, because the only cookery books previously available in Britain had been the sort Mummy owned, with titles like the *Radiation New World Cookery Book* and recipes for faggots and brawn and other brown, smelly, scraggy things that had to bubble away for hours in giant pans, and the only cook I'd ever heard of before was Fanny Cradock, who had a mad hairdo and an obsession with spun sugar. Now here was this beautiful, well-travelled, articulate woman 'sitting down quietly with bowl and spoon, eggs and all, to the peaceful kitchen task of concocting that beautiful shining golden ointment which is mayonnaise'.

'It's a very restful occupation,' I said. Kingsley Amis wrote this down in his jotter. I felt the need to add something more.

'I love making avocado soup.' Another fib. You couldn't buy avocados in Bristol. It was practically an occasion for hanging out the coloured bunting the day one green pepper appeared on sale at the greengrocer's at the top of The Mall. But I'd seen a recipe for it in a recent *Sunday Times* magazine.

'I am told,' he murmured, 'that it will make all the difference if one adds a pinch of curry powder.'

'Gosh. I'll remember that.'

'Yes, do.'

Conversation flagged. We looked out of the windows. After roughly one hundred years we reached Sonning, and I have to say the French Horn had the loveliest setting of any restaurant I had ever visited. It was beside the Thames, and the riverbanks were bright green in the late spring sun, willows shimmered, ducks quacked, and leaves rustled. All, like our clinking of glasses and chomping of smoked salmon and steak that ensued, were perfectly audible, because it was now getting on for teatime and no one was in the dining room but us. 'One doesn't eat the side salad, of course,' Kingsley Amis observed to the photographer. Well, One might not, but I bloody well tucked into the lot, because that night it would be back to Bristol, and tinned ravioli on toast.

My prize-winning entry was published in the *Daily Telegraph* magazine the following month, together with Kingsley Amis's article on me. He used 'bantamweight' to describe my appearance but I was sure it was a dig at my prose. The essay was also published in book form, with some of the other entries. I had never heard of the imprint, Pergamon Press, but at the prize-giving (at the Savoy Hotel) its chairman, Robert Maxwell, presented me with the Paolozzi sculpture. It was enormous. So was he, a bear in a suit. In the week that followed, I appeared on *Late Night Line-Up*, where I was interviewed by Joan Bakewell, and was sought out by the up-and-coming producer, David Puttnam, to submit ideas for a film.

Then came what I was really waiting for – the visit to the *Daily Telegraph* to discuss the job.

I was so excited and nervous I had reached that state where you actually can't feel anything except dreamily weird. I put on my newest outfit. The trousers were Ossie Clark blue crepe flares; the waistband was too tight to do up but that didn't matter because the matching blouse was meant to be worn loose. The overall effect being a little bland, I stuck a sleeveless Fair Isle woolly on top.

The *Telegraph* was bang in the middle of Fleet Street, and I was taken up in a very gilded lift and right through the newsroom full of men who made newspapers, and it still all seemed like a dream to me as I walked into the colour magazine department with its crammed bookshelves and huge, worn old desks behind which sat elegant people all years older than me. A woman stood up and said archly, 'Oh, have you come to rewrite the magazine?'

I had no idea how to respond, so I just gave a weak-sounding laugh, and then over her shoulder I spotted a page torn out of the magazine and taped onto the wall. It was my winning essay. Across it, in green ink, was scrawled MUCK. THIS MUST CEASE. I suddenly plummeted from age twenty to about ten, and felt completely out of my depth, something I realised I had felt ever since they'd phoned to say I'd won. I had met the magazine's editor, John Anstey, at the prize-giving, and found him completely terrifying, an authority figure, seemingly twice my height, imperious, Almighty God in Savile Row tailoring. I was so not wanting to meet him again. I didn't belong in this world of suave, sarky, grown-up people.

I kept walking, but the woman hadn't finished with me.

'I do like your jersey,' she trilled, eyeing the Fair Isle top. Second-hand ones were all the rage at the time, one having been sported by John Lennon, but as they were impossible to get hold of through the normal channels, I had knitted this one myself. However, having got fed up with all the wool-juggling involved in the complicated pattern, I had given up after the fourth repeat, which meant it stopped just under my ribs. *I was wearing a Fair Isle frieze.*

You must shape up, I told myself. You are in Fleet Street, as per your childhood dream.

'It's my bust cosy,' I snapped, moving on.

Such a relief. John Anstey wasn't there. Instead, I was introduced to Harry Fieldhouse, his deputy editor. The first thing that hit me about Harry was that his head was devoid of hair apart from some border plant-like growth each side. Had I known he had been the much-lauded founding editor, in 1965, of *Nova* magazine, a women's glossy that covered all sorts of previously taboo issues such as abortion, cancer, race, homosexuality and the Pill, my knees would probably have kept on knocking, but this comic baldness made him seem humanly imperfect and, after a cosy chat about feature ideas, we settled that my first piece would be about roadies. Then I was led to accounts to be given an advance on expenses. Forty whole pounds! Free money! I travelled home feeling the nice, crisp notes in my pocket, and gradually the strange mood of dislocation passed. I was terribly pleased with myself. I was going to be a Fleet Street journalist. I was so brilliant I was just going to walk in.

Chapter 6

Spursy

A lot of my writing life is involved with football, and added to that it has been closely associated with one club, so maybe it's inevitable that I see life through the prism of Tottenham Hotspur, a club so unique that its fortunes have generated a neologism, which cannot be said of its more trophied rivals Arsenal, the two Manchesters, City and United, or Liverpool. The neologism is *Spursy* and the *Collins English Dictionary* defines it thus:

> A Spursy performance, is to have success in reach but to ultimately chuck it away.

I think that's a much better saying than 'Make God laugh – tell him your plans.' The reason I couldn't do up the Ossie Clark flares when I visited the *Daily Telegraph* was soon all too obvious. I had stopped taking the Pill when I went home for the Christmas vacation because Mummy was a terrible snoop and would have unearthed the incriminating packet. I'd put off acknowledging the inevitable consequences throughout the *Telegraph* Young Writer hoopla but now had to face facts.

Taking up the job was out of the question. There was no such thing as maternity leave back then. You left the workforce if you were pregnant; you did not join it. Fine, I thought defiantly. I'll get on with the Great Novel instead. Naturally, I couldn't do much novel-writing at first, but the idea of a career seemed irrelevant as I floated around in maternal contentment, dreamily listening to the new Beatles LP and Jethro Tull's *Stand Up* while knitting baby jackets and looking after our little family. This included not just Jack and the baby, who we called Fred, but a huge white blue-eyed rabbit called Grapefruit. We picked him out from dozens of identically huge and white rabbits, not realising at first that the place from which we bought him was a sort of rabbit farm, and that he and his companions had been bred for the pot. I don't think he can ever have seen daylight till we brought him home. We let him lollop around our flat and, not only did he fire trails of pellets everywhere, but he blundered into everything because he was blind. To light up his life, we bought a black rabbit to keep him company. We chose a male so there would be no complications about rabbit babies. Instantly they had rabbit sex all over the place. The black rabbit eventually escaped into the garden and we didn't see him again. Grapefruit died of natural causes not long after.

The beautiful weather of summer 1970 became a rather dreary autumn. Jack was studying architecture, and his aeons-long degree course included a year spent working in a practice. He landed a job with the London Borough of Southwark, so we piled our belongings into a trailer and left Bristol.

I couldn't put The Novel off any longer. In our new Wandsworth flat, I set up my desk and little Olivetti portable typewriter, but something awful had happened. I had written since I was six, and now I couldn't string words together properly. It was like when a necklace breaks and beads spill and fly everywhere over the floor. You scrabble around but can't find them all.

At the *Telegraph* prize-giving, I had been signed up by a literary agent, a beautiful, daunting young woman called Pat

Kavanagh. She thought she was getting a new literary star. What a let-down for her. 'An excess of poetry and a paucity of plot,' she commented about my efforts.

It was a vicious circle. Not being able to add to the lustre of British writing made me even more depressed, and that made me even less able to write. And so on. It was no wonder, really, because I was too proud to ask for help. I was twenty-one, an adult, I should know what I was doing by now. Anyway, who could I have asked? None of my friends were anywhere near marriage and motherhood. They were all sharing flats, going to parties, and starting exciting jobs. Plus, my parents had been very upset and embarrassed because having a baby when you weren't married was not at all respectable. Mummy wished me to keep as much distance between herself and my son, Fred, as possible, because what would her friends say if they knew? They were not wicked, awful parents, but they were from a different generation. A month after Fred was born, Jack and I had got married, but I had done things in the wrong order.

After I had spent six months dolefully slopping around in a dressing gown, Mummy stumped up the money for a secretarial course. I heard rusty creaks. The dungeon doors were slowly opening. They would admit me to the job in the family firm, and a life hiring out mining equipment.

Well, if my mother could have an agenda, so could I. Journalists needed to know shorthand and typing. I would get my qualifications and then look for a job on a magazine. You could, apparently, begin as a secretary with Fleetway Publications and get in that way. Everyone has to start somewhere and, however lauded I had once been at the *Daily Telegraph*, I would now have to be humble.

Jack and I found a very nice childminder for Fred, and off I went to the College of Speedwriting in Oxford Street, where my brain started to come alive again. I learned to touch-type at seventy words per minute and was taught a kind of sub-Pitman's shorthand, which largely consisted of abstaining from vowels and superfluous consonants. Speedwriting, for instance, would be rendered as spdrtg.

Of course, just because you have come up with a brilliant plan does not mean it will instantly come to fruition. I started writing off to magazines, none of which had any vacancies. But there was still hope. The College of Speedwriting scanned the classified ads in the posh papers every day, and details of available secretarial jobs were passed around. One morning I spotted that the history correspondent of the *Daily Express* wanted a secretary. At least, were that to be me, I would be in Fleet Street.

I sent in my application and was offered an interview. A week later, I stepped out of the train into a world swarming with office workers, and a smell of diesel, and whiffs of stale booze and ink and hot metal. Oh, this was so much my place – everything and everyone alive and busy in the June sunshine, car horns hooting, taxis rattling, newspaper vans roaring and clattering, famous journalists striding along gesticulating with cigarettes between their fingers. Every other building seemed to be a pub, and behind the main roads was a network of alleys and ginnels and courtyards and interesting basements. It was like finding oneself in a wonderful human-sized board game.

Express Newspapers dominated the street, huge, black and shinily futuristic, but my excitement began to ebb as I was shown to some sort of library the size of a football pitch, but graveyard silent. The history correspondent had a desk between grids of towering bookshelves that seemed to go on for ever, like an Escher drawing. He was a mustily formal man with horn-rimmed glasses, and submitted me to a mustily formal interview. I decided to give him a poke to liven things up, so I told him I'd been the Young Writer of the Year. I thought he'd be impressed but it was passed over unacknowledged and we moved swiftly on to typing speeds. It did not come as a crushing blow when the letter arrived thanking me for my application but regretting to advise me blah blah blah.

What did I care? I'd spotted another classified ad. The *Observer* sports department wanted a secretary. Sport, my Favourite Thing. A department full of lovely men. The *Observer*, where I'd found my Danny Blanchflower photo. It was *like* the Danny Blanchflower photo. I had to have it. This job was my Destiny. Surely.

The *Observer* was no longer in Tudor Street, but based in Queen Victoria Street, where it occupied a wing of the *Times*'s headquarters in New Printing House Square.

I arrived in a green-and-red check Madras cotton minidress that I had made myself, and was bare-legged because it was another warm June day, and I had felt very light-hearted that morning when I got up, knowing that I was going to meet my Destiny. I was shown up to the sports desk on the fourth floor and introduced to Clifford Makins, the sports editor. The sight of him filled me with joy, because you could tell what an amazing character he was by the sheer look of him. He was short and dumpy, with a shock of greying fair hair and a sort of quizzical look, and was wearing a pair of tramp-y trousers held up with a tie. This ancient Just William immediately led me downstairs again and I followed him out of the building to a pub at the corner of the street. We sat down at one of the Black Friar's round, marble-topped tables and he asked why I wanted the job.

He wanted to know *why*? It would have taken hundreds of words to accommodate all the reasons why I liked sport and he'd probably be no less mystified by the end. How could I explain? I had no sporting talent myself. I hated playing team games. I just liked to witness people doing valiant, incredibly skilled things with their bodies. I'd rather that than go to the theatre. None of my friends shared my obsession and even the boys, who'd all been to the sort of schools where they played rugger, would look at me in a here-comes-the-football sort of way whenever I rolled up. But here . . . well, *here* . . . Further down the bar I could see all the *Observer*'s star sports-writers: Hugh McIlvanney, Arthur Hopcraft, Geoff Nicholson, wonderful journalists whose work I'd admired for years; all these *gods* like Sir Len Hutton, giant of England cricket, and Chris Brasher, the Olympic gold medallist, and Clem Thomas, the Wales rugby international. That was why. I wanted to work with them, learn from them. It would be my apprenticeship. I could yak on to them about football and racing and get all the news as it came in on the Telex on Saturdays and live sport and breathe sport and . . . and . . . It would be *heaven*.

I racked my brains. What on earth could I offer that would make Clifford hire me?

'I was *Daily Telegraph* Young Writer of the Year two years back,' I blurted. 'Kingsley Amis wrote an article about me.'

He rubbed his hands together. 'Right,' he said. 'That'll be all.'

And that was my interview over.

'Oh God, why did I say that?' I muttered, trudging over the road to catch my train home. I had ruined everything. It was a secretary these men wanted, not a writer. Someone to do their filing and type boring letters and buy flowers for the wife because they'd forgotten their wedding anniversary. Why couldn't I keep my mouth shut? After all, if I'd been that good, what was I doing trying to get work as a typist?

I'd probably never even hear back from them.

But a letter arrived very soon afterwards, stamped with the *Observer* crest.

My heart began to race. This was it, then. My hands shook as I stared at the envelope. Which contained my Destiny. If

I didn't open it, if I just went on holding it, I could pretend that I was about to be offered a fabulous job that would put my life back on the rails.

Oh God. I couldn't just stand there like a ninny. I had to open it.

Expect the worst, then you'll never be disappointed.

I opened it and then I just stared and stared.

The Observer Limited, 160 Queen Victoria Street,
London EC4.
Telephone 01-236 0202
Telegrams Observer London EC4

Dear Miss Welch,
I am writing to confirm your appointment as—

It was followed by lots of blah about salary and holiday entitle-ment, which I didn't take in at all. I would have worked for nothing and all through my holidays too. I hadn't messed up. Someone had thought I was all right. I had done something and it hadn't turned out a complete disaster. They liked me. I wasn't the absolute lost cause everyone thought I was. I had been *accepted*.

I soon found out why I'd got the job. Apparently, there had been one other applicant. She had a huge bust, so all the men had said, 'Hire her. Hire that one.' But when Clifford came back from the Black Friar and said I'd been interviewed by Kingsley Amis, the men knew at once that Miss Norma Stits was a dead duck. Clifford had made an instant decision. Kingsley Amis was one of his cronies. He might as well have been called Open Sesame.

What did I care? I had made it to Fleet Street at last.

Chapter 7

A&D: Getting There through Ambition and Determination

So, some of us were reaching Fleet Street in various ways, whether planned or haphazard, through working on local papers, doing casual shifts or freelance work, or in my case through lucky chance. But what if you had done your training, had worked hard and been given glowing references and still couldn't get in? What if you were Australian?

In August 1964, a 22-year-old Scarth Flett boarded a ship in Sydney. Included with her luggage were a ruby and diamond ring, a sheaf of cuttings and some glowing references. 'Miss Scarth Flett has proved herself a keenly enthusiastic reporter with an alert news sense. She has displayed initiative, poise and sound ability as a journalist in a variety of fields, ranging from feature work and general reporting to the directing of social pictorial coverage.' That one was from Australian *Woman's Weekly*, where she had completed her training – 'I did interviews, film reviews, TV columns, a bit of everything.' The ruby and diamond ring had been a twenty-first birthday present from her maternal grandmother. Her grandmother was a sweetheart. She'd come to live with Scarth's family in the end. Mrs Flett had the ring valued and they discovered it was paste. Granny was never told the truth.

There is a lot of space between Australia and everywhere else and in the early 1960s all the ships were going in one direction. Two other young women boarded the *Himalaya* with Scarth – her friends Susie and Suzi. Scarth's father being a P&O executive, they had a good cabin. The two Susies had come to see England. Scarth had come to get a job in Fleet Street.

The voyage to England took a month. At first, they stayed with Scarth's aunt and uncle in Camden Hill Road, off Kensington High Street, and spent Christmas with them. Then they rented a lovely flat in Tedworth Square, off the King's Road. They were right in the heart of Swinging London; music poured out of boutiques that had once been dreary tobacconists and hosiery stores; halfway along was Mary Quant's Bazaar, where you could buy her trademark black skinny rib and beige keyhole skirt, and the first minis. Quorum, stocked with Ossie Clark's crepe flares and floaty voile blouses patterned with Celia Birtwell's prints, opened just off the road in Radnor Walk; Ravel and The Chelsea Cobbler were destination stores for shoes and kinky boots (if you were a teenager back then you had to have the calf-length white ones, as worn by Jean Shrimpton).

The meeting point for Australians in London was outside Australia House, where a line of camper vans would be parked. Scarth said you'd buy a van, travel round, do Europe and come back to Australia House to sell it to the next boatload of Australians. The three of them got in a car and travelled all around Cornwall and Devon. They went to Edinburgh. They got jobs promoting Australian apples in Liverpool, going round the city on open-top buses, wearing a strange grey uniform of jacket and pleated skirt, to hand out apples at supermarkets.

They packed in a visit to the Cavern Club in Mathew Street where Beatlemania had launched; no sign of the Beatles, of course, they had played their last gig there two years previously, when 'She Loves You' had started its thirty-one-week run in the charts. Scarth had interviewed them in a hotel room in Melbourne during their 1964 tour of Australia. She and the two Susies got to see the place just in time. Bankruptcy closed it in 1965, with fans barricaded inside.

Outside London and Liverpool, England was less swinging. 'We'd go for Sunday lunch in the countryside, and always get there too late because all these places closed at two o'clock,' said Scarth. 'Nowhere to get coffee, and you couldn't get a decent glass of wine. But a friend of my father's took us for lunch at the Savoy Grill, and two tables away was Noël Coward. We were in seventh heaven! It was a lovely time.'

On 2 January 1965, Scarth began writing off for jobs. 'I didn't mess around. I sent a letter to Robin Esser, features editor at the *Daily Express*, telling him what I'd done.'

She received a prompt reply. Esser's letter was dated 11 January. 'Dear Miss Flett,' it said. 'You had better come and see me. Telephone my secretary for an appointment.'

Scarth went to see him, but it didn't come to anything. The next letter of application she wrote didn't either, nor the third, nor the others. 'I had an extra burden when I came to England,' she said. 'An extra mountain to climb. I was a bit of a novelty. People would immediately lapse into silly Australian accents when they met me. They never got it right. Oh, the jokes about, are there kangaroos in the street?' Scarth, like Flett, is a well-known surname in the Orkneys. Her parents had wanted a name for her that had meaning and couldn't be shortened. She found she was repeatedly having to spell and explain it. 'So many people thought it was Scarf. The comedians called me Necktie. Ha ha, very funny. No, there weren't many Australians getting a job in Fleet Street but that didn't deter me.'

After a few weeks, she joined a temping agency, Albemarle Appointments. She needed a bit of money. She could only take positions as a typist because she never did shorthand, so inevitably she had to accept a couple of jobs she hated, like working a company switchboard. Then, in April, Elizabeth Garratt on the *Telegraph* women's page invited her in.

'She was so nice to me. An older woman and so kind, so kind! She liked my cuttings and offered me freelance work. I had to go off and write about gardening tools for the Home page. SOMEONE HAS THOUGHT OF THE GARDENING MUM . . . STICK IT ON THE WALL. Oh goodness, a whole piece about hanging utensils on the kitchen wall. But they were really nice to me, and I had all these little bits in the paper. I was still temping with office jobs, and I went in one day and my *Telegraph* piece was pinned on the notice board!'

After a year in England, she landed her first staff job, on *Petticoat,* on a salary of £26 per week. 'Fleetway Publications were just one of the people I wrote to and it just so happened they were about to launch *Petticoat* and were looking for a beauty editor. I went to see Audrey Slaughter, the editor, with my cuttings. She was tall and freckled, with reddish hair. Quite a cold fish. I didn't want to be a beauty editor, even though I had done a bit in Australia. I wanted to be a reporter. But I was grateful for the job.'

Petticoat was Audrey Slaughter's second magazine, a weekly 'for the young and fancy free'. It cost one shilling. The front cover of its first issue promised FASHION FICTION FUN. Inside were features such as 'What Every Girl Should Know', and a seemingly endless romantic serial called 'Half-Awake Heart'; another apparently doomed-to-be-interminable feature was 'Kathy's Crowd' (*Kathy's left home to live and work in the Big City. Sharing a flat with three other girls, they're just dipping into Life and Love*). 'Problems in Living' were to be sorted out by 'psychologist Dr Roy Fraser'; the first was 'I can't stand my mother'. The magazine also contained 'an eight-page supplement to pull out and keep' titled *Your Turn to Give a Party*. Tips – called 'Life Savers' – included: 'Sort out masses of ashtrays – not all your guests will have consideration for your carpet – and remember to empty them periodically', and: 'Make sure your record player is in proper working order.' Scarth's first piece was about eyeliner.

Fleetway Publications was based in Farringdon Street, just up from Fleet Street. Scarth had her own office. It was on the third floor, looking out over a gap between the buildings. The daughter of the head of the cosmetics company Goya was drafted in as her secretary. She didn't like the job, and left quickly. Scarth didn't like her job much, either.

'I didn't even like beauty. I'd go to beauty dos. I was the youngest there. They were full of important, famous women in big hats, a lot older than me and very glamorous, like Phyllis Digby Morton.' Phyllis Digby Morton was the *grande dame* of British fashion journalism. Once she had shocked all the gentlemen on the board of Fleetway Publications when she was editor of *Woman and Beauty* by introducing controversial topics like virginity, frigidity and infidelity. 'She was quite nice to me. They all were. But I was Australian. I had no contacts. *Honey* magazine was on the same floor and their beauty editor was a lovely Scottish girl, Pat Baikie. She helped me. Frankie McGowan, the sister of Cathy McGowan, who presented *Ready Steady Go!*, was there. She helped me a lot, too – we became good friends. Once I said to her, "I need a hairdresser, to help with head shots," and she told me her sister's boyfriend worked at Leonard. That was Lesley Russell. He came to help me, and he's still my hairdresser.

'There were a lot of people on the magazine who ended up in Fleet Street. Liz Smith was the fashion editor. She was married to a very important man in an advertising agency, and went on to the *Evening Standard*. Eve Pollard, who took over from me eventually as beauty editor, ended up editing the *Sunday Express*. She used to wear bobbysox to work. Sarah Meysey-Thompson did a lot of the interviews. Frankie and I went up to Woodbridge a couple of times to stay with her mother, who ran an antiques shop.

'God, I worked hard there. "Joining the ranks of tints for sculpturing light and shade into the face are Coty's Bush Accent powder and cream . . ." All that drivel. At one point, Audrey sent me a memo about my work:

Scarth. This is getting better, but is still too much a reporter's factual account instead of a beauty editor talking.

'Audrey had a funny manner. She was clever, but she wasn't easy. She didn't like me. I think she thought Liz Smith and I were less malleable because we were a bit older. It was only Liz and I who had ever had a job previously. We were too experienced for her. I was twenty-three, not a little girl to be moulded. After a few weeks she called me in for a chat. I told her I didn't enjoy the work and we agreed that I wasn't quite suited to *Petticoat*.'

She left in June to take up a holiday relief job on the news desk at the *Daily Mirror*, 'permanent placing to be discussed'. It wasn't her niche, but it was £27 a week and she enjoyed it. There were lovely people working there. Paula James had started her career on the *Finchley Press* in London, and although the *Mirror* used her for traditional 'woman's angle' stuff on current affairs, she also worked as a foreign correspondent, going to Vietnam for the last days of the war and visiting Black Power protestors in prison in Washington, so she was a rare example in Fleet Street of a female journalist successfully operating as a serious reporter.

Sally Moore was sweet, pocket-sized and Liz Taylor-glamorous. 'She was a news reporter,' Scarth recalled, 'and then did a big shopping column.' They were both kind to Scarth; they didn't pull up the ladder. Dan Ferrari was the news editor, 'very scary, very gruff, with a big moustache and twinkly eyes and a lot of hair'. There was one nightmare piece. 'The Royal Opera House were doing a production with live animals on stage, and I was sent to report on it. I wanted to go to a party. I must have rewritten that report four times. Dan kept saying, "Do it again. Do it again." Finally, he took pity and let me go off to my party. I suppose the subs must have fixed it in the end.

'But then I was sent out to cover a fire in Smithfield. It was at a Huguenot house, owned by a gay couple. That wasn't the story, but I noticed the bathroom had two free-standing baths in it. I mentioned it to Tony Miles, the diary editor, and he said, "I think we're going to lead on that." I think that helped me a bit. It was a bit of a break after struggling on the Royal Opera House piece and I was encouraged to stay on a bit longer at the *Mirror* after the holiday relief job, but I didn't really want to. I would have been a news reporter, and I wanted to write features.'

Her next job was as a feature writer on the *TV Times*. She was one of only two women there. She liked writing colour pieces with lots of information and description, so she was in her element again. 'Ah, that was a wonderful job. I just adored it. Such nice people.' She was there for two years. 'Then I thought it was a good time to go home for a holiday. I had a Young Person's Travel Ticket which would expire if I didn't use it.

'Two of my great friends from Australia, Nene King and Tony Hope, who had worked in television in Melbourne and married in London, with me as bridesmaid, had gone to live in Hong Kong. Their old boss from Melbourne was setting up the first independent television station there and had asked Tony to join the team. I stopped off on my way home in April 1968 and had a lovely time. Sadly, while I was in Melbourne, my grandmother died. She didn't die with a fag in her hand, but practically. I used to write to her. She was never sick. In good form, smoked like a chimney, beautifully dressed, liked a drink. But she got flu, and took to her bed. The flu turned into pneumonia. We had to keep turning her. She wouldn't let us get her dentures out! Then it was as if she thought, I might as well be off now. Seen Scarth. She'll go back again. Just shrugged her shoulders. She was the dearest lady.'

'I left Melbourne a few weeks after my grandmother's funeral and flew back to Hong Kong. I got a job on the *China Mail*. It was wonderful, I loved it; I had the best time ever. I took over a daily column from a woman who was having a sabbatical. Because I was new to Hong Kong, I didn't know the gossip, so I told them, "I've got to do some interviews," and I was the first Western reporter to go into a Chinese jail, where with the help of an interpreter I interviewed a probationer.

'I worked six days a week. Sunday was my day off. It was before China took over. There were parties, everyone played hard, lots of expats working there, lots of affairs going on. People passing through. Some went on to bigger things. Like me!'

Back in London she freelanced for the *Evening Standard* and *TV Times* and later in the year joined the first *Daily Mirror* magazine writing features. But not for long. Due to production complications it folded seven months later in July 1970. Her boyfriend was due to go to Vietnam to make a documentary and it was decided that she would go too and base herself mostly in Hong Kong.

'Before we left I went to see John Junor at the *Sunday Express* with some ideas and he commissioned four. Two from Hong

Kong and two from Saigon. I was ecstatic when he used all four pieces. On my return I went to see him again and this time he offered me a staff job on features and contributing to the interview column 'Meeting People'. I was thrilled. It was a column I had long wanted to be part of. I started in January 1971!' It had taken her five years.

'It never occurred to me to worry about money,' she said. 'I never felt down. I was always sure I'd get something. It was the optimism of youth. But when you think about it, it was quite brave, wasn't it?'

Chapter 8

Jobs from Hell

Scarth Flett didn't want to be a beauty editor, and Maureen Paton didn't want to be a librarian. Maureen was the girl whose father had done a runner. She and her mother were given a home by her mother's foster sister and husband. Her mother had been forty when she was born – 'an Edwardian' – and the foster sister and husband even older: 'They were Victorians.' Her mother, as she has said, thought the best Maureen could do was be a secretary. It was the elderly couple, her aunt and uncle, who gave her the aspiration to aim higher.

She was good at English. At Leicester University, she'd had a poem in the student newspaper, *Ripple* – 'It was known as *Nipple*.' She thought about being a journalist, but as a schoolgirl she'd had a Saturday job in Watford public library, her aunt and uncle knew the chief librarian of Hertfordshire, Miss Lorna Paulin, and they wanted her to be a librarian.

Which career should she choose? 'My local paper, the *Watford Observer*, wasn't terribly good. The idea of working on that – ugh. Flower shows, hatches, matches and dispatches – it didn't inspire me.' But the even less inspiring thought of the alternative, an MA in librarianship, drove her to an interview at the *Oxford Mail*. No luck there. 'I think they preferred Oxford graduates because they knew the town. I should have explored the *Ham & High*.' But she didn't. She got a place on the MA in librarianship at college in Ealing.

'Meanwhile, I had to get shop-floor experience,' she said. 'I went to Welwyn Garden City and shared a flat with two other trainee librarians.'

It was the early 1970s. Afghan coats, maxiskirts, the break-up of the Beatles on its way, the war in Vietnam, Watergate, LSD. The other librarians were quite a collection. There was Peter, her first and last bisexual boyfriend. There was Julian, who lived with his mother. 'He was a cataloguer, very reclusive.' There was Swinging Martin. 'Medallion man, married but very flirtatious – he'd kiss you without asking.' Her personal tutor, Alan, was very nice, but there were a lot of librarians she didn't like. She became more and more unhappy and bored, and eventually got the sack for having 'a bad attitude'.

Alan, the nice tutor, said it wasn't her fault – 'You were just very unhappy.' Maureen's defection was, however, a cruel blow to Miss Lorna Paulin. 'You're the first trainee we've had to drop out of the scheme,' said the chief librarian of Hertfordshire. 'I'm very, very disappointed.'

It was the affront to her sense of order that made Edie Reilly's first job at the *Observer* such hell. Edie, who went on to become the columnist Katharine Whitehorn's secretary and right hand woman, joined the paper's promotions department in 1977. Promotions looked after the offers in the back of the *Observer* colour magazine and were very keen on silk blouses, classical music album sets and the kind of rugged pullovers photographed on curly-haired men wearing deck shoes. 'I used to wish I could get run over on the way in, I hated it so much,' Edie said. 'It was such a shambles. You just got letters of complaint from people whose goods hadn't arrived.'

She described overheard phone calls – a feigned 'Oh goodness!' of sympathy, when the details of the complaint were not even being noted down because a damn was not given. A letter from a reader said, 'This is the first anniversary of when I ordered my Guernsey.' One night, when Edie was reading through all the letters, she thought, I don't know what to do about any of them. In the end she put them all in a big envelope and stuffed them down a drain. Nobody found out.

'At Christmas we had loads of promotions and took on a trainee solicitor as a temp,' she said. 'Which he came to regret. Somebody phoned up to ask where their order was. "How do I know?" he said. "It's like asking what it's like to die! Nobody knows!" The worst was the nativity set, advertised as "Hand-carved by craftsmen in Bethlehem". Fair enough. Then they started coming back. We had so many returns that in the end we didn't even open the boxes. They just piled up on the desks and against the wall. Eventually we opened them and discovered that instead of being hand-carved they had just been hacked, because the Bethlehem craftsmen had far more orders than they could cope with. There were Josephs with splinters and Baby Jesuses with one eye.' To relieve the congestion, Edie took one home. It was cold one winter, so she used it for firewood.

Edie's boss was very skinny and always wore blouses with the collar turned up. She was, said Edie, 'a complete snob'. When Edie moved departments to work for Katharine Whitehorn, her boss interviewed potential replacements with Edie present. 'Afterwards there was a discussion about one of them and someone said, "Well, I don't know about her, she speaks badly and has an accent." My boss said, in front of me, "Well, we took Edie, didn't we?"'

Edie came from Niddrie, a district of Edinburgh. 'Later, Katharine told me she hired me as her secretary because her mother's name was Edith and because I was Scottish. If anything tricky came up, Katharine would tell me: "You phone because once they hear that nice Scottish accent they'll be fine."'

*

Having had a taste of the journalistic life at *This Is London*, Jennifer Selway graduated from UCL in summer 1974, and successfully applied for a job as an editorial assistant at *Reader's Digest*. It was not what she had hoped for. 'I was editing the jokes. You'd get this whole nine-page letter from a reader and you'd have to whittle it down to "Imagine my surprise when ..." It was a most extraordinary, bureaucratic organisation because everything had to be sent in triplicate to Pleasantville, USA, headquarters of *Reader's Digest*. There used to be a coffee trolley come round, with bone china cups – it was very genteel. I was in an office with three other women and one of them was marrying a Spaniard and spent the entire time planning her wedding in Spanish on the phone.

'I wasn't writing any features or going out on stories. It was just a matter of processing copy and sending it to Pleasantville. You came in at nine, processed the copy, drank from your bone china cup and knocked off on the dot of five. Very sedate. There was no pub culture. I was terribly bored. I thought, I can't stand this, it's so dull. Everyone said, "Oh, you must stay there, it's such good training for journalism." I probably should have stayed, but I couldn't bear it.'

Was it the job from hell? I asked.

'No, it was very pleasant. No one was nasty to me or anything. Just terribly mundane. It wasn't as if anything was happening.'

It was the next one that was the job from hell. Lots happened in that one. This, remember, was the era of Donald 'Black Panther' Neilson's kidnap and murder of the seventeen-year-old heiress Lesley Whittle. The Moorgate tube disaster claimed forty-three lives. Coaches crashed and killed a group of innocuous old-age pensioners on an outing, and Lord Lucan murdered his children's nanny because he couldn't tell the difference between her and his wife. In June it snowed. The IRA bombed the London Hilton and Green Park tube. In Yorkshire, Peter Sutcliffe murdered his first victim. Who wanted to live in modern Britain? Jennifer travelled back into the Edwardian age and became a governess.

There were two stages to this development. First, she decided that instead of going into journalism she would become an academic. Her MPhil thesis would be on animals in American literature. Jennifer had enjoyed the American lit course when she was doing her first degree and particularly liked *Moby Dick*. She had a supervisor, and was subsidising herself with a bit of teaching at a sixth-form college. 'But I didn't have the first clue what I was doing, the supervisor was ineffective and a lech, and I floundered for an entire academic year. One day my mother spotted an ad in *The Lady*. I'd be paid sixty dollars a week, all expenses included, to live in New York, where I would coach a ten-year-old girl who had never been to school. She had always been home-tutored because her mother, an acclaimed English writer and journalist, didn't want her to have an American education before she was sent off to a British boarding school.'

Jennifer thought living in New York would give 'Animals in American Literature' the shot in the arm it needed, and applied for the job. At the interview she was asked if she was fond of children. 'I was twenty-two. I tried to remember whether I actually knew any children. The students I'd been teaching were teenagers – not much younger than me. All my friends were the same age. None of us had children. Of course we didn't. The last time we'd had anything to do with children, we'd been children.'

Nevertheless, she got the job. The acclaimed English writer and journalist turned out to be Penelope Gilliatt, who had written the script for the BAFTA Award-winning *Sunday Bloody Sunday* and was now film critic of the *New Yorker*. Jennifer had not actually heard of her but everyone knew who her ex-husband was – the playwright John Osborne, first of the Angry Young Men. 'I didn't ask why the last tutor had left, and it was never specified. I don't think anyone could stand Penelope for more than ten minutes, really. But, of course, I didn't know that at the time. I was just desperate to get to New York.

'When I was given the job Penelope was in America, so in effect she had hired someone she had never set eyes on to look after her child. But I was vetted by her mother and sister. I had tea with the mother, who had this rather chintzy flat in Victoria, bred Morgan horses, and said, "Penelope is, of course, a genius." Then I had to go and meet Penelope's sister, Angela Conner, an incredibly successful sculptor. She was lovely. I'd much rather have worked for her.

'Then, while I was waiting for my US visa to come through, I was summoned to start work, not in New York but in Penelope's town house in Chester Square, Belgravia, and less as a tutor than a childminder for Nolan. Penelope wouldn't be there – she was still in New York. I didn't want to be a babysitter in London, I wanted to be a tutor in New York. I started to have some misgivings and talked it over with my mother. She thought it was a bit weird, but on the other hand was very impressed with the fact that Penelope had a house – *a whole house* – in Chester Square.'

Jennifer's visa came through at last, and she flew out to New York two days before Christmas 1975 – her first transatlantic flight. 'I felt miserable till I was on the plane,' she wrote to her parents. 'It was only a tatty little Boeing 707 and they didn't show a film. After take-off they gave us peanuts and free drinks. I had a martini. Dinner was pâté, steak and rum baba. Penelope opened a bottle of champagne as soon as I arrived – in my honour, apparently. She has been very nice, and has introduced me to all her friends . . .'

Penelope had naturally red hair and an actress voice and gestures, and wore lots of Estée Lauder's Youth Dew. She lived on 88th Street, on the tenth floor of a 1920s apartment block. Jennifer had a room overlooking Central Park. 'I could see all the way across. Snow, snow all the way to East Side. The lake was covered in it, the whole city was covered in it, and when it wasn't it was plastered in graffiti. It was a liberating thing.

'She had very good taste. The apartment was beautifully done, quite austere. White walls and white covers, nothing fussy – a style of furnishing that was to influence me. Although I was to come to hate her, I did look up to her.'

The friends Penelope introduced Jennifer to were quite something. She went to Woody Allen's New Year's Eve party at the St Regis Hotel: 'Salvador Dalí was there. He decorated the elevator for the party. Woody Allen was weedy like in the early films – nebbish. He was with Diane Keaton, who looked beautiful. He looked sad and uneasy, as though he was a gatecrasher at his own bash.

'There were banks of TV sets showing what was happening in New York that night. Everyone who was anyone was there – Norman Mailer, Leonard Bernstein, Lillian Hellman, Paula Prentiss. Richard Benjamin from *The Sunshine Boys* talked to me while looking over his shoulder for more interesting company. The first time that had happened to me, and not by any means the last.

'The next day was Betty Comden and Adolph Green's famous New Year's Day party. It was in a brownstone on the Upper East Side. I don't know which one of them owned it, because they weren't married to each other. They just collaborated and had written the screenplays for MGM musicals. So many more famous people there I didn't know. If only these people had had badges on their heads. That's the trouble with being young. I stood around, trying to look as if I was having a wonderful time, till Betty announced the buffet was open. When I joined the queue, I realised I was standing behind Lauren Bacall. After I'd loaded up my plate and was looking for somewhere to sit, this growly voice said, "Come and sit with us and tell us who you are," and it was her. Shirley MacLaine was next to her and they made space for me in between. So, on the first day of 1976 I had supper on my knee with Lauren Bacall and Shirley MacLaine.'

Among the friends Jennifer made for herself were Calvin Trillin, who wrote for the *New Yorker*, and Alice, his wife. They lived in Greenwich village. 'Nolan was allowed to play with their children and Penelope thought it would be nice if I met the nanny, Susie-from-Bath,' said Jennifer. 'Because I was the equivalent. Susie was friends with another nanny called Ruthie who worked for Laurie, who I always thought of as a white Whoopi Goldberg. She was married to a mad Israeli property developer called Zohar Ben-dov. They were a wonderful family, and Laurie was to become one of my closest friends.'

23 January, 1976
Dear Mummy and Daddy,
I've had my first disaster! The kitchen is disgusting, and Penelope told me to defrost the fridge, which was completely compacted with ice. I'd no idea how to do it, so I just switched it off and it left puddles all over the floor. Penelope was furious. I didn't know I was expected to do housekeeping as well as everything else, but there's a definite feeling that I'm a maid of all work. I have to work out how to feed three people on a hundred dollars a week . . .

By this time Jennifer had begun to wonder if Penelope Gilliatt was quite sane. 'She was a very strange woman. There was something penniless about her. She was parsimonious to a fault. She objected to me buying food and clothes for her daughter, who otherwise wouldn't have had any. She disapproved of anything that was slightly junky because she was a snob, basically. Hamburgers were terribly naff. Apparently, I should give her chicken broth, or some of the leftovers she always brought back from her lunches at the Four Seasons. Decca Mitford, Nancy's younger sister, came to lunch one day. Penelope graciously let me share scrambled egg, a glass of water and a piece of mouldy bread. I could feel Decca Mitford radiating sympathy for me. This poor girl with this madwoman. Because everything was going shit-shaped with Penelope. She was unreasonable, a total bitch.'

Jennifer endured the job for six more weeks. Then she found a note left for her in the kitchen.

> *Jennifer,*
> *Within the last few weeks I have held my tongue over the ridiculous attempts to wean Nolan from the life into which she has been carefully brought into an absurd sub-culture of jeans and sub-teenage hairdressing. You are an au pair and you need a little less arrogance if you're going to get anywhere and to make me cease regretting all the trouble I took and all the expense that I've been to, in order to get you over here and give you a decent life . . .*

'It sounded like she'd taken me out of a bad background and grinding poverty. I went to my room in a huff. Later on that night I heard a *click, click, click*. I knew it was her because that was the sound of her heels. She was fiddling with something outside the door.

'I waited and after a while she *click, click, clicked* off again. Then I opened the door. Six little pots of fruit-flavoured yogurt were piled up in a pyramid, with a note propped on top. It read, "Bedsit, petit bourgeois, tart food."

'I'd bought the yogurts because it was food that Nolan might like, rather than the leftovers in doggy bags from the Four Seasons.'

Jennifer picked up her bag and fled to the Trillins. She put the yogurts back in the fridge first.

'I didn't realise she was an alcoholic till after I'd left,' said Jennifer. 'It was beyond my scope. I'd never met anyone who was an alcoholic. Once I realised, a lot of her behaviour fell into place. Instead of assuming she was insane, I realised she was drunk.'

She spent a month with the Trillins, before going to work for Laurie and Zohar Ben-dov, who was developing One 5th Avenue, a landmark building right on Washington Square. 'He owned it and I sold some apartments for him and was given a little one to live in myself. Then Laurie said she needed a nanny for the summer on Fire Island, because Ruthie and Susie wanted to go back to England. Laurie had two little girls, Tamar and Ariella. That seemed a nice thing to do.

'It was absolutely the most hedonistic place, notorious in the mid-1970s for its gay communities. Three blocks wide, thirty-five miles long. A strip. No cars. All bicycles. The respectable people lived at Cherry Grove. It was really decadent, it was everything you've ever imagined, it was pre-AIDS. I didn't have much to do, to be honest. Laurie and I spent the afternoon drinking pina coladas. I had two little girls to look after, take them swimming once a week, put their washing in the washing machine, tidy up after dinner. That was pretty much it. I had this little cabin by the side of the shower where I slept with the washing machine, dryer and the bicycle. The song I always remember – it was on all the time – was Kiki Dee and Elton John, "Don't Go Breaking My Heart". It was absolute bliss.'

Jennifer stayed from April till the end of the summer. 'Animals in American Literature' was allowed to drift. Nothing was ever heard of it again. When she then went back to London, she resumed her journalism training on a start-up London listings magazine, *In Town Tonight*.

Chapter 9

Getting in through Magazines

I haven't talked much about magazines before, but for a large part of last century working on one was a time-honoured way to get to Fleet Street without formal training, because unless you were irredeemably dim-witted (and you would not be in Fleet Street if you were) you could pick up the niceties of 6-point bold and widows and orphans once you were there. 'I didn't have a clue what to do when I came down from Oxford,' said Lynn Barber, the author of *An Education*, 'but I had written articles for the children's page of my local paper, the *Richmond Times*, so I knew I could write for money – I was a natural writer. I was offered various traineeships but they were in the provinces and I was trying to catch a boyfriend.' (This was David Cardiff, her future husband.) She also applied to International Publishing Corporation, then the holding company for Mirror Group Newspapers and one of the UK's biggest magazine publishers. They told her she could come in as a secretary, which didn't appeal. While at Oxford, though, she had interviewed Bob Guccione for the student magazine, *Cherwell*. Guccione was about to launch *Penthouse*, a men's 'adult' magazine; it combined long and serious articles with soft-core porn. She impressed him, and he told her to come to him if she ever needed a job.

She joined *Penthouse* in 1967 as an editorial assistant on £16 a week, working for none other than Harry Fieldhouse:

'At first I was editing much more than writing and one day I thought, I suffer so much anxiety, commissioning a piece and wondering if it's going to be any good – I could do this myself. Harry took pains to teach me to write journalism. He had this fetish for cutting things, taking out redundant words, because I did have this schoolgirl thing, to yak on, and he compressed, compressed, compressed.' This was her springboard to Fleet Street, where her award-winning career as an interviewer took off. 'It was the last days of Fleet Street, but thank God I did spend those few years there. We were lots of different talents all in one room – I think that's a good way to run a magazine because everyone pitches in with ideas. We were a creative force – we were friends.'

In Town Tonight, the listings magazine that Jennifer Selway joined in 1976, was owned by David Sullivan, who was also into 'adult' publishing. It was produced in funny little offices in Aldgate East, which back then was Dickensian. 'Every surface was sticky with the glue that was used to paste typescripts onto pages before being stuffed into packages and put on the train to be sent to the printers,' said Jennifer. 'The smell of glue permeated everything. The editor was a guy called Harvey Lee – he was really nice. There was the delightfully louche Brian, twenty-six, good-looking, falling apart, black suit, ash on sleeves – he used to take me to fantastic clubs open all day. I had a little fling with him. Inevitable, really. He and I would come back from lunch and Harvey would say, "Well, it is half past four."

'We moved to better premises by Goodge Street station, and I started doing all the film coverage. Coffee and crois-sants, film at 10.30. Nibbles followed. Film at 2.30. At 6.30, canapés and drinks, and film. So I never had to buy food or see daylight. The perfect life. Then *Tonight* folded.'

Through someone she had met at a film screening, Jennifer landed a job on *Time Out*. There she did the Roundabout column – 'little odds and ends that didn't fit into any of the sections, things you might like to do during the week. I would take items from press releases, and sometimes I'd go and do something and write a little picture caption. I did film reviews, arts features, interviews with film stars and directors. Agnès Varda, the *grande dame* of New Wave – I went to Paris to interview her. She lived in a delightful house outside Paris, and I stayed there, and she was wise and wonderful.'

Between 1978 and 1979 she had three jobs simultaneously. A nice man on the *Observer*, Desmond Balmer, hired her as holiday cover on its TV guide for Jonathan Meades, 'an awkward, brilliant genius'. When Meades was sacked, she got the job full-time. Meanwhile, she was also doing PR for a porn film distributor in Berkeley Square, and working on *Time Out* as well. 'It was beaver shots in the morning, union meetings about feminism in the afternoon, and then the highbrow *Observer*. It does feel now like parallel lives because they all required different bits of me. I wore different things depending on whether I was working for the porn king or *Time Out*. Porn was a silky blouse and a slit skirt, slingbacks and a little thin gold necklace. *Time Out* meant boots, tight jeans or dungarees, a T-shirt or a black jumper. Sometimes I'd have to go into the *Observer* straight from the porn distributor's office in Berkeley Square, so I'd still be wearing the slit skirt and silky blouse.'

The porn film distributor had a bad end, incidentally. He went to prison for distributing *Nightmares of the Damaged Brain*, the first video nasty to be prosecuted. After his release he went to Cyprus. 'There was some unpleasantness,' said Jennifer, 'and I believe he's under a motorway now.'

*

Having dashed the hopes of Miss Lorna Paulin, Chief Librarian of Hertfordshire, Maureen Paton was left with having to find a job. 'I so didn't want to go home to Mother. In *Miss London*, a giveaway magazine, I saw an ad for a typist. Which I could do. It was in Victoria, at the London office of an engineering company. The chairman's p.a. who hired me was just lovely. She could see I was a bit bruised, but never asked questions – we're still friends to this day. I shared a flat in Tooting and met my husband, Liam, an engineer who wrote poetry. He ran a poetry group round the corner and within six months I'd moved in. I was in my early twenties by then, and also working on a leftie Wandsworth community magazine called *Lower Down*. The local papers despised it.

'I wasn't going to stay a typist for long. In *Miss London* I saw another ad, for an editorial secretary at Phoebus Publishing Company, in D'Arblay Street.' Phoebus published *The Story of Pop* and *Jane's Fighting Ships*, which were partworks – i.e. magazines issued in a planned sequence that added up to a full reference work. 'It was quite a place,' said Maureen. 'One assistant editor, the late Richard Green, was known as The Beast; he'd come to *The Story of Pop* from *Record Mirror* and *NME*. Although he was supposed to be mentoring me, he was a full-blown alcoholic by then and spent most of his time in the pub. Two guys of my age worked on *Jane's Fighting Ships* – one young fogey, one hippy – and played battle board games in their lunch hour.

'As editorial secretary, I was noticing things – "There's a mistake here"; "What about that?" – so I was already beginning to think like a sub. At first, I did get a little bit of frost from two other women subs towards me, the secretary, because I was pointing things out – but they did accept me later and, within weeks, the editor was saying, "You're quite good at this, I think we'll train you to be an editorial assistant." And I just felt completely at home with maverick journos, and working with words all day.'

She wrote a number of pieces under a pseudonym, and that led her to *Melody Maker*, which hired her as its first female staff sub-editor. This was the point at which the chief sub alleged that she had only been given the job because the editor had been to a conference about promoting more women. 'Oh dear,' she thought. But soon enough he was saying, 'I wasn't sure if you and I could work together. But you're the best sub I've ever worked with.'

She had set her sights on Fleet Street without local paper experience, and figured that working in features was the best way in. Still employed full-time on *Melody Maker*, she began doing weekend shifts at the *Mirror*, *Sun* and *Telegraph*. 'I'd found I had a good nose for news but I just loved writing, and features is where you can indulge that.' After three years with *Melody Maker*, she landed a job with the *Express*, as a staff features sub. It was 1979, and she was only the third woman features sub they'd ever had.

'I was labelled thick because my sister was so clever,' said Sue Peart of her days at boarding school, where she was promptly steered in the direction of sewing, cooking and dancing. 'It took me years to realise I wasn't thick at all. I got all As at O-level, and without them consulting me I was put into the Oxbridge set.'

Frantically, she rang her parents. 'I don't want to go to Oxbridge,' she informed them. 'I don't want to go to university. I don't want to take A-levels, either.' Nor did she want to leave school, so a compromise was made. If she was staying there for two more years, she might as well take A-levels. She passed three: English, French and history. Wanting to be financially independent, she went on to do a secretarial course with French and Spanish. She had always been strong-minded, she said. She knew what she wanted to do – go to London. 'Sheffield was depressed in the 1970s. London was where it was happening. I read about it in *Petticoat* every week. My parents were positive. They never pushed me. Off she goes! They never gave me any money, either. I fended for myself.'

She found a room in a house in Putney for £14 a week, and did a series of temping jobs. One was the stereotypical job from hell. 'It was in the *Times* ad department on Gray's Inn Road, and it was awful, lecherous. I couldn't bear it. I listened to a man on the phone to his wife, being jolly nice to her, then putting the phone down and going, "Stupid cow." One Friday morning I was told, "We're going to promote you because the advertising director wants you to be his secretary because you've got such a lovely telephone manner. See you Monday." "He's got the hots for you," said one of the other secretaries, like it was the most wonderful thing in the world.' She collected her wages and never went back.

Jobs, then, were easy enough to come by. She moved on to a nice one at EMI, where the boss would call in all the secretaries and play a record. 'Tell me if you'd buy it,' he'd say, and one day all they could say was, 'Play it again, play it again.' It was Kate Bush singing 'Wuthering Heights'.

Then an even better job came up. The editor of *Cosmopolitan* wanted a secretary. 'The interview was at 5.30, and I walked in there and I was just a round peg in a round hole. Deirdre McSharry was brushing her abundant auburn hair. She put on an embroidered silk jacket. She told me she was going to the theatre, and asked if I did, and I said yes, I went to everything. She never asked me about typing and shorthand; it was all about the dress I was wearing. It was from a little shop called The Vestry in South Molton Street. Far more reasonable than Browns. I think Deirdre heard the words South Molton and that was enough.

'She was very theatrical, a brilliant editor, demanding but nurturing, and I learned so much from her. If you earned it, she'd give you a chance. Deirdre had studied drama at Trinity College, Dublin and gone into rep. But she went on to be fashion editor on the *Daily Express*. She went to Leonard of Mayfair for her hair and one day she spotted a girl, slender with a long Nefertiti neck and enormous eyes in a tiny face. "Who is that young woman?" she said. It was the fledgling model Twiggy, who had been brought in by her manager Justin de Villeneuve for a fashionable haircut. She interviewed the fifteen-year-old and plastered her picture across the centre spread of the *Daily Express*: THIS IS THE FACE OF THE 60s.'

Sue had started sending off pieces to magazines – think pieces about life just out of her head, but she would get a cheque back for £25. There was, she said, the beginning of a boom in magazines and *Cosmo* broke the half-a-million sales mark. They were great days. They were all in their early twenties having a lot of fun, and over the years it was a great training ground for young female journalists. Genevieve Cooper went on to be the first woman editor of the *Sunday Times* colour supplement; Linda Kelsey was a future editor of *Cosmo* and *She*; Sally Vincent a major interviewer for the *Sunday Times* and the *Guardian*; Irma Kurtz an internationally famous agony aunt, as is Anna Raeburn, who also co-wrote the ITV television series *Agony*, starring Maureen Lipman.

Deirdre would get everyone to a meeting and ask what they'd all been doing. Had they had a dinner party? What did they cook? What films had they seen? She taught Sue that every conversation she had was article fodder.

'I was very lucky,' said Sue. 'I fell on my feet. After eighteen months she could see I was a bit of a writer and she said, "You need to get your certificate of journalism." I did a day-release course. I had to write a piece for publication. I saw an unknown actress in something and said, "I think you're amazing – can I interview you?" It was Julie Walters. I entered it in a writing competition, the Catherine Pakenham Award, and it was runner-up. The prize-winners were given lunch in the *Punch* dining room. All the editors would come and Larry Lamb of the *Daily Express* made a bit of a beeline. "Do you want to work in newspapers?" "Yes please! Yes! Yes!"'

A series of interviews took place over grand lunches: with Bernard Shrimsley, the deputy editor; with Katherine Hadley, the women's editor; with Robin Esser, the features editor. She was taken to the Gay Hussar, to drink champagne at the Zanzibar Club, to the Coq d'Argent – 'a grand place with a sommelier who would bow and scrape'. When she announced to *Cosmo* that she would be leaving, they were overjoyed for her: 'You're going to newspapers!'

'I couldn't wait, I couldn't wait,' she said. 'I was so excited.'

PART 2

The News Factory

Chapter 10

Of Mice and Men:
A Guide to the Fleet Street Newsroom

This is what it's like to be there at the sharp end. It's October 1984 and a long-delay IRA time-bomb aimed at Margaret Thatcher goes off at the Brighton hotel venue for that year's Conservative Party conference. The bomb has been placed in an en-suite bathroom next to Mrs Thatcher's room but her work ethic has kept her in her sitting room, out of harm's way. The IRA might know how to make a bomb but they haven't done their homework about her habits.

While the prime minister is unscathed, five conference attendees are killed, including a sitting MP. Thirty-one others are injured. At the *Daily Express*, a somnolent night shift (a couple of journalists and a prowling security guard) in the newsroom transmogrifies over the next few hours into a full-on Fleet Street newsroom, reporters being summoned from their homes in far-off suburbs or hauled out from under tables in drinking dens, whole pages of features being ditched, copy being ripped out of typewriters page by page and rushed down to the machine room.

'I arrived at the *Daily Express* in the era when huge national events like the Dennis Nilsen murders, the Cecil Parkinson and Sara Keays scandal and the Brighton bombing happened,' said Sue Peart. 'I went to newspaper conference from the day I arrived and that was an education, having come from *Cosmo*. You had to have ideas every morning and if you didn't you'd be fired.'

*

It's true that the big newspapers are still published in printed form, although circulations are heavily diminished. The *Independent* survives wholly online and its sister paper, the *Independent on Sunday*, where I spent lovely spells in the 1990s and Noughties, has joined the dodo and Steller's sea cow in extinction. No one's arguing about how convenient it is to jab on an app for the *Guardian* or *Mail*, but it can cause a pang if you have memories of the draught in the hall caused by two or three fat newspapers wedging open the letterbox, and the breakfast ritual of the order in which you read them. It's even more poignant for people like me who remember the bedlam of Fleet Street newsrooms in the glory days of print, the thrill of seeing your first by-line on a still-damp page proof, and the camaraderie of crowding round one small TV set to watch Red Rum winning his third Grand National or some unfolding disaster an ocean away from EC4 – if you could get a view, that is, of those blurry analogue images through the veil of cigarette smoke. That's all gone, along with the subterranean rumble of presses, and the occasional thunderclap of someone plummeting from his chair (a reasonably frequent occurrence in the days of the six-hour lunch).

Now subbing is done on screens everything is silent. There's no fiddling around with make-up sheets and rulers, no need to know the width of the letters to see if a line will fit the allotted space. You don't hear subs muttering to themselves as they tot up the word count. Indeed, for journalists who trained by working on already modernised regional papers towards the end of the 1970s, the first reaction to the Fleet Street newsroom may well, even then, have been a double-take. The equipment must have seemed as obsolete as ducking stools. Louise Court made her way in by doing weekend shifts at the

Express while still full-time on the *Croydon Advertiser*. 'I'd walk into the *Advertiser* on a Monday and think, It's awfully quiet in here, isn't it?' she said. Tina Moran left the *Bristol Evening Post* for London in 1986. 'In the provinces we were way ahead,' she pointed out. 'All my subbing training was done on new technology. In Fleet Street everyone was still putting copy in tubes and sending it up and down like they did at Grace Brothers in *Are You Being Served?*'

Oh, but call me old-fashioned. I adored those contraptions. They were like toy ski-lifts. Once you had finished with a piece of copy, you would roll it up, stuff it in a little canister and hang it on the overhead wire, which would then convey it jerkily to the machine room. Now and again it would get stuck on the way, or become detached. The hockey correspondent was an absolutely terrible writer and one night his report fell into the loo. Everyone said it was homing instinct.

But how did copy reach the newsroom in the first place? Because nothing could be transmitted electronically, every newspaper had its cohort of messengers to convey it from copytaker to relevant desk; when you phoned over your report, the first thing you had to state was which part of the paper it was destined for, so that your article would not fetch up in the wrong department. This was, in my case, a particular hazard because on seeing a female by-line a messenger could automatically deliver it to the women's pages, no matter that it was a feature on the Manchester United centre half.

Historically, messengers were known as 'copy boys' (never copy girls) and to start off as one was a recognised way into journalism. You had to have passed the School Certificate (another relic; it was the precursor to O-levels, taken at sixteen). This was how Charlie Wilson (whom I suspect is most widely known for having been Anne Robinson's first husband but was also editor of both *The Times* and the *Independent*) began his career. In the 1950s, the copy boy's duties ranged from collecting handwritten reports from courts and ferrying dispatches from sports grounds to making tea. By the time we arrived in Fleet Street, the practice had died out and messengers were regarded as members of the Lower Orders. From her early days on Londoner's Diary, Mary Kenny remembered 'Max Hastings shouting, "Boy!" and this East End urchin would come forward.'

I love the descriptions Mary and Valerie gave of life in the *Evening Standard*'s Shoe Lane newsroom around the late 1960s. Valerie recalled a legendary reporter, Anne Sharpley, bellowing, 'Marius, get your hands off my tits!' (a fellow journalist, Marius Pope, was so notoriously hands-on he was known as Pope The Grope). A Christmas pantomime was staged annually in the newsroom: 'The London *Evening Standard* proudly presents *The Wintour's Tale,* subtitled 'If the Shoe Lane Fits'. Across the back bench – the long table where the editor and other leading executives sat – was scrolled a banner that read FOR GOD'S SAKE GET IT RIGHT. 'If you spelt a name wrong, God help you,' said Valerie. 'A new boy arrived and he put a T in the surname of Patrick Lichfield, the Queen's cousin. He was sacked within days.' He had GOT IT WRONG.

When Mary arrived for her first day at work, she was immediately told to go and interview the former British prime minister Clem Attlee. Having grown up in Ireland, she had no idea who he was, and had to hurriedly mug up on the details in the library. That's something else that seems amazing now, the fact that each newspaper had a library of its own. Are there any left? If so, where are they now? I asked a friend who is a librarian at a national title. Gavin Fuller is one of a dwindling species, the human version of a white rhino:

Newspaper libraries, for those of us who are still left (the *Express* was the first to ditch its library, in the early years of the 2000s, and News International followed suit early this decade), are a pale shadow of what they used to be. When I joined the *Telegraph* there were twenty of us, and we occupied a sizeable area with, like the *Express*, hundreds of books, official publications and filing cabinets full of cuttings, a microfilm reader and rolls of microfilm covering the entire existence of the paper, plus a warehouse containing many more cuttings folders and bound volumes of the paper. Yes, we still have the cuttings and the bound volumes, but instead of being a few minutes' walk away and easily accessible they're now housed on the outskirts of Wigan, which is anything but! I'm not even allowed to keep any reference books in the office any more (I've saved some which are relevant to the paper and its history, but they're oop north as well). Cutting came to an end at the *Telegraph* at the end of 1996, due to the onset of computerisation, and now the job of the two of us left in the department is effectively database management, making sure that all the assets of each day's paper are present and correct, and editing where necessary to achieve this. Microfilms have been digitised (*The Times* was the first to go down this route, and most nationals have followed suit, the *Telegraph* being one of the last as the cost put management off doing it in-house), which does in theory make them easier to search, but practice has shown this is far from perfect (one folder I had to extract, for example, had five cuttings in it, but a search on the digitised archive only brought up three of them under the person in question's name, despite them all being present on the system). And whereas in the past we'd be the chief source of information and its provision in the paper, now internet search engines have enabled journalists to do much of this themselves, making the librarians in effect a last resort if they are unable to find what they want. One way those few of us left in the sector have had to evolve is in knowledge of searching best practice, i.e. knowing where to look for authoritative and accurate information (which quite often rules out Wikipedia . . .).

Like the good librarian he is, he concluded this with: 'Feel free to ask if you need any further info or clarification.'

When did we know the old Fleet Street was dying? Could it have been when the vending machines appeared in the corridor? It was a harbinger. That clunk of the fizzy drink can landing in the well, the spatter of small change, the *thump, thump, thump* of fist against steel when the Twix and cellophane-wrapped sandwich refused to answer our summons. Was it when the advent of laptops signalled the end of the typing three, a carbon paper sandwich of deceptively festive appearance (the top sheet was white, those beneath it yellow and pink)? You rolled it into your Remington and bashed away on the white. Really, *really* bashed, because if you didn't the typing wouldn't get through to the pink at the bottom and even the yellow would bear only a faint imprint and you'd have to do it all over again. Towards the end of the week, when the sportswriters came in to produce their copy, the place would end up festooned like confetti at a giants' wedding.

Was it when everyone stopped going to the pub and ate in the canteen instead? 'There was apartheid at the *Express*,' Sue Peart reported. 'Orange plastic chairs for journalists, brown for printing staff. All the chairs were nailed to the floor.' That's nothing – the *Mirror* even made you sign for the cutlery. The *Observer* canteen, Jennifer Selway informed me, 'was like something out of Hogarth – dark and steamy, with great big women with huge arms dishing out cabbage'.

I needed Jennifer to describe the *Observer* canteen to me because I never ate there myself, preferring the sports department's en masse excursions to Scribes in Carmelite Street or the City Golf Club, which abutted St Bride's, still famed as the journalists' church even though no journalists are around any more. Liz Morris, the lovely Welsh girl who replaced me as sports desk secretary, told me that at her job interview Ron Atkin, Clifford Makins's successor as sports editor, never raised the issue of typing and shorthand speeds. Instead he asked, 'Do you like the occasional drink?' 'You were just a secretary,' concurred Angie Mulligan, recalling her days of working in the newsroom at the *News of the World*, 'but you'd never not be invited anywhere. On Saturdays, we all went to El Vino's. It was our regime. All the men brought champagne to us because we weren't allowed to go to the bar to buy a round.' During the week, its newsroom emptied at 11.00, the hour when conference took place. 'The only person left in there was the one who had to phone the Wine Press to warn us when conference was over.'

No one eats or drinks together any more, of course; it's a social activity as remote in time as leaving calling cards. No one gets drunk in office hours, full stop. But back then? 'When I joined the *Express*, it was at its height,' said Sue Peart. 'People would drink industrial quantities at lunchtime and after work, and put in an afternoon of hard work in the meantime without apparently being any the worse for wear. Bust-ups in the pub were not unknown, and one of my earliest memories was someone being carried in literally horizontal after a heavy lunchtime session.' Wendy Holden is more succinct about her early impression of the newsroom. 'A lot of men asleep on or under their desks,' she said when I asked her to describe what it was like at the *Evening Standard* in the mid-1980s.

I am anxious not to be sexist but can't help comparing those newsrooms, populated often by men in a state of desuetude, to the womany set-up of *Cosmopolitan* where Sue Peart worked before joining the *Daily Express*. At *Cosmo*, her first job on a Monday morning had been to go to Berwick Street Market and buy a bunch of flowers for the office occupied by her editor, Deirdre McSharry. At eleven o'clock sharp she would take Deirdre a percolated coffee. On Friday nights, to mark the end of the week, wine would be served. These were Deirdre's rituals. 'They were civilised.'

The magazine was based in the National Magazine Company building at the corner of Carnaby Street – a lovely area to work. Every floor was painted a different colour. '*Cosmo* was yellow,' said Sue. 'The sun shone in and bounced off the walls.' At the *Express*, it never had a chance. 'In the newsroom itself, there was no natural light – the windows looked out onto walls. A chimney came up through the middle from the presses and when the presses started the building would get hot. It was always warm in there, and filthy. Filthy windows, filthy carpets, paper plates of half-eaten curry and chips, empty Coke cans, ashtrays. No wonder we had mice.' She remembers Larry Lamb, her editor, ambling from his office 'like a badger' and parking himself on the corner of her desk. 'He'd sniff the air and say, "Something smells a bit different round here," and it was me.'

I wish I could film this and put it on YouTube – how you actually found the entrance to the *Observer* newsroom in the late 1970s. By then the paper had moved out of its swanky front wing in New Printing House Square and was tucked away in a side street opposite the Baynard Castle, a pub that the *Guardian* opera critic Philip Hope-Wallace likened to Errol Flynn's bedroom because of all the sabres and swords that were hung on its walls. The Baynard Castle was, for my first boss Clifford Makins, an annexe to the newsroom; on Fridays and Saturdays he would decamp there at opening time and we would bring the page proofs to his table.

At least the *Express* looked grand from the outside. There was no indication that the *Observer* was published in St Andrew's Hill at all, except for a battered door, painted black, that swung open at a push. You stepped into a grim hallway lit by cobwebby bulbs. There was no reception desk, no sign of human habitation at all, not even a board on the wall telling you which department was on which floor, only a lift. This had a mind of its own. You just got in and prayed it would go up. But no matter how firmly you pressed the button marked '4', it would sink to the sub-basement, the basement and a mysterious area called the 'Mezzanine', which was like Atlantis in that everyone knew of it but had never set foot in there.

Eventually, you reached the fourth floor. In front of you was a set of saloon-type doors so scuffed that as a newcomer your immediate reaction would have been that you had come to the wrong place. Surely a national newspaper couldn't be that grotty. Inside was a scene of dystopian clutter: long tables, the surfaces of which were hidden under giant manual typewriters; typing threes torn apart and strewn like bunting, overflowing in- and out-trays, battalions of telephones with mouthpieces that smelt of the breath of the last person to use them. 'It was rather like the Wild West,' reminisced Jennifer Selway. 'Smoke coming from wastepaper bins because someone had dropped a burning cigarette in there, and the sound of banging because someone else had somehow got himself shut inside the stationery cupboard.'

Behind the sports desk, Telex machines like Daleks *rat-tat-tatted* away, spewing Press Association reports full of typos caused by bored, careless fingers: accounts of football matches abandoned due to snot on pitch, scantily shorted racing cyclists who felt every bum in the road. The Telex machines were propped against a room occupied by Fred, Reg and Tom, a team of Fleet Street old-timers who took care of the sports results; they were known as details subs. This room was formed out of glass partitions, so it resembled a vivarium of old men in cardigans.

The floor space was so huge it accommodated every department. There were parts of the newsroom I barely knew existed; as far as I was concerned, the review section and business, for example, were located Somewhere Over There or Behind Those Filing Cabinets, phrases frequently used if you were on the sports desk, which was nearest the entrance and in consequence treated as a handy information kiosk by couriers arriving with parcels of books and armfuls of clothes. Edie Reilly, in addition to working for Katharine Whitehorn – they were, with fashion, based in Round The Corner – doubled as sports desk secretary on Saturdays. 'We got so fed up with being asked the way, we put up a sign marked FASHION with an arrow pointing in the right direction,' she reminded me.

This jogs my memory, taking me back to a previous point about how everyone would eat and drink together. The fashion department boasted a cupboard big enough to accommodate an easy chair. Both cupboard and chair play a part in the following story of Edie's:

'Mary, a sub on our section, decided to take us all out for lunch. It was a real long, long lunch. I was meant to go to a friend's house for dinner and I thought I'd better go into the fashion cupboard and have a little sleep in the chair. When I woke up, everybody had gone. It was daylight outside. I didn't know if it was morning or night. I rang speaking clock and it said it was eight-something, so I still didn't know. Then it started to get dark so I knew it was night, but I couldn't find my handbag, and it got darker and darker and I couldn't find the light switch.'

Edie groped her way down to security to ask how to switch on the light. 'Oh, we've been searching for you,' they said. 'We've got your handbag.' They made her a cup of tea. She got home at about eleven o'clock.

Being Round The Corner meant the Life section – the *Observer*'s women's pages – was invisible from the newsroom. On the *Sunday Times*, the Look! section (also for women, though edited by a man, David Robson) was one floor up from the newsroom. In other words, the women's departments, staffed almost wholly by females, were more or less quarantined. When David took over as sports editor and moved downstairs to the newsroom, it brought home to him how 'incredibly masculine' papers were.

'At *Honey* [where he was editor in the early 1970s] I was the only man there apart from the bloke I brought in as chief sub,' he recalled. 'There would be a lot of debate, argument and toing and froing about what we were doing in the magazine so I was surprised when I arrived at the *Sunday Times* to see how different it was – journalists working to orders, obeying instructions, chuntering maybe but not arguing with executives, and endowing the editor of the paper with godlike importance. Admittedly it was Harry Evans, but editors of newspapers are always treated like absolute monarchs – the editor wants this, the editor wants that, the editor's decision is final.' A similar observation was made by Emma Lee-Potter, who, having completed her training in Plymouth, headed for London. Though she got her toe-hold in Fleet Street by doing shifts, her full-time job for the first two years was on features at *Woman's Own*. 'There were only two men, the deputy features editor and the picture editor. When I went into Fleet Street, it was totally different.'

But how did you feel, that moment when you walked in for the first time? It's something you still remember in spite of all the years that have passed: that excitement – 'I'm actually there!'; the tingle of curiosity. Nerves because you want to do a good job. That little first-day-at-a-new-school anxiety – am I going to fit in? Will they like me? 'The first week, they gave me a hard time, muttering, "We know how you got your job,"' said Emma Lee-Potter, looking back to when she joined the *Evening Standard*. 'If I had got my job through having a famous journalist for a mother, I would have said, but I hadn't. I'm really proud of my mum and we were really close, but no way did I want to get a job on the strength of her name. She was a feature writer and I wanted to do hard news.'

Then there was the moment you realised you were going to be one of those journalists 'working to orders'. Having finished her training, Tina Moran applied to the *Bristol Evening Post*, the editor of which was very encouraging to NCTJ trainees: 'I got my slot in 1979. It was fabulous. Absolutely great. Nineteen years old, into a big newsroom in a big municipal paper. It was a big open floor, and the majority of people were men. They'd only just all come back from the big NUJ strikes. I walk in. "Are you in the union?" I'm asked. "See that guy over there? *Do not talk to him.*"'

The man belonged to the Institute of Journalists, which was less of a union and more of a professional association; its members had carried on working during a strike of provincial journalists that had begun at the end of 1978. 'They basically broke the strike,' said Tina. 'I felt terribly sorry for this rather dignified white-haired old man. He was a total pariah.'

Your first sight of the newsroom might have brought an instant feeling of being at home in this chaotic, testosterone-fuelled environment. 'The moment I walked in, I felt I belonged,' said Hilary Bonner. She remembers 'serried ranks of desks. New boys and girls all in the front row.' (Though when Hilary arrived, it was just 'girl', because for a long time she was the only woman reporter.) 'The legends were in the back row – the best reporters, the naughtiest boys.' They were, she said, kept in line by a fierce news editor called Ken Donlan. 'He was a tough bastard, but I wept buckets at his funeral.'

Or your reaction might have been the complete opposite. Jennifer Selway felt no sense of belonging when she joined the *Observer* as TV previewer. 'I'd gone from *Time Out*, the counterculture, to being a proper grown-up,' she recalled. 'The *Observer* was such a funny, old-fashioned place. Their introduction of a TV previewer was their attempt to enter the twentieth century. Unless Clive James [then the television critic] was writing about it, it wasn't quite the thing. The TV guide was just a sort of token acknowledgement of the modern world.'

A proper grown-up. Looking back, I'm struck by how old most of these men seemed when I arrived at the *Observer* at the age of twenty-two. Old and so *tall*, an intimidating combination sometimes. Certain presences in the newsroom could, therefore, instil terror. No one made me feel more dwarfed than Chris Brasher, the athletics correspondent. Rangy, megaphone-voiced, a stranger to self-doubt, Brasher charged through life in much the same way as he won a gold medal in the steeplechase at the 1956 Melbourne Olympics, when he was disqualified for allegedly impeding a rival before being reinstated the following day. This sublime dismissal of all obstacles in his path was precisely the quality needed to found the London Marathon, which he did, with John Disley, in 1981, but he absolutely petrified me. Thinking back, I'm still ashamed that I was such a ninny – he was never unpleasant and twice put himself out to help me with advice and contacts – but even when I had graduated from sports desk secretary to reporter I still wanted to hide in the loo when he was around. In 2002 I had to interview him for a London Marathon website on which I was working. I was middle-aged, I had a string of successful plays and books behind me, I was the website editor, I had even run his bloody marathon four times. But my heart was thumping, and my hand shaking so much, I could barely pick up the phone to call him.

Jennifer, meanwhile, was terrified of Terry Kilmartin, the literary editor. A tall, handsome war hero (he had, it was rumoured, saved David Astor from a grim fate while on special ops in France), Terry was a major figure in the book world, revered for having performed the first revision of the Scott Moncrieff translation of Proust's *Remembrance of Things Past*. His gorgeous, red-haired wife Joanna contributed occasional pieces on sport; we were friends. In consequence, Terry held no fears for me.

He could be dreadfully crushing, mind. In my youthful enthusiasm for the series of novels collectively known as *A Dance to the Music of Time*, I pronounced the name of their author Anthony Powell to rhyme with 'towel'. 'Pole,' he said, quellingly. Once, Jennifer suggested a feature to him about a modern sculptor whose work had just been placed in Trafalgar Square. 'You'd have thought I'd suggested a piece on Les Dawson,' she said. 'He was so grand. He could barely speak to me. Because I was writing about TV listings, I was well below the salt. I might as well have swept the floor. I felt he just despised me – just some silly girl who did the TV preview column. I sat near the travel editor – he was very waspish and funny, and keen on betting. We sometimes had a bit of a flutter. That was as exciting as things got. Everyone would go off to have lunch at the pub without me. I'd eat on my own at the canteen. I nipped in and out of the newsroom like a little mouse. I was never aware that anyone was having any fun. Such a waste. I just felt like a little downtrodden flibbertigibbet. The subs had such power. They were all terrifying.'

That fear of falling short wasn't unique to a female, of course. All but the most complacent of newcomers would have gone through some form or other of apprehension or self-consciousness, but at the core of everything for us was the knowledge that we had an extra-hard fight for acceptance, an additional imperative to prove we were up to the job, because in Fleet Street we were not the default setting. And one thing was impossible to ignore. 'You just got used to batting off comments,' said Louise Court. 'I remember walking through the office in a tulip skirt and a person who was senior to me said, "I just want to stick my hand up the back of your legs." Me: "Ah hahahaha!" You just got used to it, as a woman. Quite rightly, young women wouldn't react that way today.'

'At the *Standard* there were a couple I was a bit frightened of,' Wendy Holden remembered. 'One pressed himself up against you in the lift. You could feel things going on. I would think, Thank goodness we've only got two floors. At the same time there was relentless scrutiny of my appearance, innuendo; you could almost smell the testosterone.' She recalled, too, being on the night shift at the *Evening Standard*. Three in the morning, munching a filthy meat sandwich. 'It's you and me, kid – how about it.' Gosh, that would be guaranteed to make her swoon.

In 1987, she was hired by the *Telegraph* editor Max Hastings. 'He seemed determined,' she said, 'to clear out all the cobwebby old men.' A parting gift from her *Standard* colleagues was a Tom Johnston cartoon. It depicts Wendy at her moment of departure. Young, attractive, immaculate, utterly self-possessed, she is walking from one building to another. The alley between the two is blocked by a pile of rubbish sacks on which one *Standard* hack has already landed. Another is depicted in the act of jumping, with a cry of, 'Goodbye cruel world!' In each window of the *Standard* building are stricken male figures. One holds a receiver: 'Hello, Samaritans!' in one hand, while another is raising a shotgun to his head. Next to him, a gentleman of the press already the worse for wear raises a bottle to his lips. At another window, surrounded by bottles, someone begs, 'Don't go, glamour girl!'

On the pavement, someone else grovels behind her, bottle in hand: 'One more drink, Wendy!' he pants. A dustbin full of empties stands behind him.

The *Telegraph* windows, in contrast, variously show an old man in an ancient woolly reading *Train Spotter* magazine, a chap in a bow tie and dinner jacket daintily sipping tea, and a Gussie Fink-Nottle type poring over his stamp album. Wendy is the only woman in the picture.

The *Daily Telegraph*, more than any other paper, had that aura of the 'gentlemen's club'. 'It was considered to be the Fortnum & Mason of Fleet Street,' she explained. 'People didn't even smoke as much. The air was clearer.'

When she walked into the newsroom for the first time, it was packed with them. Fifteen or so stood up when she entered.

These are your most immediate takes from your first days in the newsroom: the squalor because the place lacked a woman's touch, the outdated equipment, the sexism and the mixture of boorishness and excessive gallantry displayed to female intruders in a male preserve. All this could make you feel as if you'd entered a previous century. Which is as good a cue as any to look back at some of the real pioneers – the first Fleet Street Girls.

Chapter 11

The First Fleet Street Girls

The first woman to edit a Fleet Street newspaper was declared insane. In fact, at one point Rachel Beer was not only joint proprietor and editor in all but name of the *Observer*, but owner-proprietor too of the *Sunday Times*. Then, broken and exhausted in her early forties by caring for her terminally ill husband while simultaneously keeping the papers on the road, she suffered a collapse in her mental health that resulted in her being bundled away to spend the rest of her life in seclusion. A fortune beyond most people's wildest imaginings had empowered her to fulfil her dreams, but that same wealth was instrumental in her incarceration at the hands of the patriarchy at a time when women were chattels.

'I thought this might interest you,' said Maureen Paton, handing me a hardback book when I interviewed her over lunch at the Dean Street Townhouse. *The First Lady of Fleet Street* was subtitled *The Life, Fortune and Tragedy of Rachel Beer*. Written by a husband-and-wife team, Eilat Negev and Yehuda Koren, it was just what I had been looking for since happening on snippets about her online. And they were snippets; this woman has largely been pushed to one side. But we should know of her, about her struggle, her journalism, her courageous defiance of Victorian social conventions, because it tells you all you need to know about the Fleet Street we arrived in.

She was born Rachel Sassoon in Bombay (Mumbai) in 1858; the family's fortune came from opium and cotton, and her grandfather, the patriarch David, had fled from Baghdad after being banished by the pasha. Her father, also David and known as S.D., was sent to England to develop the cotton side of the business. Rachel and her mother joined him and they settled in Walton-on-Thames, where they had a country estate, and a Regent's Park mansion. One of her nephews was the war poet Siegfried Sassoon (and *much* more about him later).

She was a precociously intelligent, highly verbal child and a gifted pianist. Her father died when she was nine, leaving her a fund of £10,000 'for her sole and separate and unalienable use and benefit free from the control of or engagement of any husband'. What an escape. Had S.D. lived, he would most definitely have had her married off in her teens to some suitable chap. Instead, she grew up to be a strong, independent woman, creative and erudite, someone who refused to settle for the conventional life of a wealthy Victorian wife. She wanted a purpose.

This couldn't have been easy. Her father might be dead, but she had an overbearing mother to contend with. No chance of university for her. What man wanted a clever wife? Besides, everyone knew that intellectual activity was bad for a woman. It resulted in sterility, and mental collapse. Rachel had to stay at home. She escaped, first, by working as a nurse (and as a journalist she campaigned on issues of public health including the status of nurses). Years later, as editor of the *Sunday Times*, she spoke up for equality of education, protesting against a proposal that for a woman to be granted a BA at Oxford she should achieve honours in at least one of the examinations. Men didn't have to meet that requirement. Why should they have preferential treatment? A 'dunderhead male' could scrape in with a pass and even carry on towards an MA. That was something forbidden to women.

She resisted her Orthodox Jewish family's attempts to set her up with a suitable boy, defying them to marry out. Her husband Frederick Beer, whose Jewish father, Julius, had converted to Anglicanism, had inherited the *Observer* at twenty-one; he was the heir to a fortune. Both Rachel and Frederick were in their late twenties when they met, passionately interested in the arts and, measured by the mores of the time, slightly eccentric; they were, in fact, a very modern couple who espoused equality in the relationship. The day before their wedding, she was baptised an Anglican. She would never be forgiven by her family, who ostracised her.

When it came to the *Observer*, Frederick was a hands-off proprietor, publicly in charge, while behind the scenes Rachel's was the dominant voice. Her mind fizzed with ideas for the paper, many of them stemming from her desire for social change. Ostensibly just a contributor, she was increasingly in charge of what it published. An assertive, powerful woman who did not bother to hide her opinions or disguise her intelligence – how terrible. This was revolutionary. This was a woman with real power. It was, in consequence, anathema to the staff. One editor discovered that to brush her off left him out of a job. His successor was no fan of women's emancipation either, so off he went. When she made changes to George Bernard Shaw's copy, the playwright, spittle-flecked with rage, described her as, 'A Jewish lady who has an interest in the paper,' because along with misogyny Beer had antisemitism to contend with, none more rabid than that of the French army officer Ferdinand Walsint Esterhazy, who forged the letters that brought about the false conviction of the Jewish captain Alfred Dreyfus.

The Dreyfus affair was the hill she was prepared to die on, and it was Esterhazy who presented her with her greatest coup as an editor. The *Observer*'s story rocked Europe. Rachel's team of journalists managed to drag a paid confession from him that, under orders from his superiors, he had forged the document that framed Dreyfus as a traitor and a spy. The appalling wrong that convicted Dreyfus, and caused Emile Zola's subsequent flight to England and jail sentence for *J'accuse . . . !*, the open letter to the president of France in his defence, had turned Rachel into a dogged campaigner for his cause and gave her paper one of the biggest scoops of the age.

I walked up and down Fleet Street for ages looking for number 46, the headquarters of Rachel Beer's *Sunday Times*. She bought it with her personal fortune at a time when she decided that acting under the shelter of her husband's name was not enough for her – she wanted to be out there, calling the shots. Number 46 turned out to be a narrow building sandwiched between the newly tarted-up façade of El Vino's and Mitre House, where a 'To Let' sign hung above a computer repair shop. Only the large black lettering LONDON NEWS AGENCY, a concern long gone, picked out on the red brickwork across the upper storeys, hinted at its history.

If truth be told, it's doubtful whether she frequented the place much. Like most editors of the time, she operated mainly from home; hers was in Mayfair. Something of a Katharine Whitehorn, a bit of a prototype Carole Cadwalladr, she wrote columns that were daring, articulate, witty and prescient; she was an unflinching advocate of women's and workers' rights, and what strikes you is how much of what she wrote stands up today: 'Few among women can be lover, mother, gourmet, saint, brilliant conversationalist, a good housekeeper, mistress, companion, and much more all at the same time. Men expect too much.' 'Most men seem to think themselves so much more attractive when quarrelling.' Along the way, though, Frederick fell sick and things began to fall apart. Throughout the soul-destroying years she spent nursing him, Rachel never missed a column in the *Sunday Times* – a journalist always files – but at the end of 1901 came the tipping point. Frederick was only forty-three when he died. His obituary referred to Rachel only as 'a lady whose tastes have secured her keen interests in the conduct of her husband's journalistic career'.

She tried to carry on, but the blow to her mental health was catastrophic. She could barely speak, let alone write. Had she gone mad? The men of her estranged family were concerned, not about her state of mind but about the money. What if she squandered her estate on charities, or fell prey to crooks, swindlers or fortune hunters? What if she made some batty will? To avoid that possibility, they had her declared a person of unsound mind. ('What, really?' asked the flabbergasted judge. 'I thought she was the editor of the *Observer*.')

Her nephew, the war poet Siegfried Sassoon, does not come out of this well. Having scrabbled to make ends meet, he had written gleefully of his anticipated inheritance from 'Auntie Rachel', though he had a long wait; having been removed from the scene, she recovered to live out her days in luxurious obscurity. She died in 1927, aged sixty-nine.

Her fortune and jewels were divvied up among the grasping nephews. Thanks to Auntie Rachel, Siegfried's long-standing money troubles were no more. Her two newspapers, sinking ships without her, were sold. Though she surely would have wanted to be buried next to Frederick in the Beer family mausoleum in Highgate Cemetery, her grave was in unconsecrated ground at the Tunbridge Wells Borough Cemetery, the powers that be deeming her to be not sufficiently Christian. Siegfried Sassoon made a flimsy excuse not to turn up at her funeral. No obituary appeared in the *Sunday Times* for this woman who had been its proprietor and editor for ten years, though two weeks later one T.P. O'Connor, in his column

Men, Women and Memories, commented, 'She made something of a hash of it.'

And there's more. While I was writing this, I did some
online digging about Siegfried Sassoon and found an essay in
the *London Review of Books* (2003) by Ferdinand Mount. It
was a review of two biographies of Sassoon and one of family
members, and contained the line: 'his Aunt Rachel eventually
died of the syphilis her husband had passed on to her'. Oh,
what? Horrible, horrible. I hoped it wasn't true. I hoped it was
just a malicious comment of Sassoon's, acting on the principle
of never letting a good turn go unpunished.

Something about Rachel Beer that I would love to have learned
is whether she employed other women on either of her papers.
None are mentioned in the book, though that doesn't mean
they weren't there. It's clear from various 'how-to' books of the
time (a fairly generous span of years, between the turn of the
twentieth century and the start of the 1930s) that journalism was
becoming an increasingly popular career option. Irritatingly
so, as far as the gentlemen of the press were concerned. Here's
Arnold Bennett in his *Journalism for Women: A Practical Guide*,
griping that, 'Of all the dwellers in Fleet Street, there are, not
two sexes, but two species – journalists and women-journalists
– and the one is as far removed from the other as a dog from
a cat.' Female journalists were unreliable, they ignored deadlines; their faults included inattention to detail and a slapdash
approach to spelling and grammar; there was a 'lack of restraint
in her prose – a shrillness, a certain quality of multiloquence
. . . a garrulous, gesticulating inefficacy'. Most heinous of all
was that they 'have not yet understood the codes of conduct
prevailing in the temples so recently opened to them.'

And here's one A. Sphinx in *Journalism as a Career for
Women*, finger-wagging at the 'women amateurs crowding

the avenues where work can be had, to the detriment of the professional worker . . . [it] should be made clear to her on every suitable or unsuitable occasion that her coquetting with journalism may be speedily terminated'. 'Is the woman journalist wanted?' asks the plaintive opening chapter of another *Journalism for Women*, this one by Myfanwy I. Crawshay.

What a woman was expected to write about in this period sounds very much the same as it was in the 1960s and 70s, as do the hostile, patronising and dismissive attitudes. Below are more extracts from Myfanwy I. Crawshay:

> In the domestic field alone she has enormous scope because the man rarely enters it . . . household work, beauty culture, weather fallacies, some problems of married life or child's welfare . . .

> With the increased popularity of gossip features, the woman writer has the chance to write entertainingly of social activities and the various lighter aspects of life. Her knowledge of clothes and styles is absolutely essential for description of dress at social functions . . .

> Women have not yet had much to do with the actual direction of the policy of newspapers, although here again the feminine influence is often in evidence. What a director's wife thinks of this or that feature often carries more weight than his fellow directors' opinion, as some editors know to their cost! The feminine viewpoint has to be kept in mind at all times.

Nearly fifty years on from Myfanwy I. Crawshay, the viewpoint of the executive's wife was still considered. In the mid-1970s, David Robson was appointed editor of the *Sunday Times*'s Look! section, in all but name its women's pages. 'The Look! pages were very scary,' he said. 'Theoretically Godfrey Smith was my boss – I never saw him. I was supposed to show the pages to Harry Evans but could never see him, I think he was writing Kissinger's memoirs. Once he was standing in the next urinal so I put the pages against the wall so he could look. I got no feedback so I didn't know whether it was a fucking disaster or a triumph. Two or three pages of the paper which had bog-all to do with anything else on the paper.'

The only comment from a high-up he ever received was: 'I think your pages are very good. My wife reads them and she likes it.'

What on earth can it have been like as a woman in Fleet Street back then? In those early days, hampered by rib-crushing corsetry and seven pounds of voluminous serge skirt, she would have been one female among many men. Did she work from home, wherever that was? Or did she travel by horse-drawn omnibus or on the newly opened Metropolitan line, getting off at the north end of Blackfriars Bridge, or use the new underground station, St Paul's, on the Central London Railway? Was she that shorthand-typist who, in A. Sphinx's words, 'has worked her way up, has succeeded in distinguishing herself and gaining a position of importance in the Press'? I longed to know if her feet hurt in those lace-up boots at the end of a long day, and whether she was abused or assaulted as an unaccompanied woman in public, if she bashed out her copy on the office machine or wrote in longhand perched on her bed in a little room.

But to gain some awareness of the reality of her life as a journalist in the Victorian era, I think the best way to start is in the present, with a visit to the Tottenham Hotspur Stadium. This mind-blowingly wonderful building, opened in April 2019 and promptly garlanded with awards – unlike, I have to say, the team that plays there – boasts notable state-of-the-art features such as giant trays that will retract the football surface beneath the South Stand to reveal the artificial American football pitch below. The club shop is 23,000ft long, which makes it the largest in the world. I could go on, but as this is not a football book I will cut to the chase – there are 471 toilets, of which 84 per cent are for women.

Here I have to make a brief diversion into the mid-1970s. The provision of female toilets at football grounds was not, then, a priority. A helpful reporter from the *Daily Mail*, Jeff Powell, would stand on guard outside the gents for me so I didn't have to trek to some stinky shack the other side of the ground. But at least there was one. And all this leads up to the question that nags at me most persistently. Where did she go to the loo?

'A journalist must get about' was one of the pieces of wisdom bestowed on Mary Kenny by Charles Wintour, her editor at the *Evening Standard*. What he meant was that a journalist had to socialise, meet people, hear gossip, make contacts. A fat lot of good that advice would have been to a newspaperwoman in the latter part of the nineteenth century. This was an era when women were still regarded as 'the angel in the house'. A woman was pretty much stuck there unless she planned her journeys around the homes of family members and friends where she could use the facilities. You could only travel as far as your bowels and bladder could take it. It is known as 'the urinary leash'. The first public toilet was unveiled at the 1851 Great Exhibition. It was immediately assumed that it would be for male use. A woman would be too embarrassed to be seen entering it, surely. Indeed, a year later, when the first public waiting rooms began to appear, they were men-only. When a model of a women's toilet was set up in Camden High Street, hansom cab drivers rammed it deliberately. Public facilities, it was maintained, would encourage prostitutes by enabling them to be out on the street. Despite campaigning by the Ladies'

Sanitary Association, there were no women's lavatories in the workplace, either. As late on as the years following the First World War, some employers were resistant to the idea of installing female loos, as they believed it would enable women to steal men's jobs.

For most women who wanted to be journalists, getting a foothold wasn't easy. The National Union of Journalists set a minimum wage for its members of £8 a week. In principle, that was meant to apply to women as well as men, but the women had to get the jobs first, and few did. The NUJ resentfully allowed these pests to join, though they made sure that male spaces were barricaded against female invaders. The press gallery at the House of Commons was out of bounds. They were barred from all the men's clubs. Deprived of gossip and rumours over the chicken consommé, turbot, thick slabs of beef and the savoury, they couldn't go to the pub to get the gen either. What usually happened was that most women didn't qualify to join the NUJ. Many remained freelancers, with no steady income. It was hard to make a living when editors wriggled out of paying for their work. Surely it was reward enough to see themselves in print? It's all very well emphasising how strong, how resilient and how determined you had to be to survive in Fleet Street in our era, but just think what it took back then. From a modern perspective, these women were heroic.

I found a small amount of information online about a woman journalist whose career was contemporaneous with Rachel Beer's. This was Mary Billington, who was born in 1862. She was the daughter of the vicar of All Saints, Chalbury, in East Dorset, and her mother was a vicar's daughter. Chalbury has a hill from which you can see the Isle of Wight, and at the turn of this century a population of 140. I have no idea what life at The Rectory was like, but I suspect that if you had any go in you at all you might want to find out what the world was like beyond the hill. She became a pioneer female career journalist and I like to think of her as the ur-Fleet Street Girl; it was intriguing how much of the trajectory of that career prefigured the one we followed.

It began on a local paper, the *Southern Echo*; in fact, she was part of the founding team. In 1886, at twenty-four, she was headhunted to join its London office. Between 1890 and 1897 she worked for the *Graphic*, the first paper to target women; she was the first special women's correspondent. Her early reporting jobs seem to have been quite something; at some point during this period, she was required to dive underwater in full gear at the Royal Navy Exhibition. She travelled, filing twenty-eight reports from India describing the role of women there; they resulted in her first book, *Woman in India* (1895).

She obviously found the limitations placed on female writers frustrating at this point, grumbling in 1896 of editors' preference for men 'for the "rough and tumble" work of outside reporting'. She would never have been sent out to cover 'a murder or any revolting case'. Women journalists, she complained, were typically restricted to the 'Women's Sphere', reporting on 'frocks and frills, with laces and chiffons and other mysteries of Dame Fashion'.

In 1897, the *Daily Telegraph* hired her to look after the women's-interest page. This concentrated on the fashion news she disdained, although she did get the chance to write a weekly column focusing on women's working lives. She was in her thirties by then and I wonder if she had become worried about being judged as a hoyden – she was certainly presenting herself as ladylike. 'English lady journalists,' she wrote, 'have not so far descended to any of the vulgar sensationalism and semi-detective business which has discredited the American reportresses . . . happily, our editorial methods and our own instincts as gentlewomen do not lead us to try being barmaids or going out as costermongers on a bank holiday for the purpose of "getting copy".'

She died, not very old, in 1925. Her obituary described her career as 'a shining example to the ambitious and the independent women she thought suitable for journalism', and stated that she was 'especially kind and encouraging to young women journalists who sought her advice and assistance'. I found two images of her online. One, taken late in her career when she was pretty big-time, accompanied a brief article about her on the women's-interest page of the *Winnipeg Evening Telegraph*, and shows her looking jovial in a strange hat. It was 1920 and she had gone to Canada as the sole female delegate to speak at an international conference; the headline below the photo is PRESS WOMEN GREET SISTER FROM BRITAIN, and a short résumé of her speech is headlined JOURNALISM IN BRITAIN OFFERS WOMEN CHANCE. In the other one, she looks young but severe in a black serge jacket and ankle-length skirt, white shirt. It is the sort of thing you would wear to look completely sexless and unapproachable. I wondered if, like us, she had to make efforts to repel gropers.

A quick return to the topic of female loos at football grounds. One evening, while promoting a book on the 1986 World Cup, I mentioned this, the dearth of such things, on Terry Wogan's chat show, to his horror – you simply did not talk about lavatories on early evening television. Some good did come of it, though.

On the opening night of the new Tottenham Hotspur Stadium, when we filed into the media centre (a very twenty-first-century development) I overheard one male journo ask, 'Why is there a women's toilet?' 'Julie Welch,' was the reply.

They'd even put Molton Brown toiletries in there.

Chapter 12

Finding Your Tribe

'You have to find your tribe,' said Mary Kenny when I asked her what advice she would give to a hopeful young journalist, and I found mine at the *Observer* sports department, with which I fell in love en bloc – not just its personnel but the furnishings and fittings, the shelf of dusty *Wisdens*, the four wooden desks, the coat stand that was a retirement home for old mackintoshes, and the huge filing cabinet that was virtually bare except for the bottom drawer where Clifford, my boss, kept bottles of whisky. I was twenty-two, as impressionable as wax; for the cover blurb of *The Biography of Tottenham Hotspur*, I wrote that I was 'educated at Bristol University and the *Observer* sports department', and I've always maintained, not quite jokingly, that I was socialised by the *Observer* sportswriters. I had found my tribe, my people (and along the way the love of my life).

My only glimpse of the inner workings of newspapers had been at the *Daily Telegraph* magazine, which had been orderly and rather snooty. On my first day at the *Observer* – it was June 1971 – I stuck my handbag on the floor beside my chair and was immediately required to take down a letter to Richard Burton in my newly perfected spdrtg shorthand ('Dear Richard, I would like to offer you the opportunity to cover a game of rugby. The fee will be ten guineas, plus reasonable expenses'). I realised then and there that the *Observer* was going to be nothing like the *Daily Telegraph* at all.

151

Incidentally, Clifford received back a very nice letter from Richard Burton, saying he would have loved to do it but unfortunately lacked the time.

My working week was from Tuesday to Saturday, the hours ten till six and my wages twenty-one guineas per week. On my desk were three telephones, an ashtray, an in-tray, an out-tray, and an enormous manual Remington typewriter, so heavy that I had to send for a man if it needed moving. It had a bell, and a lever at the side with which to lash back the carriage return. I used more paragraphs than strictly necessary so I could hear it ping.

Clifford and I must have looked an extraordinarily mismatched duo, as though any moment we'd break out into a comedy routine. I tottered about in Biba's cork-soled clogs, hotpants, a boy's green-and-white striped shirt from C&A, and a darling pale green bowler hat. Clifford's workwear – I had never met a man so defiantly ill-dressed – was a baggy tweed jacket, crumpled shirt and asymmetrically fastened tie. His trousers were held up with string or old pyjama cords and hung in swags round his toecaps, while his underpants rose over the waist like a greyish-white cummerbund.

His desk was at right angles to mine, and covered with ashtrays, readers' letters, tobacco tins, make-up sheets – the A4-sized pieces of paper ruled with vertical columns, on which the pages were designed with pencil and ruler – and last week's page proofs. When not one jot of working space remained, he would sweep everything into the wastepaper bin. At 11 a.m., he arrived. At 11.45, I would hear a hiss, which was him applying breath freshener from a small bottle of Amplex. This was the signal for his departure to lunch, which by rights I should put in inverted commas, as it hardly ever involved actual food. He'd take a taxi to wherever he was going, even if it was only the five hundred yards to El Vino's.

He was divorced and enjoyed a busy love life. It involved three women, all of whom worked on the paper, so I had to operate the points system that prevented them colliding. This was complicated by two of his amours sharing a Christian name. 'Get the right extension,' he would mutter when I was required to summon one or other to the phone. The man was indefatigable. My mother came up to town on a shopping expedition, and I invited her to pop in afterwards for a sherry at the Black Friar. She was fifty-eight, an age at which a bit of male attention gives a boost, and I thought she would enjoy meeting the sportswriters. They certainly enjoyed meeting her, especially Clifford. She planned to catch the tube back to Loughton. When the time came for her to leave, he accompanied her into the street, hailed a taxi, and opened the door for her. I thought he was just chivalrously helping her in, but he climbed in beside her and off they went.

My duties weren't demanding. On Tuesday mornings I had to fill in The Ledger, a huge, heavyweight, Dickensian kind of book in which each event we would be covering that Saturday was listed, together with the name of the reporter assigned to it. Then I had to phone each reporter, post off his press pass and contact the local press agency to book a phone so he could dictate his report to the copytaker. I collected reporters' expenses from accounts, and made lots of journeys to the canteen to fetch bacon sandwiches for the subs. Towards the end of the week, I would spend a lot of the time on the phone rounding up the men. They roamed, like loose steers. There was often some emergency because Hugh McIlvanney, the chief sportswriter, hadn't filed and every pub within a two-mile radius would have to be contacted, plus various flats around town – they were known as his 'safe houses' – in which he might have spent the night. One Tuesday, as I arrived for work, Jim, who ran the reception desk, beckoned to me furtively. 'Over there,' he muttered out of the side of his mouth. 'Asking for Hugh. Can you sort him out?'

It was Eric Idle of *Monty Python's Flying Circus*. I became aware that I was gawping and hastily shut my mouth. How on earth had Hugh and Eric Idle ever found themselves in each other's company, let alone made plans for a further meeting? How would Hugh even have known who Eric Idle was? He would never have been home in time to watch *Monty Python*, let alone been anywhere near the *Observer* on a Tuesday morning. They were lucky if he surfaced on a Friday and sometimes not even then. Once he didn't even check in till the morning of Grand National Saturday and one of my predecessors as secretary had had to go to Euston and wait by the platform with his binoculars and press pass for him to collect as he raced past her for the last train that would get him to Aintree in time for the start.

'Hugh's not around right now,' I said. Eric Idle looked to be making for the exit, so I added hastily, 'but he could come in any moment. Would you like to come up to the sports desk and wait anyway?'

'No, no, just tell him I called round.'

'Are you *sure* you wouldn't like to come up?' I pleaded, because it was not often that the sports department had their very own Python come to visit, but he darted nimbly away. Obviously, he could tell that my next move would be to chain him to a radiator.

What a magic, magic place. Payday was on Friday, when Charlie Vidler did the rounds of the clerical staff bearing a wooden tray loaded with cash-stuffed brown envelopes. Charlie was a legend, rumoured to have been a butler at Cliveden, family seat of the editor-proprietor, the Hon. David Astor. He had, it was said, been given a job at the *Observer* after his dismissal for being found asleep in Lord Astor's bed. In addition to this, I suddenly realised he was the faerie-like person who had sold the twelve-year-old me that Danny Blanchflower photo in Tudor Street.

David Astor himself was a tall, fair-haired grandee whose handsome face was deeply grooved by self-doubt and intellectual agonising. (It was Katharine Whitehorn who came up with the famous comment, 'The editor's indecision is final.') His office suite was based somewhere in the building's upper region that belonged to Editorial and Comment, the section of the paper I mentally classified as Men And Their Boring Opinions. Happening on the lowlier members of his workforce caused him extreme embarrassment. If he saw you, he would cringe and pretend he was part of the wall. He belonged in a P.G. Wodehouse novel, surely.

Some of the reporters were similarly out-of-the-ordinary. Among them was Laos, a displaced Hungarian intellectual with haunted eyes. His salary was covered out of David Astor's own pocket and he repaid his debt of gratitude by delivering sandwiches, biscuits and cocktail sausages to every department at teatime on Saturdays, the day we went to press. He also provided occasional copy on Central European matters, so Clifford referred to him as Trouble In The Balkans. Another, very old, journalist seemed to have set up home on the top floor, with his own bed and pyjamas and wash things. You'd sometimes see him in carpet slippers, pattering along the corridors like an ancient pet Labrador that the Astors couldn't bear to have put down.

As for our department, *well*. The *Observer* being a high-minded paper, sport was looked down upon, a necessity whose presence had to be tolerated but not encouraged, like a randy old uncle at Christmas. Our office was situated well away from genteel sections such as Gardening and Arts, and on busy days we lowered the tone considerably, with

155

wastepaper bins catching fire owing to incompletely extinguished cigarette ends – Clifford himself started smouldering once when, absentmindedly, he stuck his pipe insufficiently tamped into his pocket – and people falling drunk off their chairs (everybody on Fleet Street drank a lot, but the sportswriters drank *a lot*).

The department's isolation meant that, while I barely spoke to any female from one month to the next, I knew an awful lot of men because I spent the entire week cooped up with them. If you were a secretary no one thought you existed and they carried on as if you were as insensate as the filing cabinet, so I was given a riveting exposure to The Male Psyche. I knew who was having girlfriend trouble, who kept a mistress in the West End, who was being chased for settlement by his bookie, and who was receiving smouldering letters from the wife of an executive on a rival newspaper (the post room steamed them open as a matter of course and it took discipline not to have a peek). The men and I all got on well. If you have, as I did, an extensive knowledge of football, you have one guaranteed subject of conversation, which means men don't have to worry about asking politely about your children or loft conversion.

There were actually two regular female contributors; they looked after tennis and show jumping, but rarely visited the office. Tennis was Shirley Brasher, wife of Chris, the terrifying athletics correspondent, but once she had been Shirley Bloomer, winner of the ladies' singles title at the 1957 French Open Championships and British number one. She was still a huge name in the sport and obviously had better things to do than lurch around Fleet Street pubs. As did the show-jumping correspondent Genevieve Murphy, a smart, merry woman who spoke in a soft, breathy Irish accent, as if she was blowing the words out along with her cigarette smoke. One Saturday she concluded four hundred words on an epic battle between Paddy McMahon on Pennwood Forge Mill and Alwin Schockemöhle on Rex The Robber in the European Championships over the All England Jumping Course at Hickstead with the line, 'The two will meet again next month in the self-same arena.' But the copytaker misheard this soft, breathy sentence as, 'The two will meet again next month in the Selsey Marina,' and failed to say, 'Could you repeat that, please?' because he was obviously in a hurry, with a queue of people waiting to file their copy. The likelihood that Pennwood Forge Mill and Rex The Robber would be swimming their way around boats didn't enter his mind. Then the sub didn't think twice about letting it through because a) he didn't know anything about show jumping, and b) he had a pile of other stuff waiting to be butchered. So it was the copytaker and the sub who were at fault, but Genevieve who looked the idiot. But what did you expect? Women in sport! Pah!

Genevieve didn't come near the office, either. It was just me and the chaps. At busy times it was like being in a Man Showroom, one which specialised in classic models such as Rugger Bugger, Wild Scot, Prince Charming, Tortured Artiste, Lord Snooty, Action Man, Mad Irishman, and a sort of super-annuated Flower Child, the columnist who did 'World of Sport', and wore flowered shirts and orange cords. Once Edie Reilly dreamed she had sex with that one. 'Standing up. I was horrified.'

I was lucky, though – they were all nice men. I heard tell of one Fleet Street boss who used to get his secretary to jump up and down so as to see her bust wobble; another who treated secretaries as his own private harem (he only ever gave the job to statuesque girls with large breasts); one who had a red-faced, spittle-flecked meltdown because his desk had been placed in a position of insufficient importance – 'You can't ask me to sit next to a sub!'

'Often you had to be the peacemaker if one man had fallen out with another,' said Angie Mulligan, my friend from the *News of the World*. '"You're going to have to say you're sorry. That's all you can do." As a woman in Fleet Street, you had to supplant your personality. You were always dealing with so many male egos.'

All the papers seemed to have a chief secretary who, while she might not work for the editor himself, attained her stature by longevity and sheer weight of personality. At the *News of the World* it was Dottie, who worked for the sports editor. Dottie loved a flutter on the horses, whizzed to and from Fleet Street in a series of amazing sports cars, and ate exactly the same lunch every day: one brown roll, six Jacob's cream crackers and a slice of Edam, with a freshly ironed napkin to spread over her lap. 'She had a sort of religious look,' said Angie. 'That kind of *quietness*. She came in one day, she'd found her husband dead, and never said a word about it.'

The secretaries to the *Observer* top brass were all forbidding but to a woman they were overshadowed by Gritta. Gritta was so eminent she received a mention in Jeremy Lewis's biography of David Astor, albeit as a 'secretary-dogsbody'. That seemed too small and mean a description for her; she was more like a monument, an institution, the one who had been there for ever and a day. She was a German refugee and had come to Britain on the *Kindertransport*; an amazing story to which, being young and shallow, I never gave a thought. To me she was just a terrifying person who hung menacingly over you with her bosom if she caught you using her Remington. It was like being under like Ayers Rock.

'She was there for about fifty years,' said Edie Reilly. 'Gravelly voice, huge bust. Her leaving-do speech was so long everyone's drink was finished and we just slid down the wall onto the floor. She'd reached the 1950s when there was a short pause and somebody started clapping and so we all joined in and she had to stop. The next day I passed her and said (lying), "I enjoyed your speech," and she said, "It was just the tip of the iceberg."'

I must say here that being a secretary in Fleet Street was not unremitting jollity. We all had our moments of terror. Angie's concerned the typing threes.

'One of our reporters typed a big feature about Paula Yates,' said Angie. 'He handed it to me, saying, "Here, Angie, tear this up." What I was meant to do was separate the three sheets so one could go to the editor, one to the sub and one back to him. But I literally tore it into tiny pieces. He went ballistic. I was so scared I hid in the loo. He was trying to entice me out – "Come on, Angie, I didn't mean to shout. I've got a little champagne waiting for you . . ."'

'I lost the manuscript for Katharine Whitehorn's latest book once,' said Edie. 'It was called *How to Manage Your Money*, and I was supposed to critique it and type it out for her. I put it in my bag and went to the wine bar after work, and when I got home I realised I had the wrong bag. I'd picked up someone else's. Helen on News had one similar, and I assumed she'd taken mine. I spent all Saturday trying to find a number for her and was then told she wasn't on the phone. I had to find her address. She lived in Clacton. So, on Sunday, a friend and I travelled to Clacton, and found Helen, and we did have each other's bag, so we swapped them over. Then the friend and I wandered about in Clacton and went to a pub. Then I realised we were quite near my sister's place so we went there and drank all afternoon. So I never typed any of Katharine's manuscript, hadn't even looked at it. On Monday Katharine rings me: "How are you getting on? What do you think of it?"

'"Oh, I don't think it applies to me."

'"Doesn't apply to you? It was SPECIFICALLY WRITTEN FOR PEOPLE LIKE YOU!!!"'

'When I did eventually confess to her I'd lost it, she went mad. She walked out of the office, she was so mad, because that had been her only copy. Anyway, a while later when she was updating *Cooking in a Bedsitter*, I was to going to type that out for her too. She took me to lunch at Le Gavroche to give me the manuscript. And then she went to the loo and turned round and shouted right across the restaurant, "AND THIS TIME DON'T LEAVE IT IN A PUB!"'

What a lot of pubs there were to leave stuff in. Every alley and side road seemed to have one, and on the street itself you couldn't walk five yards without entering a guff cloud of cigarette smoke and alcohol fumes. We drank in one or other of them every day; but, as well as that, every paper had its own special pub, and you *never* went in one if it belonged to a paper that wasn't yours. The *Observer*'s, when I joined, was the Black Friar, which was stupendous. Its back bar seemed to have been decorated in the style of the waiting room of an Edwardian brothel. It had mirrors in gilded frames, comfortable armchairs upholstered in manly brown leather, hexagonal marble-topped tables and bracing sayings engraved in brass around the walls: TOMORROW WILL BE FRIDAY; A GOOD THING IS SOON SNATCHED AT; SEIZE THE DAY. The landlord was a big frizzle-haired Welshman called Barry, who was largely genial but had back in the mists of time been a Desert Rat, one of the British soldiers who had fought in North Africa during the Second World War. One night, Brian the Saturday sub got into an argument with him and the next moment Barry disappeared through the door marked 'Private' and came back with his garrotting wire. The Black Friar was also the background for a terribly embarrassing incident, because that was where I got very drunk indeed.

I have an eidetic memory, one that retains visual images in vivid detail and, if necessary, reruns them like an old movie. Very useful for a writer, of course, but something of a two-edged sword as I can remember every asinine thing I did when drunk, even if it was half a century ago.

Now, Clifford's eclectic stock of cronies included not only Kingsley Amis, Ted Dexter and Sir Bernard Miles, proprietor of the nearby Mermaid Theatre, but a detective inspector called Pat. DI Pat was based at the local police station, Snow Hill. He was a lantern-jawed hunk with piercing blue eyes and very long legs, and he would often turn up at the sports department on a Saturday night; you'd go in there from the newsroom to fetch something and there the two of them would be sitting over a bottle of Scotch, serenaded by occasional outbursts from Pat's two-way radio.

It was a complete mystery to me how the two of them had struck up an acquaintance, but what a useful friendship it turned out to be. My favourite drink at the time was vodka, diluted with tiny bottles of Britvic orange juice. One night, it was not diluted enough. Staggering back to my car from the Black Friar, keys in hand, I spotted a police constable halfway up the street. I picked my way past him carefully, but toppled sideways a few yards later.

He caught up and ushered me into the back seat of my Hillman Imp. Then he got in beside me. He was young, and not bad-looking, and we had a nice friendly chat while I sobered up. 'I'm fine now,' I said. 'Thank you very much for looking after me.'

'I can't let you go yet.'

'I'm not going to drive. I'm going to sleep in the car.'

'Aha, but you had your car keys in your hand. I *could* book you for being drunk in charge of a vehicle. What am I going to get for looking after you?'

What?

'Are you from Snow Hill police station?' I said. 'What a coincidence! You must know my boss's friend, the inspector. He comes in to see my boss every Saturday night. He's *there now*.'

That got rid of him. But really. Not in all my twenty-two years had it occurred to me that a policeman would ask for sexual favours. I had no idea how wet behind the ears I still was.

My second near-downfall was the travel arrangements for the Newport to Bermuda yacht race. The yachting correspondent was a very decent chap, tall and tanned with buoyant, silvery swept-back hair, as if he was surrounded wherever he went by his own little cloud of ocean spray. It was fortunate that he was a decent chap because when I booked his trip out to Newport, Rhode Island, it didn't occur to me that he needed to get back. He had to stay in New York for two more nights, which might have been fun for him but not for Clifford, who was summoned by the *gauleiter* in charge of accounts to explain this colossal blow to the budget. That was something which could be laughed off, though. I went on to do something worse. Far worse.

According to Mary Kenny, in the wonderful *Something of Myself and Others*, George Orwell once said that the only autobiography worthy of trust is one that reveals something disgraceful about the writer. Oh, here goes.

One skill that proved useful to the sportswriters was my ability as a forger, and I was very cocky about it. Clifford was a good man but, being an alcoholic, his hours of work were irregular. I could replicate perfectly Clifford's signature. Thus, in Clifford's absence the sportswriters would get me to put his name to various flights of fancy.

My working week (as I said) was from Tuesday to Saturday. One day, Hugh asked me to come in on a Monday to help him compose his expenses. (This was not an invitation to see his etchings – he was inclined to let this dreary administrative task drift, and the secretary would be needed to trawl through *Observer* back numbers to find out where he had been a year ago, and with whom.) It would mean overtime – £5. As my weekly wage was £22, I accepted with gusto. After we had composed this document, I forged Clifford's signature, and then wrote my own claim for £5, duly forging Clifford's signature on that too.

I then thought, This is a good wheeze, actually, and over the next few weeks submitted similar fraudulent claims for £5 Mondays.

One day, Clifford grunted, looked up from his desk and said: 'Do you know anything about this?' He showed me a memo from our friend the *gauleiter* in accounts.

I had been rumbled. I was hot with shame and fear and embarrassment, but it wasn't the dishonesty I was ashamed of, it was my conceit. I wasn't a journalist. I was a secretary. I wasn't entitled to cheat on my expenses. I did not know my place.

Clifford covered up for me. I have no idea why he didn't sack me. Had he done so, of course, my whole life trajectory would have been very different.

Chapter 13

The Big Break: Finding a Marvellous Chap

For some years Katharine Whitehorn and I were colleagues on the *Observer*, though she existed on a more exalted level than me. Not only would I never have presumed to call her Kath (as she was known by family, friends and close colleagues), but for ten years we never exchanged a word. She was, though, the greatest female journalist I ever knew and when I started work on this book, she was the first person I interviewed.

Katharine stopped writing for the *Observer* in 2013; for some years she had also been *Saga*'s agony aunt, but her by-line had disappeared from that too. I knew she would have passed her ninetieth birthday, but would she be willing to be interviewed? To find out how to get in touch, I contacted her publisher. They referred me to her son, Bernard Lyall, who kindly gave me her email address.

As I started to compose an email to her, I wondered whether I should remind her who I was. What to say?

1. You once gave me a useful tip for the book I was producing on etiquette. (It was that you should never replace a spent match in the box, because the owner of the matchbox would think they had plenty left but then, on going to light up, would discover a box full of duds. This was, of course, in the days when everyone smoked.)

2. The first time you ever spoke to me was when you expressed interest in the Kaffe Fassett needlepoint cushion I was working on to pass the time as we waited in a studio to be filmed for some TV ad for the *Observer*. It was the early 1980s. I think you were going through your kind of Must Mentor The Young Ones phase because you also invited me to a talk you were giving at the British Medical Association (you were witty and magnificent).

3. In 1984, while you were away on holiday, I deputised on your column, and did it rather better than I might have. You wrote me a gracious letter with a coded warning, i.e. thanking me for *keeping it warm till you returned*.

4. The last time we met was at Random House in 1994 when you and Edie Reilly came to the launch of my first novel. Which was kind because obviously you got invited to dozens of book launches and it must have all got a bit tedious in the end, going to the fag of trailing into town to drink the publisher's cheap wine where someone else is getting all the limelight.

I then realised that this was becoming All About Me, so I just emailed to ask her if she would talk about her life in journalism with me. Unfortunately, my request was excessively gushy.

'Great heaven, stop being nice to me!' came the response. 'Of course, I'd be delighted to discuss all that with you.' It sounded as if in spite of her great age she was much the person I remembered.

She invited me to her house (Hampstead borders, lovely), where she lived with a cat and a carer; her husband, the thriller writer Gavin Lyall ('He was a super person to be married to') died in 2003. Like all the people I interviewed subsequently, she was smartly dressed and had put her make-up on – not one of us had Let Herself Go. At this point, though struggling, she was putting up a good front.

Before I went to see her, I did my homework by rereading *Selective Memory*. It was for the fourth time, and remained as wonderful. Here's the potted history, accompanied by some of her comments when we met. Started as a publisher's reader at Methuen, three years, no progress. Taught foreigners on the side to make some money. Went to Finland, ran a pub. 'I keep changing jobs,' she said. 'I thought, I must really get into a job that changes a lot itself.' So she went to America, bought a $20 typewriter in a Church Aid shop and decided to become a journalist. Came back to England, took a job on *Home Notes*, a long-defunct magazine for which she had to write 'Real Love Stories'. A friend who worked on *Picture Post* introduced her to the great photographer Bert Hardy; he used her as his model for a feature called 'Lonely in London'. The photos made her famous. 'You were beautiful!' I burst out, and she said, 'Any journalist, girl or boy, will work with what they've got. It was useful for finding someone to talk to.'

Anyway, *Picture Post* gave her a job; that's where she trained. 'A marvellous place; you did everything with a photograph and a chap was teaching you the whole time. I always did my learning from chaps.' Then *Picture Post* folded. She got a job on *Woman's Own*. 'Awful – I had to interview girls in factories. But I earned lots of money.' Was sacked by *Woman's Own*. Was taken on by the *Spectator*, and that was when it all really started. She wrote a column called Roundabout, which appeared at the back of the magazine and it caught the eye of George Seddon, women's editor of the *Observer*. He was looking for a female journalist capable of bridging the gap between women's writing and what would have been, at the time, regarded as 'serious' writing – i.e. the stuff that men wanted to read, about politics, business and sport.

So she moved to the *Observer* and worked with George Seddon.

'At that time, you either behaved like a man or you were put in a place where you didn't matter. With George, you didn't have to be like a man. He was perfect because he was married but he was gay, so he was on both sides of the fence. If you think how women were at the time and how the chaps were running everything, George was the perfect person. He took the women seriously and let them write what they thought was important. Not what a bloke would write – that women need even thinner bras. You had to find a man who would help you and George was a marvellous chap.'

As I got up to leave, the hands on the clock were at twelve on the dot. 'Would you like a gin and tonic?' she said.

I hate gin and hardly ever drink alcohol now, but had one anyway, because it was her.

As per Lynn Barber's dictum that you must always be nice to young journalists at the beginning of their careers because they'll end up your editors, I always say yes if trainees ask for an interview. It's generally in the form of an online question-naire, and invariably one of the questions is: How did you get into football reporting?

As you get older, you develop a different perspective on time. Now I am describing how I came to be a football writer I see everything happened very quickly, whereas when I was the sports desk secretary the struggle to get anywhere seemed to last as long as the Crimean War.

My lunch hour consisted of a tub of cottage cheese and an orange at my desk, along with my knitting, a copy of *Petticoat* magazine, and the *Daily Telegraph* crossword. The phones never rang in the afternoons and Clifford rarely reappeared, so I just got on with trying to become a journalist.

The whole sports department seemed to be writing books. Ron, the deputy sports editor, had just typed the final full stop on his second, a history of the Canadian Mounted Police. Clifford was co-writing a detective thriller with Ted Dexter, the former England cricket captain. Murder in the cricket team! They were dropping like flies. Every other chapter seemed to begin with something like: 'Chadders was found dead in the morning.' (It's called *Test Kill*, by the way, and copies can still be found online. It's jolly good.) The only one who wasn't writing books was Arthur Hopcraft, who was writing play after play after play. I still had grandiose ideas about the Great Novel but, when I sent her anything, my beautiful, daunting agent Pat Kavanagh swiftly disabused me of hope. All right, then, I thought, I'll have a shot at doing some features for *Honey* and *Petticoat*.

This was a useless idea. Sex and emotion. Boyfriends. Parties. Flat-sharing. Holiday romances. I was rubbish at every topic I tried to address. I could not write that sort of stuff with any conviction. My concerns were no longer the same as those of anyone else of my age. Of course, those concerns would have made interesting copy – the trauma of having risen so high and crashed so low, the challenges of being married with a baby at twenty-one when you know nothing about babies or even being married – but how could I have gone public with all that? My mother had kept Fred's existence secret from her friends. What if any of them got to see what I had written?

It had been a blisteringly cold winter. Nothing seemed to go right. We had a beautiful cat called Pud-Pud, black and white and hairy, a very maternal lady. She had been our Bristol cat, sleeping next to Fred in his baby basket, which now would probably be regarded as child abuse, but our flat had been very cold (we couldn't afford to heat it properly) and she kept him warm. Love in a cold climate, indeed.

One day she disappeared from our Wandsworth flat. At first we didn't worry because she had done it before, and generally returned twenty-four hours later pregnant, in due course presenting us with a new family of kittens, of many and various hues but always appealingly fluffy so there was no difficulty finding them decent homes. But this time she didn't come back, and didn't come back, and then one morning, setting off to work along the snowed-up street, I spotted a patch of black among the white in the gutter. I hurried closer, thinking wildly that she must be having a lie-down. But she had been the victim of a hit-and-run driver.

No more kittens. No more Pud-Pud. But what was I to do with the body? I couldn't just leave her to be flattened by passing traffic into scraps of fur when the thaw came. There was a communal garden behind our flat. We would bury her decently. I went back inside and found a cardboard box and then, as often happens in tragic events, dark farce intervened. Pud-Pud was frozen rigid. I could not curl her up into her cardboard coffin, even after a few karate chops. So I put her in Fred's outgrown pram and wheeled her in a sort of cortege to the vet, who agreed to do what was necessary.

Eventually, after a few weeks, my luck changed. Bob Houston came in on Saturdays to provide the Football Round-up, which mopped up all the matches we weren't covering and was brightened up with suitable snippets, such as the time someone let a ferret loose on the pitch at Watford. He was known as Big Bob, and this wasn't at all ironic – he was a massive, maliciously witty, ferociously talented Scot with a huge girth and a bull-like poll of curly black hair. You could imagine him charging over the border, barefoot on his pony, bonnet on and plastered in woad. His real job was that of editing *The Miner*, magazine of the National Union of Mineworkers. Before that, he had been something important on *Melody Maker*. Now, in his spare time, he had launched a rock magazine, *Cream*. He offered me some work.

I went to gigs and wrote one or two features, but mainly I had to write reviews. They were all blues-rock and folk and country albums by women artists I'd never heard of, singing boring, waily, rattly songs, which seemed to be the only kind of woman-singing that was approved, whereas I was a fan of the work of Laura Nyro and Judee Sill, who were women who sang about what it was like to be women. And how could I let on that I actually adored Elton John and, even worse, quite liked the song that won the 1972 Eurovision Song Contest, which was Luxembourg's entry? It was a dramatic *chanson* sung in French by a woman moaning that after her lover had gone, she'd just been a shadow of her shadow, which, coming as it did after Pud-Pud dying and my career not going anywhere, chimed perfectly with my mood. How could I even admit to these erudite musos that I'd watched the Eurovision Song Contest?

I was at the stage where I thought clever writing involved being withering, and I was keen to show off. Cue a debut album by Bonnie Raitt, about which I was very scathing when I was meant to praise her skills as a bottleneck guitarist. I didn't even know what bottleneck guitar meant. Strangely, my opprobrium didn't prevent her from going on to win countless Grammy Awards and being nominated as number 50 in *Rolling Stone*'s 100 Greatest Singers of All Time. Shows how much I knew.

The budget was tight. Bob was commissioning eminent writers such as Clive James, now the *Observer*'s television critic, and Richard Williams, who went on to present the BBC music show *The Old Grey Whistle Test*. They obviously had to be paid. This meant I could not be. My function was to bulk out the pages, but Bob had given me my start, and he was nice about my writing, so I didn't mind working for free. And oh, I was so excited when the issue of *Cream* came out with my by-line in it. I really thought, for a moment, that now I'd had something published Clifford might give me the chance to write for sport. I raced into the Black Friar to show him. 'Yes, very good, Julie,' he snapped and waved me away. I had learned nothing from the expenses debacle. I still didn't know my place.

Then I had something new to worry about. Clifford announced he was leaving, so there would be a new sports editor and then what would happen to me? He would be bound to want an efficient and scrupulous secretary who remembered to book return tickets and didn't try to defraud the *Observer*. Thank heavens when they decided to give the job to his deputy, Ron Atkin, who had dark curly hair and a lovely smile and who I liked very much. Though even that didn't help, really, because he was just as reluctant as Clifford to let me have a go at writing.

But soon I stopped minding, because *Honey* accepted one of my short stories, and then it accepted another, and then, most thrilling of all, Pat sold another of my stories to *Transatlantic Review*, a proper literary magazine. It was read by someone called Richard Hall, one of the high-ups at the *Observer*. Mr Hall actually descended from Olympus to the sports department to say nice things about it.

This was one of those sliding-doors moments because my first thought as soon as the higher-up had left the sports department was, Now I don't have to be a secretary any more. I can leave and get on with The Novel.

That was the point at which Ron said, 'Why don't you try writing something for us?'

I went to Dorset to interview a fourteen-year-old high-jumper called Ann Gilsom, who was lovely, and so was her mum, with whom I bonded over tea and custard creams.

The piece got in the paper. I took the page proof home, still damp, to keep for ever. Two weeks after that I was sent to Roehampton to interview an Australian girl, Dianne Fromholtz, who was living with her mum and sister in a camper van in a car park while trying to qualify for Wimbledon. They were lovely too. They told me about the thunderstorm that had broken out in the middle of the night, and it pelted down so hard that when anyone wanted the loo they had to drive the camper van to get there. I always like that sort of detail because it's human and it always goes into my copy.

So, another by-line in the *Observer*. Not for long. It was whisked out of the paper so soon after it appeared, it must have got whiplash. At the time, I shrugged. I just thought it had to make way for something more newsworthy. The following week started as a normal Tuesday. I arrived at ten, entered the Saturday reporting assignments in The Ledger, informed all the reporters, booked phones for them and posted off their press passes. The prospect of a tub of cottage cheese and an orange alone at my desk wasn't enticing, so I suggested to Ron that we pop out to the Black Friar for lunch.

'Can't,' he said. 'There's a meeting. It's about you. Go and wait for me in the Old Bell.' The meeting had been convened by the father of the *Observer*'s NUJ chapel, so something significant and, I suspected, not terribly nice, was about to happen to me. Apart from anything else, the Old Bell was a neutral pub. More than that, it was not a day pub. It was a night pub. You fetched up in there in the dregs of the evening after you'd already been to two or three other pubs, accompanied by whoever was still capable of movement and picking up survivors from other battalions on the way, like in the First World War. Why was I being told to wait there?

I pulled my face into a sort of smile. 'Can't I wait in the Black Friar?'

'Better not.'

The enormity of what was happening hit me. Usually the sportswriters treated me as part of the team, and if they were going out drinking I was always invited. Now I felt like an incomer to one of those strange rural villages where they sacrifice chickens by the light of the full moon. I didn't belong with them, not really. They were going to go to the chapel meeting and then they were all going to go to the Black Friar, and if I was sitting there waiting to hear the verdict, and I'd been bombed out, how embarrassing would that be for them?

I sat at my desk for a while in the empty office, fuming. Well, if Ron was going to sack me I'd rather it was in St Bride's churchyard where no one went, rather than in the Old Bell where I might start raving and carrying on, and everyone would witness my humiliation.

With that thought, I tucked my handbag under my arm and headed to St Bride's.

Whatever Mary Kenny's old headmistress, Mother Annunciata, might have said, your fate is never entirely in your own hands, and there will always be people who are *for* you as well as *anti*. Luckily for me, Pat Kavanagh was also the agent for Clive James and Terry Kilmartin, both very influential figures on the *Observer*. They spoke up for my cause (I expect Pat would have had something to say had they not), as did David Astor. So, when after another fifty or so years, Ron tracked me down, it was to say, 'You're all right.'

Sort of. I had to resign as secretary and apply to join the NUJ, and then I could be a freelance contributor. But how could I join the NUJ if I wasn't a journalist? It seemed I had to send them cuttings of everything I'd had printed so far, and then they'd decide if I was worthy. Thank heavens Bob Houston had given me all that work on *Cream*. Even so, the cuttings were pathetically few and I was dreadfully worried that I'd be turned down. But Ron wrote the NUJ a letter on official *Observer* paper saying he would guarantee me regular employment, and I didn't even have to wait very long for my acceptance to come through. I was now an accredited journalist.

Usually in life what you do is slog away and slog away in a such-is-my-lot fashion, but just once or twice something so magically opportune happens that it almost makes you believe in fate. One evening not long after all this happened, I went drinking with Ron and the *Observer* football reporter Arthur Hopcraft in the Black Friar. It was just before the start of the football season and Arthur was very gloomy. How could he not have been? He lived on his own in a bungalow just outside Stockport. It didn't have enough windows, and the décor was rather peculiar. There were dark green tiles halfway up the living-room walls, which made it look like a giant public convenience. I couldn't be in there more than half an hour without feeling glum.

I tuned in to hear him saying, dramatically, 'If I ever have to report another football match I will jump under a train.'

Which should, of course, have been a matter of great concern to me, but on one level I was thinking, Oh, Arthur, what a load of melodramatic bollocks, and on another level I was thinking, He's going, he's going, they'll need another football writer!

Also, I happened to be sitting opposite SEIZE THE DAY.

'It might be fun if you sent me to cover a game,' I said, turning to Ron.

'Yes, that's what I was thinking,' he said.

I had found my Marvellous Chap, my perfect person. And that is how I became a football reporter.

How I came to carry on being one is a longer story and needs a chapter in itself.

Chapter 14

Girl in the Press Box: Stunts and Tropes

Whenever I told people what I did for a living, their first response was, 'That's a very unusual job for a girl, isn't it?' From August 1973 for the next thirteen years, I was Girl In The Press Box – the first female in Fleet Street to report football. I now know there were plenty of young women who loved football and who would have given anything to earn their living watching it and writing about it, but unlike me they weren't lucky enough to be given the golden chance. And it was truly golden, a fantastic opportunity, the one that made my name because for a long time, till Sue Mott started reporting it for the *Sunday Times* in the late 1970s, I was the only one, and I revelled in it, even if, occasionally, I did find myself considering whether on meeting new people I might cut to the chase by handing out business cards that said: 'Yes, it is an unusual job for a girl. No, I can't get you tickets for the Cup final.'

Oh, the thrill of seeing my name entered in The Ledger, alongside the match that I would be reporting that Saturday; of being given a press pass that would provide free access to the game, and of being able to charge expenses for my train fare and Refreshments On Journey; of ringing up a club and saying, 'This is Julie Welch of the *Observer*. Could I speak to [insert name of latest Chelsea starlet or revered international],' at which this god would come to the phone at my command, because it rapidly came home to me that for most of my childhood I had been bound in invisible but increasingly limiting ropes of Girls Just Don't Do That Kind Of Thing, and now I was living a life for which almost any man in the country would have given all.

There were joys like being allowed to walk on the pitch at Wembley (commonly referred to as 'The Hallowed Turf'); eating mushy peas at half-time from a plastic cup with a spoon chained to a giant enamel jug filled with hot water at Nottingham Forest (once the peas had been scoffed, the spoon was to be replaced in the jug for a hurried rinse before the next customer); being interviewed by the Radio 1 DJ who introduced me as 'the prettiest football reporter' (admittedly the competition was weak); moments of pure happiness when just being alive and a young woman, sitting in the late summer sun waiting for the teams to come out while 10cc played over the PA, was enough; and always, always, that first glimpse of floodlights poking into the sky and the feeling I got when I saw the stadium. I'd think of all the people it had contained over the years, this receptacle for their hopes and dreams and disappointments and rapture. Even when the ground was empty, the emotions were still there, like a watermark.

The first player I interviewed was Tony Currie, who played for Sheffield United and England. At the time he was hot, christened 'The New Günter Netzer'. (If you don't do football, here's a brief explanation: Günter Netzer was a West Germany international, an attacking midfielder who had an outstanding talent for long, sweeping passes from inside his own half and had taken the last World Cup by storm. Tony could pass like that too, but the key fact was that they were both blonds with the same hairdo – a shoulder-length pair of curtains.)

I was apprehensive travelling up to Sheffield. Would I be able to do a good job? It was uncharted territory. Females just didn't interview footballers. What would Tony Currie make of it all? Would he be rude or try to grope me? I felt a bit scared. Tony was waiting in the front hall at Bramall Lane. He looked a bit scared too, poor boy. Well, he was only twenty-one. He could be my little brother. I started feeling rather tender-hearted towards him. Anyway, he was sweet and chatty and I got a lovely piece out of it.

As the weeks wore on, I realised how at home I felt in these surroundings. Managers, players, coaches, people who ran the front office, people who made the tea and swept the ground, they were all lovely. Norman Hunter was especially lovely. He was the Leeds United and England defender with the reputation of being football's Hard Bastard, an ogre; his nickname was 'Bites-Yer-Legs'. I bearded him in the Minotaur's Den, otherwise known as the reception area at Leeds United's Elland Road stadium, where he arrived straight from training, showered and floppy-haired in trackie pants and clutching a tin of Johnson's baby powder. He was older than Tony Currie, and amused to be interviewed by a young lady, whom he addressed as 'pet' throughout. He talked about what losing was like, how sometimes it made him close to tears, how football made him emotional. Thinking about it now, I was asking questions and putting in details and descriptions that wouldn't occur to a man. The piece went the 1970s equivalent of viral, being read out on radio and included in anthologies.

There were special, sometimes hugely amusing, moments that I couldn't wait to recount to the sports desk. Making my first visit to White Hart Lane, the Spurs stadium, as a reporter rather than a fan, I didn't know where to enter the ground. I was directed to an oak-panelled hall. Spotting a door marked 'Press', I pushed it open and barged in, only to be confronted by a line of my fellow reporters facing the urinals. On another Saturday, after a match at Derby County, I was standing with the rest of the press pack in a bleak car park,

177

the kind of location in which managers gave their post-match press conferences back then. When someone asked why a Derby player had been booked, Dave Mackay, Derby's player-manager, fixed me with a terrible eye. 'It's a man's game,' he growled. 'If the referee's a cunt, you call him a cunt.' I wrote this down very carefully in my notebook, and after that Dave was no trouble at all.

Then there was Crystal Palace v Middlesbrough, the third, and most important, football match I ever reported. It was 4 September 1973. Oh, what a day. Crystal Palace played at Selhurst Park. I'd never been there before. It was in Norwood, southeast London, crammed near the bottom of White Horse Lane below rows of terraced artisan housing that looked like tightly permed grey hair. Forewarned of the difficulty of find-ing somewhere to park, I took the train. This, by the way, is germane to what happened – I'm not just moaning about transport problems.

My report wasn't needed till six o'clock and dusk was falling when I left the stadium. Most of the press and supporters had exited long since; I was a dreadfully slow writer. There is nothing more calculated to lower the spirits than walking through a deserted car park on a carpet of discarded litter. Faced with the trudge back to Gipsy Hill station I decided to take a taxi.

From the top of White Horse Hill I had a very good view of suburban Surrey, that time of day when the sky is deep violet and the buildings and treeline velvet dark and romantically dotted with lights, but not those of taxis saying 'FOR HIRE'. I waited and waited, getting more and more dispirited. Then a Mercedes drew up beside me and the passenger door swung open. 'Would you like a lift?' said an Irish voice.

I remembered reading an article a few weeks earlier about a small-to-medium-grade TV personality who had just been nabbed for kerb-crawling, and for a moment that's what I thought the owner of the Irish voice was up to. But then I had a better look and realised it was the icon of my girlhood. The man whose Christian name I had adopted in his honour when it came to choosing nicknames at my boarding school. Danny Blanchflower!

Danny hadn't played for Spurs since 1964, but he didn't have to go off and open a pub like other retired footballers because he already had a second career going as a journalist and author, and now he worked as a sportswriter for the *Sunday Express*. But I had been so busy concentrating on the match and then faffing around with my report that I hadn't noticed him in the press box.

I hopped in.

'I used to watch you play,' I breathed.

'They all say that,' he said dismissively.

What was I expecting, a round of applause? How would I feel in years to come if someone young said to me, 'I used to read your match reports'? I'd feel old, old and past it, my best days long gone.

I imagined the rest of the journey would pass in awkward silence, but no chance of that. He kept up a stream of persiflage all the way back into town, because Danny, I discovered to my delight, could rabbit away for Great Britain and all I had to do was sit back in the wonderful pale leather passenger seat and let the words of god wash over me all the way back to Fleet Street.

Later I told Arthur Hopcraft about it. 'He'd probably run out of other people to talk to,' Arthur said, crushingly.

When I made my debut as a football reporter I had thought there might be a bit of a fuss, but that it would soon die down. What a hope. I was the journalist who had become the story. The following week the phones started ringing in the *Observer* sports department. Was Julie a man's name like Hilary or

Shirley? enquired one puzzled reader. A couple of men wrote in to ask me out on dates. I appeared on *Pebble Mill at One* in Birmingham, where jokes were made about me chesting down the ball, by the first of a bunch of middle-aged men who said it because they thought this line was somehow fresh and witty, when in fact it revealed them to be among the most unattractive, tedious clots you've ever left the room to avoid. The BBC invited me onto the *Today* programme, where Fritz Spiegl, a humorist, read out a pre-prepared essay complaining that there was too much flowery reporting creeping into football these days, taking as his example something I had written the previous Saturday (Spurs v Newcastle United; Spurs lost 0–2) about the Tottenham striker Alan Gilzean, whom I had described as 'tossing his head like a shampoo advertisement'. You had to know what Alan Gilzean looked like to appreciate that because he had as much hair as a snooker ball. Mr Spiegl, too cultured to pay attention to football except when he was mocking a rookie female reporter, did not get the joke.

I thought it was a bit off to be reading out this finely crafted essay in front of the studio guest he was being rude about, but far from tactfully closing him down or inviting me to respond, the lady presenter smiled at the smirky old fart dotingly. I was still a bit gormless at that stage and had no idea that you didn't have to be a ravishing beauty for an older woman to find you a threat, you just had to be young.

And, unwittingly, I had created a new female trope: Girl In The Press Box. This was the heading on a reader's letter published in the *Observer* at the end of that September.

I feel I must write to congratulate you on your new lady football reporter. This revolutionary venture promises to be the happiest in sportswriting for a long time. Julie Welch's entertaining reports promise to lift football reporting to a level of literature comparable to the best cricket writing.

I consider that anyone sentenced to review a match between Norwich and Arsenal deserves applause for producing a report of any kind. Miss Welch's is quite memorable.

E.V. Hughes, Reading.

I was convinced someone in the office had composed it till I was shown the handwritten original, complete with address and date and postmarked envelope. Its publication on the letters page, complete with my potted biography and a photo, just increased the hoopla. I had, in fact, begun to feel rather unnerved. All I was doing was writing football reports. Then again, it's hard to remember – well, at least I find it so – that as little as fifty years ago, women were only allowed to be certain things. 'Rather a strange girl, isn't she?' the political writer Anthony Howard observed to my agent, Pat Kavanagh. Pat scoffed at him, but I was mortified. Yes, I was abnormal. Mentally abnormal. That must be it. But there was nothing I could do about it. It wasn't like being fat. I couldn't diet off the mad bits.

By this time, the backlash had begun. One journalist was so vocally outraged at my presence that I dreaded sitting anywhere near him. He was very grand and had always regarded himself as the star and now I was taking all the attention away from him. On and on the old shit went, saying I was only doing it as a stunt, that what I wrote was gimcrack, rubbish, that I'd soon be found out. 'Oh, everybody hates him,' said my colleagues. 'Just ignore him.' But they had no insight into what it was like to be subjected to this continual verbal harassment, how could they have?

I was horrified by the antagonism I had unleashed. In an attempt to provide a football version of *Private Eye*, a group of smart young guys started a magazine called *Foul*. I thought it was nicely done, funny and entertaining, at least until I flipped through the issue in which the comic strip 'Miss Julie' was introduced. There I was, caricatured, some of my more pretentious phrases lampooned, along with the implication that I slept with footballers. It was libellous, but I didn't have the guts to call them out. I felt it was my fault, for writing fancy nonsense. I had stepped outside the permitted boundaries, for being female, basically.

There's nothing like a barrage of trolling for making you drain rapidly in confidence, and by the end of autumn I had begun to shake with fear when I had to walk into the press box. I dreaded letters of complaint from readers. I had plenty of appreciative letters too, but no kind words would sink in. Nor did it matter that I had the most tremendous support from my colleagues on the sports desk. I knew they were being teased – being upstaged by a woman, how shameful. It meant nothing to me that Hugh McIlvanney went around proclaiming, 'The Lady [Hugh's nickname for me] can write most of us under the table.' I had always been a very healthy person. Now I felt ill in my body and my mind. I had a lump in my throat all the time and a pain in my chest, as if my heart was broken, but I didn't dare go to the GP. He would tell me I had cancer. I would die. That would be my punishment for stepping out of line. I began to long for the end of the season, when I wouldn't have to walk into that press box every Saturday and endure the disdain and hostility. I still saw my future as a novelist and playwright; and I had just received my first commission from a drama producer at the BBC. That would give me the excuse I needed to step away.

Then the *Daily Express* wanted to interview me. They sent along a hack known as Tommo. Tommo looked a bit like Jack, my husband, so I mistook him for a nice person. Virtually the first question he asked me was about my colleague, Peter Corrigan, the chief football writer; perhaps he was hoping I'd trash him. But Peter, like all the others, had been incredibly kind and helpful to me.

'Oh, he's the sweetest man!' I gushed involuntarily.

'Peter Corrigan's a sweetie!' Tommo chortled, scribbling it down.

'Don't put that,' I said between my teeth. 'It's not what I said.'

'You can't stop me! Peter Corrigan's a sweetie!' he giggled.

I was so angry, my teeth so clenched, that I practically had to prise them apart. With him, because he was trying to turn me into a figure of fun. With myself, because I'd walked straight into the trap and I couldn't bear it.

What could I do? If I walked out, he'd just make something up out of spite. So I just answered yes or no to the rest of his questions without further elucidation, and when the snapper arrived to take a photo I refused to smile for him. They never used the piece.

I went on being angry for a long time. They thought I was only doing it for a stunt and I'd soon go away and stop bothering them. If that's what they all thought, more fool them. It was true that I myself had resolved to do this for no more than a year or two before returning to what I thought of as Proper Writing But now I wasn't going to give up, not ever. This was my crusade. I was going to prove the sexists wrong.

Before I go any further, a few words about stunts. When, in 1896, Mary Billington dived underwater in full rubber gear, a newspaper staple was born. She was, I now realise, the prototype Girl Reporter. She did stunts. These entailed dispatching a young woman to try out something outré or faintly ridiculous to test out public reaction. When Mary Kenny joined the

Evening Standard in 1966, she was the only female on Londoner's Diary – not to mention the only one, apart from Max Hastings, who hadn't been to Eton. He was an Old Carthusian. The diary was packed with Old Etonians – 'terribly nice, really', she said – but they had the society contacts and she didn't, so she had to think of a strategy. 'I positioned myself as the Wild Irish Girl, with a kind of flamboyant and reckless personality. It's an Irish trope, how we've always been presented: the Edna O'Brien template, the enchanting young Irishwoman living the London life. Somebody once asked Valerie Grove (in my hearing) what I was like as a young journalist and she replied, "Mad! Absolutely mad!" A fair description, probably. Being the Wild Irish Girl was, in a way, being different and that, in itself, was also an advantage. You use what you can if you haven't been to Eton.'

'They liked to have a girl around because they could do stunts with them,' said Sue Peart. The year the Sinclair C5 was launched, she was the one who had to drive it. The C5 was a small, battery-operated one-person vehicle the colour of half-mourning, which was portentous, because it looked like a carpet slipper on wheels and was about as useful. It was the full-on wintry January of 1985, and after a glitzy unveiling, the press were let loose to have a go. What a disaster. Batteries ran down, engines went *phut* and even those that achieved some sort of motion lacked the oomph to climb the alpine slopes of central London without their driver resorting to the pedals. 'I was the one who had to take it over Waterloo Bridge, in the snow,' said Sue.

No, she didn't think it remotely beneath her dignity. This was one way of managing the woman-in-a-man's-world thing – be a good sport. There were, though, limits. In the 1980s, rubber frocks became a thing – punk era fetish-type garments that looked impossible to get into and were redolent of underground S&M parties and fantasy role play. Louise Court was told to go out wearing one – 'by a woman who shall remain nameless' – to test the public reaction. 'It was all right to ask me to do that as long as I was going to be the one who wrote about it,' she said. '*But* she wanted to send out a male reporter to do the story as "he was a hilarious writer" – insinuating it wouldn't be funny if I'd written it. I couldn't believe a woman said that. But I wasn't brave enough to stand up for myself.' Instead Louise pretended she had a rubber allergy, and they had to hire a model to wear it.

The point to be made here is that roles for female journalists were limited. You were told what to write by men and your career progress was decided by men. That was the way it was and had always been. An example is what happened to Mary Stott, initiator of *Guardian* Women. She was born in 1907, and at seventeen she went straight from Wyggeston Grammar School in Leicester to the *Leicester Mail* after her mother, Amalie Waddington, who contributed a recipe column to the paper, persuaded its editor to give her a job. Being unable to join either the Typographical Association or the Correctors of the Press Association because neither accepted women members, she was 'tolerated as a temporary copyholder'. When she was appointed women's editor at the age of nineteen, she wept. 'It was because I thought my future as a proper journalist was ended, as indeed it was. I didn't want to be a woman-journalist, I wanted to be a journalist.'

In 1945, having spent twelve years editing two pages of the weekly *Co-op News* (they were devoted largely to reports of the women's co-operative guild and children's books), she was offered a job as a sub on the *Manchester Evening News*. The staff, she reported, were 'totally devoid of sex prejudice, and there was no discrimination in the allocation of work'. She felt she was a real journalist at last, not a woman-journalist.

Five years later, having become the most senior occupant of the subs' desk, she was sacked for being female. The post of chief sub-editor was up for grabs, and it had to go to a man.

Even towards the end of the twentieth century, when a handful of pioneering women – Wendy Henry, Eve Pollard, Rosie Boycott – were appointed editors, there existed, at the apex of the pyramid, another man, the very powerful proprietor, who could dispense with you at will. It goes without saying, therefore, that this was the most obvious aspect of the Fleet Street we entered. We were outnumbered, and we needed to develop tactics to overcome that and make sure our voices were heard.

Chapter 15

Outnumbered:
How to Survive and Succeed in Fleet Street

Nothing says you don't belong like excessive politeness. As we've already recorded, fifteen of Fleet Street's finest stood up when Wendy Holden walked into the *Daily Telegraph* newsroom for the first time. I'm also reminded of the experience Maureen Paton had while working as a sub on the *Express* in the early 1980s.

Her workload often involved going down to the stone – the part of the presses where fresh proofs were laid out on a metal table so a sub could make any necessary cuts and corrections. It was virtually unprecedented for a woman to be a stone sub and, as one printer was struggling to make the metal fit into a forme, he muttered, 'It's as tight as a nun's twat. Sorry, Maureen.'

It was just one of the ways in which men dealt with our gradual, and then accelerating, encroachment on their territory during the last half of the twentieth century. You would think, too, that it was highly preferable to what happened to Angie Mulligan some years later at the *News of the World*.

This man, a high-ranking figure at the *News of the World*, at one point developed an illness apparently so debilitating he needed help putting his socks on. Angie, a senior personal assistant, was summoned. 'He came in barefoot, holding them,' said Angie. 'I knelt down to put them on and when I looked up he'd whacked his todger onto the coffee table and said, "You can't do something about this by any chance, can you?"'

'Mr [Name Redacted]!' she yelled. 'Put it away!'

'I'm sorry,' he said sheepishly. 'I don't know what came over me.'

I love how she retained the formal address.

We worked with and for all kinds of men; kind, decent and encouraging men; powerful men, tough bastards and legendary brutes; cads, lechers, dinosaurs and misogynists. Among them, you might, as I did, meet the love of your life. You could find the ally who helped launch your career, which is how Wendy Holden's took flight in the early 1980s. Her first job after completing her training was at Fleetline Court Reporting Agency, where she had eighteen months of providing inquest and general court reports. Not only did she find it fascinating but she made useful contacts at the big court cases.

'I got to know freelance Fleet Streeters,' she said. 'They were earning a great deal more than I was. John Lamb, who is lovely and I'm still friends with, suggested I try the *Evening Standard* because they were hiring freelances.' By then, Wendy was already married; she was nineteen when she met Chris Taylor (later a picture editor at the *Mirror*) and three weeks later he proposed to her. 'I'll marry you when I'm twenty-one,' she had said, and was good to her word. Through John Lamb's tip-off the freelance work at the *Standard* led to the next step up; in 1985 she landed a job on the staff. 'Sixteen thousand pounds a year. Chris and I opened champagne, we couldn't believe it. We'd just moved into our first house. Men like John Lamb made up for the gropey ones.'

As well as this kind of lifelong friendship, you could form the perfect platonic relationship – that which involved an Office Husband. This happened to Jennifer Selway when she worked at the *Daily Express*. 'David Robson and I were "married" for a long time,' she recalled. 'He says we had lunch every day for ten years. Provided you don't have a sexual relationship with that person, it's amazing, because you spend longer with them than you do with your own family, and neither of you makes an effort for the other person so they're like a spouse, and if you're sitting next to each other for eight hours a day and get on, it's an amazing level of intimacy, isn't it? I think everyone thought we were having an affair, it was just assumed – we'd go off to lunch together, we'd come back together. But we weren't.'

'I found there was a huge camaraderie,' said Emma Lee-Potter, one of only four women on the news desk at the *Evening Standard*. 'Deadlines were shockingly intense; and I never felt as a woman I was treated any differently. In my experience, we were all very supportive of each other. The hours were so terrible I don't think we had the energy to be nasty to each other, and the men were really nice. One of the reporters had done every foreign job, so he was senior. Once I had to do a difficult cold-calling interview and when I put the phone down I sighed, "Oh, that was really difficult." He just said, "I feel like that every time. Sick."'

It did often seem to be the senior men who were the most helpful, perhaps because they were already established in their careers. At the *Sunday Express* magazine, which she joined in the early 1980s, Lynn Barber was reunited with her mentor Harry Fieldhouse, formerly of *Penthouse* and the *Daily Telegraph* magazine. 'My other great mentor was its editor, Ron Hall, who came from the *Sunday Times*. He pushed me to do bigger, more ambitious articles, cover stories. At the *Indie on Sunday*, I had Ian Jack, who was very valuable, though he was always trying to protect me from myself – "That's too mad, too off the wall"; "I really don't think you come out of this in a good light." Now,' she said sadly, 'I have to censor myself.'

In contrast there were the ancients who thought having women around was going to ruin everything. According to the former *Mirror* editor Roy Greenslade, when the first female sub was employed at the *Daily Mail*'s Manchester office in 1968, one rebarbative veteran complained that a woman's presence would spoil the culture of the newsroom because they 'wouldn't be able to fucking swear'. To which end, Maureen Paton, in her first job as a sub, was warned to 'be careful – women journalists (especially subs because they're the last defence) can't always recognise double entendres'. But as she went on to say, 'Some of the most foul-mouthed journos I've ever met have been women.'

'A newspaper office was four-fifths men,' said Louise Court, comparing it with her later experience in women's magazines, editing *Best* and *Cosmopolitan*. 'In magazines, there would be just a handful. I had some wonderfully supportive male colleagues, bosses and friends but there was far more bitchiness from male colleagues on newspapers than I ever experienced from women on magazines. I remember some men saying, "Well, I'm not going to be told what to do by that stupid bitch," when women were promoted to more senior positions: I was told by a friend that as a young woman it was a nightmare trying to corral all these old Fleet Street warhorses set in their ways.'

'My time on Fleet Street, like Maureen and Louise, who were both in Showbiz, coincided with a kind of cultural shift in what constituted news,' said Sue Peart. 'It was the start of the celebrity culture, where we tracked celebrities' clothes, their rackety lifestyles, their relationships, their marriages – celebrities were making news (in a way that "news" wasn't making news in quite the same way). Celebrities seemed to achieve the longed-for circulation "needle-swing". And there was Diana, of course, who was a kind of royal celebrity. So we young women entering journalism who loved clothes and pop music, and went out to concerts and clubs and cinemas and theatre and pubs, and the wine bars that were springing up all over the place to cater for us, were influencing the news in terms of what "girls like us" wanted to read, and what sold newspapers.

'Newspaper editors were watching the boom in women's magazines, and how these magazines were achieving huge circulations, and they wanted some of that action for themselves. They *had* to feminise in order to attract that market. Women had their own wages and salaries, and they were choosing to spend their money on magazines . . . Newspapers had to reach out to women if they were to survive long-term, even if they did it while holding their noses. The only way they could do that was by allowing us to enter their portals, and take us seriously.'

'When I was on the *Daily Express*, I switched from subbing to writing, and then to television and theatre reviewing alongside feature writing,' said Maureen Paton. 'That led to a bizarre confrontation at someone's leaving party with a *Daily Star* reporter I didn't know. He came up to me and aggressively told me that he could do a better job than me as the *Express* theatre critic. He was so rude and abusive that I slapped him – first time ever for me, and I had only had one glass of wine! – and he then slapped me back, much harder. At which point, his male *Daily Star* colleague, who had been anxiously watching us, intervened and stopped any further slaps.

'It seemed to earn me Brownie points with the male journos when I told the story around the office. A lovely *Express* sub called Stewart, whose immediate reaction was "Never hit a woman", even though I had hit the *Star* man first, went on to nickname me "Slugger" ever afterwards! So there were certainly kind and gallant men among the boorish ones. But would the abusive reporter have said what he did had I been a man? I wonder.'

Time and again, though, we come back to the most immediate hazard – gropey men. 'I'm like someone in an H.E. Bateman cartoon,' observed Jennifer Selway. 'The only woman in Fleet Street who was never groped. The only time someone asked me to his flat "to discuss work", he said, "I'd really like to go to bed with you," and I was like, "Oh yes, come on!"'

Nor did Sue Peart suffer these unwanted attentions at the *Express* and, later, the *Mail on Sunday*. 'The male journalists were big, interesting, clever personalities who when they saw a woman were more interested in showing off than sexual harassment,' she recalled. For most of us, though, knee-patting, bra-twanging and buttock-fondling – what my mother called 'getting familiar' – was just an insidious background element to life, like that not-quite-sub-aural piped music in lifts and bad restaurants. It was, of course, exacerbated by the drinking culture – men were more hands-on when (another mother-ism) they were 'a little worse for wear'.

Oh, but really. If you are young and female now it must be difficult to comprehend what comprised appropriate behaviour and conversation in the workplace back then, when it was entirely run-of-the-mill to be felt up. In fact, I suspected some men thought it was rude not to do so. In my early weeks at the *Observer*, bare-legged in my summer dress, I happened to be standing beside the desk of my first boss, Clifford Makins, when he reached out and clutched my thigh. It seemed an asexual, almost chivalrous gesture – I had placed it there, so he felt he should acknowledge it, rather as he would doff his hat.

'If you've been in journalism a number of years, you must be a pretty strong character,' commented Tina Moran. 'A married news editor who made a play for me used to refer to me as The Fridge because I spurned his advances. I thought, What is it with these blokes? You sad, sad little men.'

'There were a lot of very much older men,' said Wendy Holden, remembering the reaction when she joined the *Daily Telegraph* in 1987. 'They didn't rate me at all in those early days. Then they respected me because I was computer savvy. They'd come to me again and again – I ended up writing an idiots' guide and that was the turning point. I wasn't just eye candy.

'That ilk of man – they were still schoolboys. University. Newspapers. Politics. Cricket played all day long on the TVs. Imagine if the women in the newsroom had started watching Gok Wan. I was in my twenties, and at the High Court and the House of Commons, the leering was so disgusting. You'd walk down these corridors – heads would pop out. The only other women around were secretaries so to have one representing a newspaper . . . they were stammering, virtually unzipping their flies. If they made a lunge, I punched them. Several are now MPs.'

Described like this, it sounds like a nightmarish place to have worked. In fact, Wendy did not look at it like that. 'Max Hastings [her editor] pushed me out there. He wanted people to see that this was a new era. He sent me to report on the Gulf War – it was pioneering in *Telegraph* terms. They were very happy days. It was an extraordinary time.'

There was one recurring occupational hazard: 'Being propositioned by the person you interviewed,' as Valerie Grove put it – she had to deal with 'Rolf Harris on a sleeper train'. 'I had to interview the mad German actor Klaus Kinski when he appeared in *Nosferatu, the Vampyre*,' said Jennifer Selway. 'He stuck his tongue down my throat in the 20th Century Fox boardroom in Soho Square.'

'When I was on *Melody Maker*, where I also did interviews and reviews alongside subbing shifts, a musician smilingly suggested continuing the interview at his home over dinner,' said Maureen Paton. 'Naïve as I was, even I realised that was a bad idea. Though it wasn't as bad an idea as another *Melody Maker* experience of mine – smoking dope and drinking Guinness with the late singer-songwriter John Martyn in a pub round the corner from his record company, Island. I was sick as a dog on the tube platform afterwards. A valuable early lesson in not trying to ingratiate myself with the interviewee by trying to match their macho intake.'

When she worked on *Petticoat*, the then 24-year-old Scarth Flett went to Paris to interview Omar Sharif, described by the critic Kenneth Tynan as, 'The only full-blooded romantic hero at present working in the British cinema,' and by Clive James, then TV critic of the *Observer*, as 'a box of dates smouldering with passion'. Sharif was filming *The Night of the Generals*. Scarth stayed with a friend, Robyn, who was working as an au pair. The interview took place in a restaurant.

'I began interviewing. My suspender broke. He didn't know, but it put me at a disadvantage. It was well-known that he was a very keen bridge player, so I asked him why. "Because it's a very good filler," he said. "After dinner and before fucking." Nobody used the word "fuck" then. I was a little girl from a teenage magazine, so he tried to shock me. I showed no shock. I didn't blush. I thought, Keep going. "Oh, right," I said coolly. His chauffeur-driven car dropped me off at Robyn's afterwards. He wouldn't let me get out till I'd kissed him and agreed to go to dinner. I gave him a peck on the cheek and got out. I didn't want to have dinner with him. I thought, If I do that, I'm giving him the green light. So when he rang to arrange it, I got Robyn to say I wasn't well.'

I recall only two incidents clearly, perhaps because they were the ones where I found it difficult to cope. Bill Grundy was a television presenter notorious for a 1976 interview on his Thames TV *Today* programme with the Sex Pistols during which band member Steve Jones used the f-word on air for the first time. After that things escalated. Though *Today* was only a regional programme, headlines were made.

The appearance I made on Grundy's show was so innocuous I've no idea now why I was on, though I won't forget what happened afterwards. He offered to show me the way out of the studios Repetition, which I thought was very nice of him till he grabbed me in the lift. I was so taken aback it didn't occur to me to smack his face. It had been very casual. I felt as if he had blown his nose on me. I was so embarrassed and ashamed. I didn't admit what had taken place to a soul. I didn't even *know* this was sexual assault. It had happened before, with men who were friends of my parents. When I told my mother about those men, she said they had done it to her too. It was repulsive, but you couldn't make a fuss. It was just something men did.

It happened at one football match I was reporting, too. The manager of Stoke City FC, Tony Waddington, was boozy, saggy and middle-aged – no Adonis by any stretch of the imagination. He liked to join us in the press room after a game and, one Saturday, he seized me and gave me a huge snog.

Nobody took any notice. They all carried on yakking and smoking and drinking the free whisky. What did I do now? If I reacted, everyone would look at me. This must be my fault, I thought. I've been chatting to him, he'll have taken something I've said as a come-on, or perhaps I've been boring him and he just wanted to shut me up.

Now, most clubs gave the *Observer* a seasonal press pass, but not Stoke. We had to ring up and ask for one whenever we wanted to cover a game, and collect it from the main gate when we reached the ground. It was a nuisance, and all the other national papers seemed to have seasonal passes. We had begged and begged for years, but were always left out. When I returned from Stoke that night, I told everybody about what Tony had done. At the beginning of the following week Ron dispatched a letter to him:

> *Dear Tony,*
> *Once again I must ask your club to give us our own press pass. Until you accede to this request, I must ask you to stop kissing our reporters.*
> *Yours sincerely,*
> *Ronald Atkin,*
> *Sports Editor*

Tony rang Ron up the moment he read the letter and laughingly agreed we could have our press pass. So that was him warned off, in an immensely stylish way, and thank goodness I had my *Observer* colleagues to protect me. The next time I went to Stoke, Tony playfully asked if I would like to come up and see his European pennants. Ha ha ha, no thanks. 'All very jolly and no harm done,' was my attitude at the time. But I've wondered, since, why I found it easier to brush off Tony's assault than the one inflicted on me by Bill Grundy at Thames TV. I think it was that, while Mr Grundy was just a boozy, disgusting old television presenter, Tony Waddington a) made me laugh but, more importantly, b) was a football manager, so I was prepared to give him absolution. Those were different times. It just seemed like the price I had to pay for having such a fantastic job. Thank God the climate has been so seismically shifting. Now, whenever I learn of a powerful man being called out, I think, Yes! You go, girl!

Now we come to the man who either directly or at several removes could influence your career for good or bad. There was,

I suspect, a lot left over from my childhood in my attitude to editors. For much of the time, my father was a remote figure who, though affectionate enough, took very little interest. From that I concluded that my presence in an editor's life would be similarly irrelevant; why on earth would this deity want to have anything to do with me? Far healthier was the attitude expressed by Lynn Barber. 'I've never signed up for the idea of editors as gods,' she said. 'My favourite interview was always me with a rather rude older man who expected to intimidate me, like my father. If he spoke at all, it was to shout and often a lot of bollocks. So I felt really comfortable interviewing John Junor.'

John Junor – known to the inmates as 'JJ' – was the *Sunday Express* editor-in-chief, and notorious for his prejudices, frequently inveighing against immigrants, socialists, homosexuals and men with beards.

'He was thin and tall and powerful,' says Scarth Flett, whose job for many years was as celebrity interviewer on the column Meeting People. 'Big ego. His way or the highway. Politically I wasn't a supporter of the *Express*. John [Pilger, Scarth's husband] always caused controversy. Some for, some against, and people always felt the need to tell me. JJ wasn't a fan! There was one programme of John's that he didn't agree with and he felt the need to tell me so acutely he chased me down the steps to the loo.'

Stand up to him, she was advised by the columnist Peter Mackay. If she was unhappy, just go in and see him. 'And it worked,' she said. 'You could go in and fight. I didn't always get my own way; sometimes you'd win, sometimes you wouldn't. But you knew where you stood with him.' An example she gave was of the time she had to profile the British film star Diana Dors.

'We talked about babies and nannies,' said Scarth, who, when the interview took place, was only just back at work after the birth of her son, Sam. 'She was a really good actress. She'd had a hell of a life and I'd written that she was one of the nicest people I'd ever met.

'You wrote your piece and it had to go to JJ. It would come back with a comment – "Excellent", "Good" or "Words Please". If it was "Words Please", you'd have to go and see him. I had to go and see him about Diana Dors.

'John Junor said, "You can't say she's the nicest person you've ever met."

'"Why not?"

'"Because having said that, you'll never be critical of her if you need to be."

'I didn't always give in and Junor liked me better for it. In this case he was right. I shouldn't have put my heart on my sleeve. But I'd gone to him as a very young journo from Australia, and he thought I was okay.'

Did it make a difference, this being picked out by the editor as a young journalist? It must have done if you worked hard and justified his judgement, as did Wendy Holden when she was hired by Max Hastings. We've learned, too, that Larry Lamb was 'quite proud' of his protégée Sue Peart, whom he had hired as a feature writer from *Cosmopolitan*. I particularly like this story of Sue's about 'the time Larry called me into his office, poured me an enormous tumbler of whisky and said, "I want to promote you to deputy features editor" (no preamble). I'd read in *Petticoat* (my bible!) that if you were offered a promotion you should ask your boss for "time to think about it". So I said to Larry, "Oh, I think I'll need some time to think about that." He glanced at his watch and said, "I'll give you five minutes." And walked out of his office, leaving me alone with my tumbler (which I literally had to pour into the pot plant . . .). Five minutes later he walked back in. "Well, have you thought about it yet?" Yes, I had. Embarrassing . . .'

Someone else who went to an editor as a very young journalist was Mary Kenny. I am intrigued by the bond between her and the *Evening Standard*'s Charles 'Chilly Charlie' Wintour. Mary, though, defrosted him.

Charles had a streak or two of radical chic, she said. It was the era of anti-Vietnam War demonstrations, and in 1968 Mary took part in London's, marching – complete with Vietcong flag – behind the political activist Tariq Ali to the United States embassy in Grosvenor Square. 'Anna Wintour (she was seventeen and walking out with Christopher Hitchens) was on the march too. Charles said to me, "For God's sake, keep an eye on her. She's not very sure what to wear . . ."

'The march was all mounted police, students, radicals, blah blah blah. Charles said, "Mary, I'll meet you afterwards at the Dorchester for tea." So I went for tea at the Dorchester carrying this Vietcong flag.' This memory is now the cause of self-recrimination: 'What a plonker I was. What a silly billy.'

The most interesting moment, though, stemmed from Mary's decision at one stage to leave the *Standard* for another job. She did return to the *Standard* later, by the by, but at this point she had been in a relationship with Bernard Levin, then the youthful, brilliant drama critic of the *Daily Mail*. 'Bernard Levin broke my heart. He was a very attractive person, just a scintillating personality, very clever. He took me to all sorts of grand places like Glyndebourne. Gave me ideas above my station. I didn't know enough. He dumped me, which was a heartache. I was miserable. In 1969, I got offered a job as women's editor of the *Irish Press*. My personal life seemed to be going nowhere so I took it up.

'Charles Wintour was very disapproving. He actually said, "It makes me feel suicidal to think of you going back to Ireland," which was strong meat coming from Chilly Charlie.'

*

Let's go back, now, to the most obvious aspect of our working lives and how we managed it – that of being surrounded by men. According to the former *Mirror* editor Roy Greenslade, the renowned fashion journalist Felicity Green, who in the 1960s earned a reputation for effortlessly getting her way as associate editor of the *Mirror*, explained that she had taken the advice of the paper's editor Lee Howard to 'let men leave the room with their bollocks intact'. This was the stratagem that Tina Moran espoused when she joined the *Daily Express* from the *Daily Mail*'s Femail section. Her editor there had been Tessa Hilton and, when Tessa left to edit the *Sunday Mirror*, she took Tina with her. 'She was an inspiration,' said Tina. 'She was great. She taught me you don't have to be authoritarian, bossy, a bully. Just build a nice pleasant team around you.'

In the late 1990s, when the *Daily Express*'s Rosie Boycott was one of the pioneering women editors, Tina was called in for an interview. 'I thought it was for a post on the magazine, but it turned out she seemed rather fed up of the old men in cardigans and wanted me to be deputy night editor, on the back bench.' A woman in authority on the night desk! Whatever next? 'I knew I was going into an unprecedented situation,' Tina said. 'I thought, What's the worst that could happen? I completely fuck this up and I get to spend more time with the kids. So, win–win, really. The second day the night editor had a cold. He was snuffling away. I went out and bought him a box of tissues. That completely wrong-footed him. No man would have done that. It was my white-flag moment. It was strategic. I got called "Mum" – in a most affectionate way. They're never going to be rude to or angry with Mum. Fine. It worked for me. I won over some of the guys and they started to respect me. I was unsure of some of the elements of the job but I got the rest of the desk onside. I didn't walk around all guns blazing, because in the end I needed the help of the team.'

'Use your femininity,' was Sue Peart's tactic. 'They're like horses, they don't like to be startled. So I was really transparent all the time. Never take them off-guard. I used to have a scented candle in my office. They'd come in from the newsroom jabbering and frazzled, then their shoulders would drop and they would take a deep breath and say, "It smells like a spa in here." I learned that from Deirdre McSharry. Brush your hair, apply lipstick, literally spray with fragrance. It disarms.'

How, though, should you act among the men who were your equals as colleagues? Not to ask for special treatment was Emma Lee-Potter's way of going about it. 'At the *Standard*, reporters had to do nights – midnight to 8 a.m. You would be monitoring wires, talking to foreign correspondents round the world, getting them to file for the first edition. When I arrived in 1984, women didn't do nights. I'd never come across that. I'd been to a co-ed school; I didn't want to be treated any differently. It would be three in the morning, in the huge, empty *Express* building, with one security guard emerging every few hours, but I was more scared of not doing the job properly than anything else. There were four of us [women] and when we asked to do nights the men used to laugh at us! But we insisted.'

Oh, and take everything with a pinch of salt. 'Have a great sense of humour,' said Tina Moran. 'I learned that from my dad on the road. Even if you don't feel like it, if you can seem to be laughing it off it makes things easier.' What also helped was wit. When Hilary Bonner worked on the *Sun*, a colleague was the legendary news reporter Harry Arnold, who at 4ft 11in tall was dwarfed by Hilary's stature. Once, impassioned by drink, he informed her, 'One of these days I'm going to give you a right seeing-to.'

'Well, if you do and I find out I'll be very cross,' said Hilary. The riposte found its way into *Private Eye*'s 'Street of Shame' and was not only widely applauded but lucrative. 'It got me a new contract,' she said, 'and an office BMW.' It also earned her the ultimate gesture of approval from her colleagues, the naughtiest boys. 'I received a proper letter, handwritten, from The Back Bench That Matters, offering me the opportunity to join them on their bench. I thought it was a great honour. I'm not sure the news editor viewed it with great approval, but it was such a mark of acceptance, I can't tell you.'

Chapter 16

The Highs and Lows of Being a Journalist

One of the best aspects of working in Fleet Street was that feeling of being at the centre of everything. Even if you weren't directly involved in reporting the story, you loved the drama of news. If you were in the pub, for instance, you could always tell when something big had happened because of the sudden abandonment of drinks and rush for the exit: the death of Elvis; the upstairs–downstairs drama of Lord Lucan's flight after murdering his children's nanny Sandra Rivett; the fatal launch of the space shuttle *Challenger* – all were instant emptiers of the saloon bar. And whether or not you were able to summon up the emotion appropriate to the event, your overwhelming feeling was that of excitement.

Even better, of course, was to be right there in the news-room as something triggered it into frenzy, quite often at the most inopportune time possible. 'On the night in 1987 when Fred Astaire died, the news came through in the early evening, after the first edition had gone to press,' said Sue Peart. She recalled writing the obituary feature with Larry Lamb perched on the corner of her desk: 'He was pulling the sheets out of my typewriter as I typed, dropping them into the copy tray for the typesetters to collect.'

It was more frantic still when several big stories broke

on the same day. She remembered, too, the night two years earlier when Lamb called her into his office and asked which of three deaths they should put on the front page: the Brixton riots flaring up again after police accidentally shot someone's mother in her bed; the body of Samantha Novak, 21-year-old daughter of Shirley Bassey, found face down in the River Avon near the Clifton Suspension Bridge; and Laura Ashley, the Welsh designer who had sparked a fashion revolution with her flowered dresses and skirts, who had fallen downstairs to her death in the middle of the night. Sue felt the Laura Ashley story should occupy the front page. 'So many of the young women of my generation felt an almost personal connection to Laura Ashley, and her death was so sudden and shocking. It felt like the end of an era.' She was disappointed when Lamb went with Brixton. 'Although I lived quite close to Brixton, the riots – which were very contained to that area – seemed a long way away from my world. As a story, it was vivid, but it felt remote.'

Wendy Holden remembered her first week at the *Daily Telegraph*, when she had to cover the Jeffrey Archer trial of 1987. Archer's life already had an oh-where-do-you-start narrative and at this point, having stood down as an MP in the 1970s after financial scandal left him bankrupt, he had reinvented himself as a best-selling novelist (school of Airport Paperback Fiction) and had been deputy chairman of the Conservative Party until scandal brought about his resignation. The latest episode in this extraordinary life involved his suing the *Daily Star* after they ran a story claiming that he had paid for sex with a prostitute, Monica Coghlan. The case is probably best remembered for Archer's wife, Mary, Standing By Her Man throughout the case, and testifying to their happy marriage. The judge's closing instructions to the jury are repeated here just for the joy of it:

Remember Mary Archer in the witness box. Your vision of her will probably never disappear. Has she elegance? Has she fragrance? Would she have, without the strain of this trial, radiance? Has she a happy married life? Has she been able to enjoy, rather than endure, her husband Jeffrey? Is he in need of cold, unloving, rubber-insulated sex in a seedy hotel round about quarter to one on a Tuesday morning after an evening at the Caprice?

'I told my mother to look out for my stories in the paper,' said Wendy, 'and she told all her friends. My first piece for the *Telegraph* was the front-page lead about Jeffrey Archer's semen. She didn't talk to me for a week.'

You might conclude that a journalist's life boiled down to this – the excitement, the privilege of being involved in big stories, the cachet of being able to reel off great anecdotes after the event. Often, though, it wasn't like that at all.

'Hard news was really tough,' Emma Lee-Potter told me. 'You'd get in at seven, complete with your passport – it was drummed into you that you had to have it with you at all times. If there was a big foreign story, you'd get sent on it. One morning I got to the office and was immediately sent to Nairobi.'

Her future husband was living in her flat and she got a message to him: *Gone to Nairobi, don't know when I'll be back.* The background to the story was this: in 1988 Julie Ward, a publishing assistant and amateur wildlife photographer, had gone missing. She was fair-haired and attractive, with a lovely smile, and twenty-eight years old when her remains were found in a Kenya game park. 'Her father was flying out and I had to get the same flight as him. It was quite daunting, having to search through hundreds of people for a bereaved father – "Is there someone called John Ward on the flight?"

'You were sent out all the time. All the stories I was on – the King's Cross rail disaster, the Manchester air disaster – meant a lot of time interviewing bereaved people. It was never a matter of, "Help, I've got to do that; help, I'll have to knock on that door." I just did it. It could be hairy if you were doing backgrounds to crime stories, going to scary parts of London on your own. But I was far more terrified of the situations I was in because of the timeframe – your first deadline would mean you'd have to file well before 7.30 in the morning. It was so demanding, so pressurised.'

Did that pressure get to you in the end? When Mary Kenny arrived at the *Evening Standard* in 1966, Anne Sharpley was *the* ace reporter. Reputedly the best ever in the Beaverbrook empire, Mary said. 'She was ruthless, hard-boiled, what P.G. Wodehouse called a twenty-minute egg. She didn't only have to get the story first, she had to sabotage everyone else's.' Once she gave Mary the jaw-dropping advice to 'always sleep with the Reuters man, darling, because the news desk checks your copy against Reuters, and you'll have filed before him'.

Sharpley's triumphant besting of her rivals at Winston Churchill's funeral in 1965 was regarded as a classic. Once the ceremony was over, the race was on to get to the nearest phone. She was wearing a pencil skirt which impeded her movement, so she simply stepped out of it and left it in her wake. Having dictated her copy, she vandalised the handset so the competition would be unable to use it. The consequent delay in their filing meant their copy missed the first edition. She got the front-page splash and rather than being abominated for her lack of fair play was applauded for her enterprise.

'I slightly hero-worshipped her,' said Mary. 'She was in her late thirties, and someone once said she "looked like she came out of the same sort of box as Princess Margaret". She was red-lipped, dark-haired, glamorous and absolutely fearless. She would play the femme fatale card if it suited her. She had that Princess Margaret smile. A confident, educated Englishwoman. She wrote a memoir which, she said, was to be published in 2028 because everybody involved would be dead.

'But she sacrificed all her personal relationships for journalism, and then in midlife, in the 1970s, she had a nervous breakdown. She was sent to write about a day with a fisherman. She looked at the fish and suddenly felt a terrible panic attack. About her whole life. It was the pressure to be best. All those tough years – she crashed under the crush of them. "It's all been a chimera," she said.'

'It wasn't something you could stay doing,' said Wendy Holden of her years as a war correspondent for the *Daily Telegraph*. 'You'd either die, divorce or become an alkie. Sometimes all three. I was in Kuwait for nine weeks, Baghdad for eighteen months, solidly, with my notebook and camera. There were times I didn't think I was going to make it back. After one frightening journey to Basra, where our helicopter was forced to land and the rebels were closing in, I wrote a farewell note to my husband and put it in my shoe. But in the Middle East, shoes are coveted – they would have been taken off me. It would have been better to have put it in my knickers.'

Why, I asked, did she keep on doing it?

'It's very addictive,' she explained. 'You're suddenly a big cheese. Max Hastings would have me picked up at the airport to dine off drippy beef and claret with the great and good, and then I'd be dispatched to appear on *Woman's Hour*. But I'd seen too many dead bodies. I saw someone being murdered – a young woman, by three men in Iraq. I tried to get the driver to stop and he locked all the doors and drove through a red light to get away because otherwise we'd both be killed. I was in pieces.' A reporter for the BBC World Service was so concerned about her that he called the *Telegraph*. 'She needs to get out,' he told them.

She made a conscious decision to walk away. She couldn't face it again. Unlike Anne Sharpley, her sense of worth was not wholly bound up in her life as a journalist and the organisation for which she worked.

'I was able to walk away because I was happily married,' she said. 'I did go back once. There were decomposing bodies. The Iraqis would take us to a torture chamber. It was designed to shock us. It was so gruesome and grisly. I suffered PTSD, and had nightmares for years. If I'd carried on, I would have gone mad, and I would definitely be divorced.' When she set off for Iraq for the last time, Chris, her husband, had burst into tears. 'Please don't go,' he'd begged.

'I've got to go,' she said. 'This'll be the last time.'

She cried all the way to the airport.

But horrific, barely imaginable events do not happen only in countries far away. Clare Arron reached a turning point when she covered the trial of the two Merseyside children accused of murdering two-year-old James Bulger in 1993. 'It was such a horrendous crime, and the pain and horror was etched on his parents' faces,' she said. 'I had had to walk the route the children took, and photograph it, and then I covered the case. As a photographer, that meant waiting outside Preston Crown Court every day, getting glimpses of the comings and goings, photographing the police vehicles with the two boys inside arriving and leaving and the onlookers screaming at them. I particularly remember the night of the verdicts and the judge listening to argument – mostly from tabloid editors – for the two boys to be named. I stood in the dark outside, willing him not to name them, but he did. When that happened, the story immediately went from James Bulger to a frenzy of finding out about the two boys.

'It was a very important case to me. What I was aware of there – the breakdown of society in some areas, inequality of opportunity, the damage to children by parental neglect – reflects some of the reasons I left newspapers to become a social worker.'

At the opposite end of the scale were the kind of light-hearted snippets that Mary Kenny had to provide for the *Evening Standard* in the late 1960s. Though trivial in nature, they could sometimes cause both soul-searching and trepidation. 'I had to phone the Archbishop of Canterbury at seven in the morning,' said Mary. 'It was known as the Gestapo method. You rang them before breakfast so that a) they thought it was urgent so they had to come to the phone; b) they were slightly caught off-guard, and would blurt out anything. Then you'd have to ask these frightfully footling questions. I got through to a butler or someone at first, and heard him say, "My Lord, the *Evening Standard* is on the telephone for you." I was nervously telling myself, "Look, he can't bite your head off, you're not asking if he has a mistress." Then I thought, Oh dear, he's going to think the Queen Mother has died. And then Michael Ramsey picked up the phone, and I had to say, "My Lord, what side of the bed do you sleep on?"

'He was adorable, most courteous. "Oh, my dear young lady," he said, "I shall have to ask my wife about that." Such Christian forbearance. When you think he could have said, "Get lost, you silly minx."'

That injunction, 'get lost', or its more vehement equivalent, was often to be heard if you were involved in doorstepping – trying to get an interview with someone without prior arrangement or agreement. This might involve confronting them in a public space, such as their workplace or outside a courthouse, but traditionally entailed approaching them at their home.

Journalists are popularly supposed to be ruthless, callous types, who ditch any tendency to basic humanity at the merest whiff of a story, but is that universally the case? Louise Court had her first experience of doorstepping early on, when she worked at the *Epsom & Ewell Advertiser*. 'A man had hanged himself. We got it from the police calls. The opposition paper had published it first with the headline – HANGING HORROR. I was sent round to talk to the bereaved woman.

'I parked up, looked at the house, and prepared what I was going to say. She opened the door, I introduced myself and gave my condolences and she cried out, "Go away, you vulture!" It was awful. The widow was broken. Of course I felt terrible and thought, Did I have a right to go uninvited and knock on that door? *But* that person *could* have wanted to talk. You can never know how someone's going to react, whether you'll be welcomed. Journalists in dramas are always vile and disrespectful, but if you're like that in real life, nobody would tell you anything. As a journalist, you have to be respectful and be able to justify it to yourself. I think you have to establish a moral code.'

'The way journalists are portrayed in fiction – aggressive, foot-in-the-door – no way would you get an interview like that,' concurred Emma Lee-Potter, who is the author of *Interviewing for Journalists*, a highly readable textbook that covers this and other issues. 'You have to be empathetic, charming.'

'Being a woman, you were often sent out on really sad interviews because you were a softer touch,' said Tina Moran. 'But as a woman you'd get a better story. I had no problem with that at all. You had to drink and eat to get the interview. Perched on a chair. Tea with milk floating on top, soggy biscuits. You'd sit there with tears in your eyes while she told you about her little boy.'

This empathy, this ability, developed early in girlhood, to read people is one reason why women are regarded as being better at interviewing than men. How true is that, really? 'I think a lot of interviewers – especially men – have an agenda,' said Lynn Barber. 'They're not really interviewing a person, they're trying to have a discussion; whereas I genuinely want to interview. I think actually the reason I'm a good interviewer is that I'm *not* a good judge of people.' She referenced the relationship she had with a conman as a teenager that formed the basis of her autobiography and film, *An Education*. 'Because of that experience, I have a distrust of people. I need to get it explained to me. It's this quality of nosiness – once I start asking I can't stop. There are some very good men interviewers but broadly speaking I prefer to be interviewed by a woman.'

'I like talking to people and I'm interested in them,' said Scarth Flett. 'I did very thorough research, checking things that other journalists had written – sometimes the cuttings were wrong. It was just natural interest. You'd talk about their bloody book or movie and then some of them were quite happy to chat away. Sometimes they thought that once you'd turned the tape recorder off it was all systems go, so you'd get better quotes. But even when I had a tape recorder, I was scribbling along. People preferred it in my experience. They thought they could say things that wouldn't be recorded . . . though if someone said, "Please don't print that," I never did.'

Scarth's big thing was that she always put in what she'd like to read: what their house was like, how they looked. 'You always talk about their eyes,' someone teased her. She made friends with the subs – 'I could say, "You can't do that, that's not the same. You can't alter up my copy." Sometimes you had to bite the bullet, but they were quite wary of me because right from the beginning I checked my proofs. I didn't want my quotes reorganised and things written in. I never got anything wrong. A lot of people wrote rubbish and didn't check their facts. I always told the truth and I never misquoted.'

All celebrity life of the 1970s and 80s, everyone newsworthy and famous, from socialites to hell-raisers, can be found in the pile of cuttings Scarth showed me. She got the actress Sarah Miles to disclose she hadn't had sex for four years, and the racing driver James Hunt to admit he was pleased when his first wife, Suzy, ran off with Richard Burton. Michael Heseltine, three years after storming out of a Cabinet meeting at the height of what was known as the Westland affair and resigning as Margaret Thatcher's defence secretary, confessed to her that he missed the power. She would also be sent to interview politicians just because JJ wanted to find something out. 'If the truth didn't quite live up to his expectations, he didn't always run the piece,' she said.

Ron Atkinson, then manager of Manchester United, was popularly known as Mr Bojangles. He was renowned for his sunbed tan and ice-cream suits, and was usually photographed with a bottle of bubbly in his hand while his wrists and fingers twinkled with bling.

'When I went to see him, I said, "Where's all that junky jewellery?" He kept it in a drawer!'

Kirk Douglas wrote to thank her. She has kept the letter, a page of writing paper printed simply with his name at the top and dated 13 April 1987.

Dear Scarth,

I like that name – I meant to ask you how you got it.

I hope you had time to get a good interview. They certainly had me on a treadmill.

By the way, I mentioned our interview to Michael. He remembers you well.

All my best wishes to you,

Kirk

The letter was hand-signed. 'He liked me because I had a dimple,' she said.

An interview did not always go how you hoped. 'Now, tell me about your childhood,' said Mary Kenny to Eamonn Andrews, the presenter of the TV staple *This Is Your Life*. 'Why? Were you too lazy to look up the cuttings?' he retorted.

I lost most of an interview with Ron Atkinson because I stuck the tape recorder on a table at a high-ceilinged restaurant and when, later, I went to transcribe it discovered everything had been obliterated by the clatter of cutlery on plates. At one point, Scarth's husband John Pilger had upset the journalist and *Private Eye* diarist Auberon Waugh. Later, both were at the same party, and Waugh chased him around the room. After Waugh's wife, Teresa, wrote a book, Scarth arranged to interview her at home in Somerset. Then the publisher rang: 'I'm sorry, Mrs Waugh doesn't want you.' 'She thought I might say something nasty about her,' said Scarth.

She went to the USA to interview Susan Sarandon. Instead of giving her Susan Sarandon, the PRs shoved her in to talk to Sean Penn. Who she hadn't researched. Embarrassing.

'All the American journos were asking soft questions,' she said. 'I noticed Sean Penn had "LOVE" tattooed on his hands. "Oh, when did you have that done?" I asked. "Was it when you were married to Madonna?" The room went silent. He just laughed and said yes. Well, I didn't have anything else to ask him.

'I had to interview Kathy Crosby, Mrs Bing, at a house in Green Street. I found a famous PR was sitting there. We waited. Then a minion came in and said to the PR, "Mrs Crosby won't come down while you're here." So she had to leave with her tail between her legs.

'Another PR would say, "Whatever you do, don't ask about such-and-such." So you'd leave that till last. I was going to interview Andy Williams at the Dorchester. He allegedly had a thing with Ethel Kennedy, and the PR said, "Oh, whatever you do don't mention Ethel Kennedy, he'll shoot you."'

Oh, bugger that, thought Scarth. 'At the end of the interview, I said, "You'd better get your gun out now."

'"Why's that?"

'"I hear you don't want to talk about Ethel Kennedy."'

She couldn't stop him talking after that.

There's the interviewee who's quite potty. The socialite Olga Deterding, who inherited an oil empire from her father, was famous for affairs with two TV personalities of that era, Alan Whicker and Jonathan Routh, both of whom left her. Routh had scarpered only three weeks before Scarth went to interview her in the penthouse flat overlooking Green Park. Scarth described her as 'a slender woman with a taut face and long, red hair that she pushes back constantly with small, capable-looking hands, empty of rings . . .' 'She was a bit mad,' said Scarth. 'It was hard tracking her down and, when I did, she said she'd like to have copy control. Mostly you said no to that, but I thought, Fuck it, I don't care, and told the features editor I didn't mind. They humoured her, and I got the piece. A strange lady. Yves Saint Laurent had made this big sheep and it was hanging in her apartment. She'd scattered raisins underneath to look like sheep poo.'

She mentioned the raisins in the piece and what they were meant to be. That was the one thing that didn't get past the subs.

I interviewed Alan Hansen, later an articulate and authoritative pundit on *Match of the Day*. He was famous for having four A-levels, and was in the early stages of his career as a centre half when I went up to Anfield to write a profile on him. While we were talking in the players' lounge, one of his team-mates strolled in and growled out a not-very-nice suggestion on what he, Alan and I should get up to afterwards. Alan briskly told him to go away, but for the rest of the interview and till my taxi drew up outside he stuck resolutely by my side, rather as he man-marked opposing strikers.

I interviewed Bobby Moore, who was polite and handsome and impenetrable. It was at Southend, where he was making one of his final attempts to succeed as a manager, and I could get nothing out of him that wasn't bland. A few days later came the announcement that he'd split with his wife, Tina. There had been nothing in his manner to suggest this seismic change in his life, no tells or shiftiness. He had the most impressive self-control. A man who could have kept the Second Coming secret if he'd been required to do so. Twenty years later I helped Tina write the story of her life with Bobby. She was warm and generous and funny, a very intelligent woman who was still stunningly attractive at sixty. I liked her much better than Bobby.

But some of the players and managers I met and interviewed were people you will never have heard of, because football in the 1970s and 80s was not big-time as it is now. The players and managers were all lovely to me. I thought then it was because of my in-depth knowledge of football, but of course most of them just liked being interviewed by a babe – I was a novelty. Who cared? It meant I got the interviews when others did not, and of course I wrote about them differently, as if they were rock stars and actors. I could describe what they looked like and get them to talk about their feelings. Dangerous ground for a male sportswriter but they could tell a woman. What was it like to be a footballer? What was it like to be a man? I really wanted to know.

Lynn Barber once had six months of interviewing foot-ballers, and hated it. 'They were thick,' she told me. I never thought so, though most were undereducated: gifted children who had been courted by clubs since their age was in single figures and after that all they did was dream football, football, football till school leaving age. Malcolm Macdonald, a bright boy who played as striker for Newcastle United and England, didn't find it surprising. 'You're in a classroom trying to concentrate on a diagram of spirogyra when all you can think about is how to make the left-back overlap.'

There were only two rules in Fleet Street. One was that you must always buy your round. The other was that a journalist always files. This inbuilt compulsion gave a routine and a struc- ture to your life, and a discipline that made you shove even huge emotional pain aside while you did what you had to do. Maureen Paton had left her feature writer's job on the *Daily Express* to become a successful freelance feature writer when her husband, Liam Maguire, was diagnosed with advanced prostate cancer in 2004. She kept quiet about it for a long time – that was what Liam wanted as well. Then he went into a hospice and she realised she had to front up. She was doing a lot of work for Sue Peart's *You* magazine and rang Rosalind Lowe, its features editor, on her mobile. 'Sorry about ringing in the evening but I've got to tell you something.'

'What's the matter, what's the matter?'

'My husband is very ill and may not last much longer,' she said, 'but I want to keep working and he wants me to.'

Liam died in January 2006. Sue Peart and her team were incredibly kind. 'Work will help,' she was told. It was a male colleague who said that to her. 'And it did.'

At other times, the internalised imperative to file could give you an almost absurd indifference to your personal safety. Emma Lee-Potter worked on hard news at the *Evening Standard* during the years that Princess Di was in her heyday, and covered a lot of her visits abroad. 'I went out to the Middle East with her, and at one point had to cover a falconry display in the desert,' she recalled. 'Other journalists didn't need to file as early as me. I needed to catch the first edition, so I left the press pack. A couple of men offered me a lift to the hotel – men I'd never met before. I'm literally on my own in the desert. How stupid is that? But I was more scared of missing the deadline. *I've got to file!*'

Did I ever get in dangerous situations while I was working? Some aspects of football in the 1970s and 80s were horrible. Fans fought and rioted, local residents were intimidated and frightened, stadiums were shabby and old. I existed in a bubble, of course. I had the press box to sit in, and going to and from grounds I was more or less invisible to the all-male throng because they were all so wrapped up in their chest-thumping and horn-crashing that no one noticed a small female hurrying along – I was just part of the street furniture, like a traffic island or a bin. Once, a Scotland supporter, enraged after defeat by England at Wembley, exposed himself to me and tried to get into my car – thank heavens for the automatic central locking system of my Ford Capri IIS (not to mention the salary that meant I had been able to afford to buy a sports car). But I experienced only one moment of mortal terror. This was when I became swept up in a football crowd funnelling through the narrow subway from Witton station to Villa Park. My legs left the ground and I was carried along like driftwood. It would only take someone to stumble and fall and there would be a tragedy, surely.

I thought, once I found my way out, that my reaction had been disproportionate, but it was only a few years before the loss of lives at Heysel, Hillsborough and Bradford. Little attention was paid to our safety, because football supporters were, in the 1970s and 80s, regarded as a dangerous and verminous mass of oafs and scum, not defenceless and largely harmless human beings who went out to watch a game of football.

So what was it like to set out to report something you expected to be joyous and thrilling, but to find yourself a witness to a disaster? It was the end of May 1985, and the showpiece of the football season – Juventus v Liverpool in the European Cup final. Most of Brussels two hours before kick-off was simply enjoying the last of a sunny day. In a taxi from the station to the ground, as you passed La Grande-Place you noticed it was heaving with drunk Liverpool supporters. There were shopping trolleys laden with beer. It was Whitsun in the UK, so they'd been there three days on the toot.

From the press seats at Heysel Stadium, trouble was visible behind one of the goals. It was divided equally between Liverpool and Juventus supporters, only a feeble mesh fence separating them. The Liverpool fans were penned into one tiny area and, as the ground filled up, they flattened the fence and forced the Juventus fans to retreat. Then, when they fled along the terraces, they couldn't get out at the front or the back. The *Observer* photographer, Eamonn McCabe, went to take photos. You could see the fans were being squashed against a waist-high, concrete retaining wall. It gave way. Eamonn waved up at the press box and made a throat-slitting gesture.

A troop of Belgian mounted police came trotting on. They just stood there. You were astonished by how little concern was shown. Somebody got hold of some railings and carted away a body under a flag. An arm flopped out.

It was like watching a horror film unfold. You just sat there, helpless.

You phoned over a holding piece to the news desk.

Phil Neal, the Liverpool captain, went out onto the pitch to try to calm the crowd. You remembered Bill Nicholson, the Spurs manager, trying to do the same thing when fans rioted at a European game in Rotterdam in 1974. He was shouted down. It never worked.

You felt a moment of self-disgust. You were just a paid voyeur. Then you phoned over another holding piece.

Two and a half hours had passed when they decided to go ahead with the match. It was appeasement by entertainment. But there seemed a kind of depravity about the whole thing, about letting the game go ahead, about Juve's Michel Platini wheeling around in triumph after scoring the winner, about Juve parading around, doing laps of honour with the cup.

You phoned over a match report.

It was a matter of pride, not crying. But in fact you didn't feel any urge to cry anyway. You just snapped into job mode. This is what's happening. Make a note of everything you see. Put the words together. File. You're just engrossed in the task.

But some were in floods. Emlyn Hughes, former Liverpool captain and a lovely, bouncy, giggly man, came up to the press seats afterwards to be interviewed for TV, crying buckets. You weren't. You phoned your office to check if there were queries then went down to look at the scene. The dead had been taken away. Most had died through lack of oxygen in the seething crush. All their shoes were lined up at the edge of the pitch.

'The night of the Heysel Stadium disaster I was downstairs in the pub,' said Sue Peart. 'Someone came running down – "Sue, Sue, something's happened." I raced back to the newsroom. People were gathered in silent groups, watching TVs. My job as features editor was to get people out there, make decisions. It's like being in a whiteout, skiing down a mountain, you're unaware of time. It was about two in the morning when I came out into a silent Fleet Street. No taxis. Nothing. Oh my God, how am I going to get home? I stood at the bus stop opposite the *Express* and the *Telegraph*, waiting for a night bus.

'Lights were ablaze. Everything else was black. It was just these two buildings. It was a factory. Every window lit. You could hear the humming.

'I became aware of someone next to me. The bus arrived in the early morning mist. So I got on. Behind me, someone said in plummy tones, "I'd like a single ticket to Charing Cross." It was William Deedes, the *Telegraph* editor. I was in awe of him. Dare I go and say, "Bill Deedes, I hold you in awe?" We rode all the way to Charing Cross. Him and me.'

'The phone rang in my tiny little flat in Lavender Hill,' said Emma Lee-Potter. 'I was in my nightie. "Victoria station, meet the people coming off the boat train. There's been a football disaster in Brussels."'

In March 1988, in a military operation, three members of a Provisional IRA cell were shot dead in the forecourt of a Gibraltar petrol station by undercover members of the SAS. They became known as the Gibraltar Three, and Clare Arron was sent to cover the funerals.

'It was a heavy day,' she said understatedly. 'You're covering three funerals in an atmosphere of anything-can-happen, and then Michael Stone of the Loyalists comes up the motorway and starts shooting. I carried on taking photos. I stood there. A lot of people lay on the floor. I didn't know where the other photographers were – we had a lot of film taken off us by the IRA. I thought, Now how am I going to manage this? I hoped they wouldn't go into my pockets. "Is that all?" they asked me. I said yes, knowing it wasn't. That was the moment I knew I could do stressful things.

'You have to get rid of your film, develop it and wire it, or go to the airport and get someone to take it back. I got in a car with a stranger. He said, "I'll have to take the back roads because I haven't got any tax." He took me to the airport.

Another photographer took my film for me and the *Telegraph* used it. And the other *Telegraph* photographers didn't get any pictures.

'After the cemetery I went to the hotel bar. Everybody was in there, including two photographers I knew quite well. One I liked and one who was an absolute creep. The one I liked walked over. "All right? I heard you were crying."

'Not a tear. I'd been busy doing my job. I didn't know what to say. Where's that come from? That was not very nice. Then the other guy, the creep, walked behind me and stuck his finger right inside me. In my jeans. Nobody even noticed. What a fuck of a day. Jesus.'

You don't know where to start with this. It's just speculation, but perhaps to appear models of manly fortitude, they needed the counterpoint of fluffy feminine crying. After all, wasn't that what women were meant to do? Just like they were expected to be nice and smiley all the time? Even when someone cops an unwanted feel?

In the next section we'll look at the behaviour expected of us, at sexism, and the other issues that affected us as women in Fleet Street.

PART 3

Women's Interest

Chapter 17

Sexism

'Neither at *Penthouse* nor the *Express* did I discover discrimination, but at the *Independent* it was rampant!' said Lynn Barber, who joined it in 1990. 'The really odd part was that I encountered sexual prejudice for the first time in my life! Sons of vicars, not top public school, in their forties, talked about cricket – and because I'd come from *Penthouse* and the *Express*, I was Miss Naff. They always seemed to regard the sports pages and books pages as sacred. When they launched, the market research came back: "You're not attracting women," and forty men would go into a huddle and say, "Should we have a fashion page?"'

Sexism – bias, prejudice, stereotyping, discrimination. Whatever the best definition, it was hard to avoid, and if you were a female football reporter it just went with the job. Sometimes it even made me smile. The *Rothmans Football Yearbook* of 1977 stuck my name in a list of 'the men who travel Great Britain covering football'. During my first season as a reporter, I went to Stamford Bridge to interview Chelsea's new starlet, Ray 'Butch' Wilkins. He was just a boy, only eighteen, with a teenage mop of hair the colour of dark mahogany, but great things were expected of him. (He did go on to captain Chelsea and England so he didn't disappoint, except in the matter of his hair, which in the later stages of his playing career fell out abruptly and almost all at once as if someone had snatched it off his head.) At Stamford Bridge, I was shown into an office where Butch was waiting. Some minutes into the interview I realised we had company. The assistant coach sat through the entire thing, in case I was a femme fatale sent to compromise their protégé.

'After the Romanian revolution I was assigned to go there for three weeks, travelling all over the country,' said Clare Arron. She was accompanied by the author Patrick Leigh Fermor, who was old and frail, and just recovering from cancer of the mouth. 'He was quite unwell at times,' she said, 'and I had to make sure he was warm enough and ate properly. The working conditions in Romania were difficult, and it was winter. No one knew where we were, and there weren't any phones working. One night, in a cold hotel in Transylvania, I piled all the clothes we had on top of him and just hoped he would be okay. When I got back to the office, the foreign editor told me they had sent me because they knew I would look after him.'

That kind of sexism was sweetly funny. The other sort wasn't so much. When I'd triggered that demarcation dispute in 1973 and the *Observer*'s NUJ chapel voted to allow me to join, the father of the chapel was not gracious in defeat. 'So,' he said, the next time I saw him. 'You managed to swing it, then.'

'What?'

'We thought you and Ron were in collusion,' he said.

No matter that I was an award-winning writer, that my work had been published in top magazines and that I had a burgeoning second career as a writer for television. There was no way I could have got this job on merit. I had obviously slept for it.

'You just got used to it, as a woman,' said Louise Court. 'Certain senior men saying, "Let's go out for a drink, discuss a few ideas." Many were being genuinely helpful but not all of them. I was never in a compromising situation. But if a woman did do well, there would often be rumours. Someone told me there was a rumour about me. I said, "Well, either I must be really bad in bed or it's not true because why am I earning less than everyone else!"'

You might think that kind of attitude must have died out. Surely. No, not a bit of it. 'It's a familiar excuse,' said Lynn Barber. 'She got the job because she's his girlfriend. You can't be a successful writer because you're someone's girlfriend – it's ridiculous.' In fact, I heard it expressed only recently, by someone wondering rhetorically, of a woman presenting a football programme on TV, 'how many dicks she had to suck to get there'. The speaker was young, and female. It isn't only some men who feel the need to diminish a successful woman.

You would not, for instance, have found much evidence of female solidarity in Fleet Street – not in what Katharine Whitehorn termed 'male subjects': news, business, politics, sport. Well, why would there be? There were so few roles for women to go round. You wouldn't want to encourage the competition.

'At the time I never thought about it,' said the photographer Clare Arron, 'not in any massive way. Colin Smith, the picture editor at the *Telegraph*, was very nice, and still a friend. I took him a photo of black kids tree-planting. Next day, Colin said, "That's the first time the *Telegraph* has had a photo of black people in the paper." You thought, How could that be true? There's a glass ceiling if ever there was one.

'But elsewhere, even should you get regular work, there was definitely a sense that you were The One Woman.' She remembered what a Press Association photographer had told her: 'I know they took me on because they had to have A Woman. Although I have great affection for my colleagues at the *Telegraph* and had a great time working there, I had always wanted to work at the *Guardian* but could never get past the picture editors. At that time the *Guardian* did not have a regular woman photographer, nor did the *Independent*. They really were more sexist in attitude than the *Telegraph*, which is the opposite of what most people would have assumed.'

'It was pull-up-the-ladder,' said Angie Mulligan of her experience on the tabloids. Wendy Holden said much the same thing. 'I never got on with the female executives in Fleet Street. I felt they'd broken through the glass ceiling and then had it reglazed. There was no helping hand. No acting on Jack Lemmon's advice: When you get to the top of the building, be sure to send the elevator back down. The attitude was, "Well, I'm here so I don't want anyone else here." One day I was in the ladies with another senior editor. I was thirty-two. She looked across at me. "Do you wear foundation?" I thought she was going to compliment me. "Well, you should," she said.'

Maureen Paton had a theory about this. 'When gays came along in Fleet Street, they didn't like each other because they thought there would be a quota,' she observed. 'One was closeted. The other was out and proud and in your face. And they detested each other because – as far as I know – they were the only gays on the paper and they thought each was exceeding the quota. I think women might have thought along the same lines.'

And there's another point to be made here – how different standards are applied to females. 'Women are judged doubly,' said Wendy Holden, 'for performance and for how they look while they're doing it. We were surrounded by some revolting caricatures, fleshy, stinking, balding, repulsive, and yet they felt they had the right to tell you you've got childbearing hips. And they're standing there with beer bellies, and food stains all down their front. It was just how it was. They didn't think they were being cruel.'

Sometime in the 1980s, the *Express* showbiz editor Victor Davis told Maureen Paton, 'You're going to have a great career.' And that was so encouraging, it was wonderful: 'He'd had a tough climb himself, so he wasn't someone who gave out praise lightly,' she said. 'In later years I got quite friendly with Jean Rook [the *Daily Express*'s Voice of Middle England columnist] and Victor said I could step into her shoes tomorrow. Lovely, but you have to have your heart in something like that. I didn't want to keep criticising women for what they were wearing. "She's showing her knees, those clothes are far too young for her." It was the men that corralled them into it. I preferred to criticise men – the feminist in me coming out. I didn't want to do that Glenda Slagg thing. Women are human. They're allowed to have as many faults as men.'

'I only worked briefly for the tabloids as a freelance but I was largely given more photocopying than the men,' said Wendy Holden, 'and I was automatically handed any books on fashion, the royals, flowers. When you were sent on a serious story, you were told, "Look nice, sweet-talk them into it." Basically, telling you to go and sleep with somebody. Getting to places men couldn't.'

This assumption – that Wendy would merrily agree to being used as a honeytrap – was closely related to another issue: the unwanted male gaze. 'Nigella Lawson was very shy,' said Wendy. 'She never went to the pub with the rest of us and seemed to wear black virtually from head to toe. There were a couple of women like that in my early days on Fleet Street – they kept themselves on the periphery, and rather than face the testosterone would virtually be in full yashmak. Frankly, I didn't blame them.'

'During the James Bulger trial I was standing outside the courthouse with a *Times* reporter,' said Clare Arron. 'Traumatic and horrible, and I was fucking freezing. "Well," he said, "I'm sure you've got enough fat on your thighs." I don't have. Who do they think they are? It kind of comes out of nowhere.'

In my case, because I was the only woman in the press box, I started off by muting the more obvious signs of my gender as much as possible. On match days, I wore bulky sweaters (not that there was much to hide) and trousers – these out of sheer practicality, since getting to your allotted seat in the press box often entailed rudimentary parkour, climbing across seatbacks to avoid squeezing past crutches in case they, um, stood to attention. One Saturday night, as I drank my post-match vodka and orange in The Cockpit, a reporter called Lindsay Vincent sidled up to me, grinning.

'You're butch, aren't you?' he said.

What did he expect me to do? Apologise for insufficient simpering? You should have told him to fuck off, everyone said, but I was too upset to think straight. It pained me so much. 'No! Far from it!' I wailed, and off he went to snigger with his mates at the other end of the bar.

Several of the stories I was told were about men stabbing you in the back. When Louise Court was a celeb writer and pop correspondent on the *Daily Express*, one got her into a big row. 'I'd known Siobhan Fahey of Bananarama since before she was famous. When she married Dave Stewart of the Eurythmics I'd been invited to the wedding as me, not as a reporter. It was my private life. Meanwhile other reporters had received tip-offs about the wedding and where it was, in a chateau in France. I went there with my friends. The guests were bussed in. I lay on the floor of the coach, not wanting to be seen by the journalists waiting outside. Months later, my news editor found out I'd been there and ripped me to shreds. I found out later I had been stitched up by a male colleague.'

The theme of male antagonism also featured in Jennifer Selway's early career. 'When I was a TV previewer on the *Observer*, my colleague Desmond Balmer waved a piece of paper at me and said, "Have you seen this?" It was a press release from ATV. Some bastard who'd had the hots for me at *Time Out* but who I'd rejected had written a TV play about the adventures of this girl who came to work for a listings magazine. It was about me, and the tone of the play was really spiteful.

'The play had been recorded. It was all in the bag. I made a complaint, informally, to the ATV press office: "This is completely libellous." That really put the wind up them, and they dropped it.' Not long after that, there was a piece in *Private Eye* about hackettes who go running to their lawyers complaining of something written about them they don't like.

'But I sort of thought, as you do: "I've brought it on myself. This is my fault. I overstepped the mark. This is my punishment for it." I'm still quite angry about it. Getting done over by the bastard who wrote the play. Getting done over by *Private Eye*. So you get clobbered again, just for standing up for yourself.'

I think we've forgotten – or are too young to have experienced – the entrenched sexism that meant it was completely normal for women to be barred from places or institutions. As the owner of a vagina, I was not allowed to join the Football Writers' Association. This, too, was a time when a nice 'girl' didn't go to the pub unless she was with a man. In 1972 I walked into the Black Friar on my own and bought a drink. Even in Fleet Street that seemed an act of defiance.

I tracked down an informative column in the *Guardian*, written by its women's editor Mary Stott. It hasn't a date on it but the smeary, inky type suggests that it's late 1960s vintage:

More women than ever before are going into pubs. Good thing, bad thing? Most of us would be hard put to give an objective answer. All sorts of conditioned attitudes get in the way . . . pubs are places for men to escape from their wives; the mingling of the sexes should be kept to well-defined limits; no lady goes into a pub on her own . . .

Etc., etc. No lady was permitted to drink beer from a pint glass, either; she would only be allowed halves. Pubs were traditionally 'male environments', and a landlord was entitled to refuse her service. It wasn't until 1982 that it became illegal. Imagine that. But it's just one example of how women were constructively excluded. Sometimes, of course, the barricade was unofficial. As we've already seen, the absence of loos was a standard ploy for keeping women out of male spaces.

At least El Vino's provided one. It was down in the basement and opposite the men's; the adorable Philip Hope-Wallace, opera and theatre critic of the *Guardian*, referred to the area as *entre-deux-loos*. The opportunity to pee was about the only concession El Vino's allowed us. We couldn't enter via the front door. We couldn't go up to the bar and buy a drink. We weren't tolerated in the front bar at all. They didn't want women in there. Our handbags would get in the way. Anyway, banning us from the front was an act of chivalry, so they claimed. It was to ensure we weren't jostled at the bar.

Even so, this exclusion wasn't necessarily accompanied by resentment. I never gave it a thought. Being taken there felt as if I was being afforded a treat. I was in El Vino's! I'd arrived! So what if I had to sit in a back room? It was all part of the romance of Fleet Street; it seemed as if you were just taking part in some quaint custom. Besides, when you sat in the back you had Philip Hope-Wallace, gay, cultivated, funny and mischievous.

He had his own table, positioned under an elderly oil painting of the Widow Clicquot. Here he would tootle away telling you naughty stories, lacing them with the occasional 'fuck', like the sixpence in an old Christmas pudding. 'We loved it,' said Valerie Grove. 'Philip was a gorgeous man and it was a privilege to be on his table. He used to buy champagne.' This was probably because it was the best thing to drink there, as the wine was quite horrible, but it all added to the glamour.

'El Vino's was a very special place and listening to Philip was a university education,' said Mary Kenny. 'It felt as though we were like the children of the Bedouin tribe, sitting in a circle at the feet of the elders, listening to their stories. Tom Driberg was another colourful Fleet Street character. He was also gay, and always suspected of being a Russian spy.' She remembered Philip saying languidly, 'I think Tom would tell you it's always invaluable to have a fifty-pound note in your pocket, to serve as a bribe.' Then, said Mary, he would raise his voice: 'Another bottle of the Widow!'

History does not record how Philip reacted one day in 1970 when a group of women journalists tried to enter via the front. Probably he simply sat there and called for another bottle of the Widow. But the invasion caused a sensation; it made the next edition of the evening papers and the tabloids featured it the following day (A STORM IN A SHERRY GLASS, tittered the *Daily Mirror*). It went down in Fleet Street folklore. Not everyone later alleged to be present was actually there. Someone who was mentioned, in Anne Robinson's autobiography, *Diary of an Unfit Mother*, as having taken part was Mary Kenny, who was in Dublin at the time being women's editor of the *Irish Press*. In any case, she disapproved strongly. 'I was slightly under the influence of Marxist feminism at the time. I thought it a bourgeois protest. Unserious. Not applicable to the working class.'

Among those involved, though, was David Jenkins, Valerie Grove's first husband. 'He led a whole posse of women from *Nova*,' she said. 'I've got a photo of him being manhandled by Van.' Geoffrey Van Hay was the bar manager. Starchy Mr El Vino sent him out to defend the territory. Van wore a white collar (detachable), dark tie and striped trousers. He was a policeman's son from the Elephant and Castle, but along the way this master of assimilation assumed posh vowels and fluttery, effete mannerisms (we were flabbergasted when he married and, in rapid succession, fathered three sons). He was actually a very nice man, but of course he was The Enemy, and when the crowd of women journalists burst through the front doors and demanded their equal rights, he took the brunt of it.

'Ladies aren't being served today,' he uttered prettily in his finest pantomime dame mode. Poor man, he didn't have a hope. In the scuffle that followed, someone made a wild grab at his tie and dragged him around, at which a political cartoonist called Willi poured jugs of water over them.

A fat lot of good the march on El Vino's achieved. Once the spilt water was mopped up and the buttons sewn back on Van's shirt, everything returned to how it had been. The men went off chuckling to write in their memoirs about 'the monstrous regiment' and 'liberated ladies' entering 'this citadel of masculinity'. Oh, ha ha. Even the nice men thought it was funny. They had no idea what it was like not to be allowed in places.

This particular prejudice against women lasted until 1982, when the journalist Anna Coote and lawyer Tess Gill succeeded in a long-running sex discrimination case – it went to the Court of Appeal – against the wine bar. All three appeal court judges had to declare an interest in the case as they all drank there. El Vino's reacted with the sourest of grapes, the then manager Jeremy Jones declaring Coote and Gill would not be served there at any time. 'They are not welcome.' His successor, Paul Bracken, said he would serve all women who 'genuinely wanted a drink', but not 'those who want to make trouble or a feminist point'. Too bad. We had long deserted El Vino's by then. Van had left to manage a wonderful club, Scribes. Philip Hope-Wallace followed him there. He would fall asleep in a comfortable chair in the back bar. It was more comfortable than his seat under the Widow Clicquot.

Chapter 18

The Penis Premium:
Glass Ceilings and the Gender Pay Gap

Ms Monopoly is the name of a new version of the famous old board game, where the rules have been rewritten. In this one, women make more money than men, female players start with more cash than their male counterparts, and earn more than the men each time they pass Go, which hasn't of course been the case since Never BC. Launched in the US, the object of the exercise is to teach children about the gender pay gap. It's the world in reverse – most estimates say that, although the gap has been getting smaller over the years, progress has sputtered to a halt and women still earn somewhere between 79 and 85 per cent of what men rake in for comparable jobs.

Ms Monopoly was launched in September 2019. Four months later, at the Central London Employment Tribunal, Samira Ahmed, presenter of BBC's *Newswatch*, won a case against her employer for sexual discrimination. The case – centred on pay inequality at the BBC – was brought after Ahmed discovered that, in 2012, she was paid £440 per programme. A fellow presenter, Jeremy Vine, meanwhile, earned £3,000 for presenting *Points of View*, a programme of comparable length and content. The BBC was unable successfully to explain away the differential. They claimed that Jeremy Vine was more of a celebrity and it was nothing to do with his being a man. Ho-hum.

Rewind back to the mid-1970s, when women's tennis had become symbiotic with the feminist movement and I was writing about Billie Jean King, who in 1961 as a bespectacled seventeen-year-old had bounced into the British national consciousness (and became one of my Girl Crushes) by winning, with eighteen-year-old Karen Hantze, the women's doubles at Wimbledon. They were the youngest ever pairing to achieve that title. That was just the start of it. By the end of the decade, the women's game was booming and one of the big-name events was the Pacific South West Tennis Tournament. It was run by Jack Kramer, a one-time Wimbledon champion who was now a tournament promoter, TV commentator and a gentleman adamantine in his resistance to the notion propounded by King that women players deserved to be paid as much as the men. King had a good case; the women received just 15 per cent of the prize money in spite of their final attracting the same number of spectators as the men's.

This yawning disparity triggered the Virginia Slims Circuit, a tennis tour, originally with nine elite female players, that later became the Women's Tennis Association Tour, as it remains today. To help with publicity and organisation, they enlisted Gladys Heldman, the influential publisher of *World Tennis* magazine. 'You've come a long way, baby,' was the slogan used to advertise tournament sponsor Virginia Slims, a long-gone brand of cigarettes designed to be a female-friendly way of giving yourself lung cancer and heart disease. Heldman is reputed to have said to King, 'You do the tennis and I'll do the smoking.'

When I interviewed her, King had just founded the Women's Tennis Association, which demanded – and got – equal pay at the US Open. Enter Bobby Riggs, another one-time Wimbledon champion and a grandstanding sexist who claimed that women's tennis was inferior. 'I'm fifty-five,' he said, 'and

I can still beat any top female player.' He challenged King to play him. When King refused on the grounds that it was just a gimmick, fatuous, an excuse for Riggs to make money (he had an unfortunate gambling habit), the world number one Margaret Court stepped up. Riggs beat her in two easy sets on Mother's Day in California. Inevitably, this humiliation was dubbed the 'Mother's Day Massacre'.

This wouldn't do. King announced that she would take Riggs on after all, and they met at the Houston Astrodome late on in September 1973. It was one of the most-watched televised sports events in US history. Exhibition match, 30,000 at the stadium, 90 million viewers worldwide.

'I thought it would set us back fifty years if I didn't win,' said King. 'It would ruin the women's tour.' She won in three straight sets and pocketed the $100,000, winner-takes-all prize money. The head-to-head 'Battle of the Sexes' became the eponymous film.

Rewind even further back, to 1968, and fly across an ocean to Dagenham in Essex where 187 women worked in Ford's flagship factory. The women, who sewed car seat covers, were classified as 'unskilled' workers, though male employees performing the same or similar jobs were classified as 'skilled' workers.

This was a time when people still thought a woman's primary job was keeping house and looking after the kids. Work was something secondary, for pin money, supplementary to the income brought in by the male breadwinner. The women were paid 87 per cent less than the men. Even teenage boy floor sweepers were paid higher wages than the women were. The women walked out, bringing car production to a halt. Thousands of staff were laid off. As the strike fanned out across the UK, women on the picket line were jeered as they raised a banner that read: 'We want sexual equality.' Unfortunately, imperfectly unfurled, it read: 'We want sex.' You can just predict, can't you, the delight of the Fleet Street photographers. Women organising to ask for equal pay was a threat, and how do you deal with a threat? By making fun of it.

Anyway, after intervention by Barbara Castle, Secretary of State for Employment in the Labour government, the women eventually accepted a deal for 92 per cent of male wages and returned to work. The episode ultimately triggered the introduction of the Equal Pay Act in 1970, established to outlaw discrimination in pay and conditions between the sexes. Except it didn't, of course, not absolutely.

How does all this relate to Fleet Street in our era? In 1973, the year of the 'Battle of the Sexes', Felicity Green was appointed publicity director of Mirror Group Newspapers; as the first woman to take a seat on a national newspaper's main board, she really did smash the glass ceiling. Deservedly so; it's all there in her book *Sex Sense and Nonsense*, how after joining the *Mirror* in 1960 she became executive women's editor across all three Mirror Group titles, in the process turning the daily paper into the go-to read for style. This was fashion as news, as business. She put it on the front page, showcased the hairstyles and clothes we wanted to wear, at prices we could afford. In the late spring of 1964, she hit us with a centre spread featuring *that* dress, the pink gingham one that launched Biba. It had a little keyhole fastening at the back, sleeveless, rollneck, and a matching headscarf: it was 'Yours for 25s. including the kerchief'. The accompanying story was about career girls making a financial success of their burgeoning fashion businesses. Biba – Barbara Hulanicki – had been struggling with the fledgling mail-order business she had set up with her husband, Stephen Fitz-Simon. Green asked Hulanicki to design a simple summer dress with a headscarf to match that she could offer to

Mirror readers. She thought they might sell 2–3,000, but they sold 17,000 in the pink and another 5,000 in the blue. 'We had emptied the UK of pink gingham,' Green said.

When she championed Mary Quant's miniskirt it brought her the threat of the sack. 'How long are you going to carry on putting these ridiculous clothes in my newspaper?' demanded Cecil Harmsworth King, the chairman of the International Publishing Corporation, which owned the Mirror Group newspapers.

'As long as they're news,' Green replied. 'And what will you do if I carry on putting them in the paper?'

'I'll arrange for you to be fired,' said King. She outlasted him; he was terminated for plotting to overthrow Harold Wilson's government via the front page of the *Daily Mirror*, while she went on to be given that seat on the board. 'She'll be the first director to powder her nose before a board meeting,' trilled the *UK Press Gazette*. Five years later, Green discovered that a male journalist, newly appointed as a director, was being paid £30,000 a year. Her salary was £14,000. 'So I left,' she said. 'Everyone was astonished. Apparently, I was supposed to be honoured simply to be a director.' Being the best isn't good enough. She was female, therefore worth less. It was the penis premium.

We talked, in the last chapter, about sexual discrimination; in spite of journalism being one of the professions that ostensibly offered equal pay, did it really? Yes, when you're talking about the non-executive roles, reporting, grunt work, subbing jobs and the like. And we were certainly not underpaid compared to women and men out there in the land. Three among us, Wendy Holden, Maureen Paton and Louise Court, were main bread-winners in their marriages. But compared to our male Fleet Street colleagues, there was one glaring disparity, particularly in the 1970s. When it came to being promoted to senior roles where the biggest salaries came in, guess who got the job?

Why didn't more of us have the courage of Felicity Green and kick up a greater fuss? There are two ways you can answer that. One is that, unmarried and with no dependants, she could afford to walk away – especially as, with her talent, she would immediately be snapped up elsewhere. The second reason is this. When, in 1975, moonlighting for the *Telegraph* magazine, I wrote a piece on Pan's People, the dance troupe on *Top of the Pops*, I asked Ruth Pearson, one of its members, how much they earned. 'We never talk about money,' she demurred. 'It's unladylike.'

You get the picture. Many girls of my generation were socially conditioned not to mention something as vulgar as money. Which led to us finding it difficult to ask to be paid more, which meant we continued to be underpaid. And because we worked for lower pay, we considered ourselves to be of lower status.

One day in June 1974 I was staring at my little Olivetti portable typewriter trying to think of an intro when a Gordon Someone of the *Daily Mail* rang to ask if I'd like to work for them. I said I might, and we arranged to have lunch at Inigo Jones, which was *the* new restaurant in Covent Garden. This choice of venue immediately predisposed me favourably towards the *Mail*. When, a few months earlier, the *Evening News* had offered me the job of chief sportswriter, the wooing took place in a grotty pub off Carmelite Street. No thanks.

At the time, I had no job security at the *Observer*. I was paid on a per diem basis, match by match, feature by feature. If there was nothing for me to do, if I was unwell and couldn't work, if I had to take time off because of childcare commitments, I earned nothing. If the sports editor took against me – well, that didn't bear thinking about. And now the *Daily Mail* was offering me a staff job at £5,000 a year.

But the *Observer* was familiar. They were tolerant. They put up with the lack of formal training that made me struggle sometimes to shape copy. They let me use long words (some of which I didn't quite know the meaning of myself). Along with the lack of indulgence that I would find at the *Mail*, working for a daily would be much more demanding than a Sunday paper. I would be on call more and would have to travel a lot, and Fred was nearly five, and about to start school. But it wasn't even that that gave me pause. I knew with total certainty that they didn't want me for the beauty of my prose. They wanted me as a gimmick, their Girl In The Press Box, as if I were a talking dog or something. They'd rewrite my copy and put in all sorts of ghastly clichés, and they'd discover how hopeless I was at getting stuff in on time and – most important of all – how unglamorous I was. They'd get fed up with me after six months. Then I'd be back where I started.

Honestly, what a coward. I'm sure I could have done it. But, anyway, I turned them down. Not before going back to the *Observer*, of course, and telling them about this amazing offer.

I did get a proper freelance contract out of them. It was half what I'd have earned at the *Mail* but I loved the *Observer* so much I didn't mind. The contract stipulated that I had to produce a certain number of features and reports per year. My fee for each feature, when it was first arranged, was twenty-five guineas. The male freelances were paid thirty. I was worth five pounds five shillings less than the men.

Chapter 19

Climbing Up the Ladder

How, in Fleet Street back in the day, did you get your foot on the next rung on the ladder? One aspect of sexual discrimination worked in our favour – where a few of us were concerned, anyway.

It would have been churlish, for instance, to have moaned about some of the less enjoyable aspects of football reporting when it brought me fame and opportunities *because* I was female.

One of the themes we've already touched on is The One Woman, and a must-have in the late 1960s and early 70s was The Girl Reporter, the template for which was the *Evening Standard*'s Maureen Cleave. In 1969, the author Hunter Davies, then editor of the *Sunday Times* Look! pages, offered Valerie Grove the role. She was, at this point, Valerie Jenkins, and at the interview Davies said, 'You're married. How old is your husband?'

'He's twenty-five,' said Valerie. 'He's gone to work on *Nova*.' But what a funny question to ask. If she'd been a man, he wouldn't have asked the age of the wife, surely?

The offer from the *Sunday Times* brought a dilemma. Should she take it up or stay at the *Standard*, where she was so happy? 'My pa said, "You should go. Nobody ever thanks you for staying,"' recalled Valerie. 'But Charles Wintour countered the *Sunday Times* offer with £2,250 p.a., and I stayed at the

Standard. Hunter Davies gave the Girl Reporter job to Jilly Cooper instead.'

At the *Standard*, Valerie added feature writing to her Londoner's Diary brief. In due course she faced another dilemma. What do you do when you have a well-known by-line, part of which is now defunct? Divorced and remarried to her fellow journalist Trevor Grove, she wasn't Valerie Jenkins any more.

'It was the end of my maternity leave with my second daughter,' she said. 'I decided to change my name to Grove instead of keeping my first husband's name. Charles Wintour said, "Bad idea. You've written as Valerie Jenkins for ten years, you've written a book under that name – it's like starting out all over again." And he was right.' But in 1980, she was appointed the *Standard*'s literary editor, and she carried on with that and the feature writing for another seven years and two more children. Then came another decision to be made.

One morning early in 1987 she received a phone call from Andrew Neil, then editor of the *Sunday Times*. 'He'd liked a piece I'd written about Edwina Currie – I think he mistook me for a political journalist – and offered me a job.

'New technology was bringing in new newspapers, and various people from the *Standard* were being recruited. I felt I was being left behind. I thought, I turned down *The Times* in 1969 and I'm about to be forty and this could be my last chance. I succumbed.

'I was *very conscious*, that first day at Wapping, that it was totally, utterly different from Fleet Street and all that it meant. It was such a hideous, windowless, modern, silent office, and nobody talking or going to the pub or lunching. I went back to Fleet Street that first Friday, and rejoined happy, noisy *Standard* and *Telegraph* folks at Mother Bunch's under the railway.'

Oh God, what have I done? she thought.

*

Not everyone felt these emotional ties. Jennifer Selway had been at the *Observer* since 1979 and was still its TV previewer, her abilities going unrecognised. She found an outlet for her energies with additional freelance work, writing for *Woman's Journal*, *Options* and *19*, and providing pieces for the *Mirror* and a weekly TV column for a magazine. 'None of it exactly Pulitzer Prize-winning, was it?' she said.

There was, too, one humiliating incident soon after the birth of her second child. 'I came back from about half an hour's maternity leave, at which Simon Hoggart [then the *Observer*'s political writer] tried to get me sacked. He was annoyed because he'd been on *Did You See . . . ?*, a programme about TV, and I'd missed it out of the Sunday listings. It was a mistake. A bad mistake. But nobody died. He didn't complain to me – he just went straight to the editor, Donald Trelford. Who didn't sack me. He just ignored it.'

But working at the *Observer* just got worse and worse. As Fleet Street started to break up, the paper left St Andrews Hill to operate from various strange premises. Marco Polo House was a post-modern building set in a dip on the other side of the road from Battersea Park; Hugh McIlvanney observed that Marco Polo would have had trouble finding it. Then the *Observer* merged with the *Guardian* and moved into its headquarters on the Farringdon Road: 'We were stuck in the attics.' Another move took place, to a new building, where it continued to be the *Guardian*'s poor relation.

When new editors took over, Jennifer was still overlooked. 'Jocelyn Targett came to run the arts pages. Justine Picardie was his sidekick. They made my job even less important than it had been. They got different people in to write the previews, like Hilary Mantel, so I was basically just doing the listings.'

Then Nigel Billen, a colleague she'd always got on with, left for the *Daily Express*. He offered Jennifer a job there. 'It was *lovely*,' she said, 'to get out.'

At first her role was broadly similar to the one she had at the *Observer*. The Last Word was made up of a few pages of arts and TV coverage at the back of the paper. After that, she was made associate editor of the Saturday magazine.

Real success didn't begin till her mid-forties, though. Then everything took off. 'In 1999 they asked me to edit *Parent* magazine and *Get Up & Go* (or, as we called it, *Fuck Off & Die*).' They were monthly magazines – giveaways in supermarkets and at garages. 'My first editing gig. We had no budget to speak of so we used to photograph things on our desks. And it was good fun really. Then *Get Up & Go* closed, then *Parent*, because they weren't making any money, and I was made assistant editor on Comment and Features. And, for the *Sunday Express*, I did a column about the domestic travails of a fictional character called Lucy Cannon (loose cannon, get it?).'

She was, by now, an editor and columnist, well-established at the paper. 'Hugh Whittow took over after Peter Hill left and I loved Hugh to bits,' she said. 'He was the best boss ever, a proper *Sun* reporter, been everywhere, done everything, stories about every scam that ever happened. If you had a bottle of wine with Hugh, you'd end up telling him everything about your life. He could charm everyone. It's a great gift for a journalist to have.'

She finished up editing the comment pages and looking after the star columnists. She also wrote the leaders. She wasn't particularly at one with the paper's politics, but it was a part of the job she enjoyed very much. 'You can be a complete psychopath, say the most terrible things, and no one will ever know it's you.'

*

'There's a fork in the road,' said Sue Peart. 'Writing got me in, and you either go forward that way or the other way towards an executive role. I'm naturally bossy and nosy and like knowing what's going on, so I was much happier on the executive ladder.'

You can't help feeling that Sue would have succeeded whether male or female, but what's relevant here is that she entered the workforce at a time when the middle-market papers, the *Mail* and the *Express*, had editors acute enough to realise that women constituted an important part of the readership. One such was Larry Lamb, who nurtured her early career. 'He was so paternal. He wanted to teach me about Fleet Street, which I was so grateful for.' Her job when she arrived was that of assistant women's editor. From there she became deputy features editor before moving to the *Sunday Express* magazine, first as deputy editor, then editor. She was there for seven years.

Inevitably, though, regimes change. In 1991 Eve Pollard took over as editor, having previously been in charge of the *Sunday Mirror*; she was, by the by, the second woman in modern times, after Wendy Henry, to edit a Fleet Street paper. But, said Sue, she wanted her own person at the magazine – 'So I was out!'

For the next six months she worked on the *Daily Mail*, before being contacted by 'the late, great Brian MacArthur' on *The Times* about editing its Weekend section. Three years later she was head-hunted to be deputy editor of the *Mail on Sunday*'s *You* magazine by its editor, a big, blonde, redoubtable Australian called Dee Nolan. This involved being interviewed at seven o'clock one evening by David English, chairman and editor-in-chief of Associated Newspapers. 'I raced over to Northcliffe House from *The Times*, and went up to the sixth floor, where I was met by Ena, David's remarkable PA. Ena showed me into his vast office, where he leapt up from his desk and asked me if I enjoyed *The Bill*.

'We then sat on the sofa and watched *The Bill* together. As the closing credits rolled, he said, "Well, it's been lovely to meet you – I'm happy to say the job is yours."' She took over as *You* editor in 2000 and held the post till she stepped down in 2018.

'One of the things I felt most privileged to have had an involvement in (however loose) were the big stories that happened over the years,' she said. 'Mostly they were shocking, unexpected things – Diana's death, 9/11, 7/7 – huge stories that newspapers had to make sense of literally as the story was breaking. Nine-eleven was fascinating from a newspaper point of view – unique in that there were practically no eyewitness accounts; everyone was either incinerated or made it out right away. There were hardly any casualties taken to hospital – extraordinary. I saw real frustration during that story. It happened on a Tuesday, the worst day for a Sunday paper simply because no one really knew or understood what was happening and people were either very alive or very dead. It boiled down to a story about clear blue skies, gleaming planes and buildings crumbling to the ground. So most of the papers just did picture stories. Pages and pages of pictures. It was hard to write about.'

That journey from being a secretary at *Cosmopolitan* to involvement in the biggest stories of the age to executive editor of a national newspaper tells you everything you need to know about her sense of purpose and commitment. 'My experience of sexism was a bit like the menopause,' she said. 'I never had any symptoms. But I did work hard. If you work hard, muck in, do anything, they respect you.'

*

When Tina Moran left the *Bristol Evening Post* for Fleet Street in 1986, she was in her mid-twenties and had already got herself married and unmarried. 'He was a film cameraman. His dad knew my dad. He was doing a lot for brand-new Channel 4. But he was away a lot, and going to London was a perfect escape. No kids. Straightforward. I was the one who wanted out. We're still friends. I didn't tell a soul at the *Post* what was happening. My attitude was, I leave this at the door.'

Those first days in London were a time of glorious free-lancing, hanging out in the Punch Tavern, doing morning shifts at the *Evening Standard* then running upstairs to work at the *Daily Star*. On Saturdays she would go out reporting for the *Sunday Express*. 'I loved it,' she said. 'I love work. I love the money. I was knackered but I was earning £30,000. This is what you do. You put yourself out there.' To which end, she went out to Madrid to work on the launch of *Hello!* after spotting an ad in the *UK Press Gazette* for a Spanish-speaking sub. She was in Madrid when the *Mail* rang to ask if she would like to do maternity cover.

So she went back to England, and started on Femail and stayed there. The *Mail* back then was still in its old building on the corner of Carmelite Street and Tudor Street, and she was a sub going down to the stone at night. 'One hundred per cent men. They were just pussycats. They'd do anything for you.' By the time she was at Femail her partner was Justin Davenport, who became crime editor of the *Evening Standard*, and she can clearly remember it, the miscarriage at work. 'I went to the toilet and realised what was happening, but we had pages to get out. Fundamentally that was the priority. My other concern was that it would affect my chance of promotion and I thought, Oh shit, they'll know I'm potentially trying for a family. I'm not the childless career woman I appeared yesterday.

'Tessa [Hilton, the editor of Femail] could not have been more wonderful. She scooped me up and put me in a taxi, organised everything, called Justin. I got successfully pregnant with Hannah a couple of years later. I worked beyond my due date because I didn't want it to be seen impacting in any way, shape or form on my performance. There's nothing different about me now just because I'm expecting a child.

'Back then your job was held open for six months while you were on maternity leave. I spent the whole summer frantically trying to find a nanny. I enjoyed earning money, I missed the office. I couldn't imagine staying at home full-time. I needed the buzz of office life. I had asked if I could do a job share – two days a week as a sub – but that was not encouraged. It had to be full-time or not at all.'

So she just went back. She got a fabulous nanny who arrived in the mornings and was prepared to stay for ever. Most of Tina's money went on childcare, of course. Working at the *Standard*, Justin started early and finished early 'so it was ships in the night'. Her work routine was the guideline. The family had to fit in around it.

Almost as soon as she was back from maternity leave, the *Sunday Times* hired her to be one of the assistant editors on *Style* magazine. 'It was glorious. Alison MacDonald, the editor of *Style*, was brilliant – she'd get up from her desk and, between hers and the editor's, she'd have come up with ten ideas. She was an amazing ideas machine. But Alison left *Style* while I was on maternity leave with my second daughter, and I wasn't a fan of the man who replaced her.'

So it was back to the *Mail* for a few shifts and then Tessa Hilton took her to the *Sunday Mirror*. 'Tessa said, "I want you to be chief sub of *Mirror* magazine. You can leave at six every evening." I'd never have asked for that in a million years. *But* . . . I could get out of there and have a life. I wasn't going to say, "Oh don't be so silly, Tessa, I'm going to stay till midnight."'

After twenty-eight years together, by which time she had gone to the *Express*, she and Justin were divorced. 'But I got to be number three on the *Express*, an executive editor. I can't think of anything more I would have achieved if only I'd been a man. I think you've got to be a bit alpha male. Give as good as you get. It's game-playing – office politics, strategy, mind games. I think men are quite easy to read. Life's hard enough as it is. Why go out of your way to make enemies? You can't get out a paper on your own.'

Did the marriage break-up, I asked, change her attitude to others going through the process? 'I found it difficult over the years,' she said. 'Not in the sense of being unable to have sympathy, but . . . well, I got through this, why can't you? I loved every single day of my career. My only regret is that my dad died three months before I joined the *Daily Express*, so he never saw me get there.'

Chapter 20

The Sweetest Thing: Marriage and Motherhood in Fleet Street

December 1989 was the month of the Romanian uprising, the start of the explanation of why the freelance photographer Clare Arron got married and why she got out of Fleet Street and went to Scotland. The uprising was part of the wave of revolutions that resulted in the end of communist rule in Central and Eastern Europe. The Christmas Day film footage was eye-opening: dictator Nicolae Ceauşescu's execution by firing squad at a military base outside Bucharest (the cameraman was fractionally late making it into the courtyard; he got there just after the last gunshot, but the footage went round the Western world – the flopping bodies of Ceauşescu and Elena, his wife, who had insisted on standing against the wall with him; together they'd sung 'The Internationale').

Reporting from war zones meant heavy stress, maximal for photographers who, if unable to develop their film and wire it back to Fleet Street themselves, had to find ways of getting to an airport and persuade someone to take it back for them. The young freelance Ian Parry had badgered the *Sunday Times* to send him out to Bucharest to cover the chaos, the firefights in the streets, the water jets and police beatings. He'd spent several days there taking pictures of the city in the aftermath of Ceauşescu's overthrowing, photographs of soldiers with flowers in their arms, of funerals for people killed in the revolution. Flights of military and civil aircraft had been banned from take-off, but he'd got wind of a plane leaving for Belgrade on the 28th to collect blood supplies for the wounded; from there he would be able to pick up a flight to London. It was a one-off chance to get his film back, and he was taking everyone else's with him. The plane crashed, forty-three miles west of the city, most likely brought down by an anti-aircraft missile. He was killed along with everyone else on board.

Clare Arron was driving back through France after an assignment. She switched on the radio and there it was, the news. It was a massive shock, the culmination of two draining months of work. A month before the fall of the Berlin wall, she had covered the visit of Soviet Union leader Mikhail Gorbachev; in the street riots that accompanied it, she suffered a cracked rib when she was attacked by a member of the Stasi. 'Ian was my very close friend,' she said. He was twenty-four, she was twenty-six. Ian's death really affected her. After Christmas, she had to cover the first elections in Romania. 'In my madness I got married two months after that. He was another photographer. It was stupid of me. I wasn't in the right frame of mind at all. Everybody should have said, "Go and do something else." He'd been married a few times before. We both knew straight away it wasn't going to work.'

The fall-out left her in turmoil. 'After the divorce I needed a clean break. I moved myself to Scotland, rented a little house, immersed myself in work. The *Telegraph* gave me loads, and a friend who was setting up Scottish *Daily Mail* gave me lots too. I really appreciated all the work I was getting, but it wasn't my comfort zone, so I decided to take a job with the *Glasgow Herald*. While I was there, I could do voluntary work to get on a social work course.'

She married again and started a family after newspapers. It wasn't something she ever thought she was going to do. Her second husband was a photographer and he changed jobs too and became a helicopter pilot. 'I was thirty-six when we had our son, and a social worker. Compared to "I'm a journalist/photographer", I've become invisible.'

She still takes photographs in her head.

Clare's experience is a classic example of the starter marriage, an expression first coined in a 1994 *New York Times* article by the journalist Deborah Schupack. She defined it as an early and child-free first marriage that lasted less than five years; the parameters were later widened to include children. The point was, we were a new breed of young women, ambitious and financially independent. We could make choices denied to our mothers' generation. We didn't have to stay in a marriage if it turned out we'd made a mistake (though, of course, that went for husbands too).

Jennifer Selway was twenty-five when she married Rod, a cool Australian with very long hair at *Time Out*. 'We got married in a ridiculous manner,' she said. 'I'd known him a few months, and we'd only got together properly two weeks before the wedding. Mad.'

A couple of years went by. In 1982 they were still kind of together. 'He'd gone to live in Australia, and rented a flat in Sydney,' said Jennifer. 'I was on the brink of being in love with someone else. Then in 1983 he came back – and went back to Australia again. But then I discovered I was pregnant.

'I spent the summer being pregnant on my own and perfectly happy. And then Rod came back *again*, which was a bit of a bore. Luke was born early in 1984. I left Rod three months later and went to Folkestone with Luke to live with my parents. But we stayed friends till he died a couple of years ago.'

She carried on as a working mother. 'The childcare I had was Rolls-Royce. My parents were marvellous, both of them. It was very nice, really. Very comfortable. I had all my washing done. But Rod and I had had a flat. He bought out my share, giving me enough for a deposit for another flat, a three-bedroomed one in Maida Vale. It was nice. Twenty-eight grand. It would be worth a fortune now. I was a single parent with a flat and a mortgage. I didn't know how I was going to pay it. It was a total leap in the dark. I had a nanny called Keira who didn't last long. She was awful; bovine and truculent, and thought she knew best. Alison was kind but a bit wet. I suppose it was a struggle but I don't remember it as such. I never had any money but I managed.'

She met Jonathan Bouquet a year later, in 1985, on a press trip to the South of France – 'Armagnac country'. At the time he was with the *Mail on Sunday*'s *You* magazine, though later he moved to the *Observer*. They got married in 1986; Henry was born in 1987, and Amelia in 1993. Which pre-empts the question I was going to ask: How, as a woman working in Fleet Street among the old men in cardigans, did you find someone to love?

It was 1966, and Scarth Flett was working as a temporary holiday relief reporter at the *Daily Mirror*, trying to get at a copy of *Who's Who* in a cupboard when a voice behind her said, 'I think we've got something in common.'

Oh dear, she thought. She'd been told when she joined the *Daily Mirror* that they had another Australian working for them, but he was supposedly away at the time. 'What's that?' she asked The Voice coolly. 'But it was a lot of the attraction,' she said.

John Pilger was very tall and blond and tanned, and had just returned from a reporting assignment abroad. He had come to England from Australia in 1962, and a year later started working for the *Mirror* as a sub. He shot through the ranks:

reporter, feature writer, then chief foreign correspondent. He was the *Mirror*'s star reporter.

'I was twenty-three, he was twenty-seven,' she said. 'Fleet Street wasn't full of Australians. He was from Sydney, and I don't think he had a girlfriend at the time. My boyfriend in Australia had gone to Europe a year before me. He met someone on the ship, so that was over.'

Their first home was in a tiny flat in Long Acre, off Covent Garden, in the building in which Sally Moore lived, the pocket-sized news-reporting Liz Taylor. She was going out with another news reporter, but that had to be kept secret because you weren't allowed to have a relationship with anyone who worked for the same paper. It was John's flat first, and Scarth moved in with him later after she'd left the *Mirror*. They got married because she wanted a baby. In 1973 when he was on his way back from Israel, she went to the airport to meet him and announced, 'I'm pregnant!'

'I got married when I was on the *Sunday Express* magazine and that was a bit of a disaster,' said Sue Peart. 'I left the *Express* to go to *Times* Weekend and in those days you didn't get maternity leave unless you'd been there two years. My baby was due twenty months after I joined.'

They told her she could have two weeks' sick leave and two weeks' holiday, and she said that would be wonderful, thank you very much. She had to hire the nanny before the baby arrived. She had four weeks off, then went back to work. Two months later her husband walked out without warning.

Her boss was Brian MacArthur, 'a very experienced journo and a lovely, kind man'. She told him her husband had left but he wasn't to worry – *Times* Weekend would come out as usual. An hour later the phone rang. The editor, Peter Stothard, wanted to see her.

'I went up to his office,' she said. 'Big paintings. Big desk. I went to sit in a chair and he said, "No, no, no, Sue. Sit on the sofa," and he came and sat down beside me, in his red braces. And said he'd just heard the most awful thing had happened to me.

'"No! Don't worry! Everything's fine! *Times* Weekend as normal!"

'"I'm not worried about *Times* Weekend. I'm worried about you. Are you okay?"

'"Yeah . . . I suppose so."

'"Have you got any help? Are you okay for money?"'

What a hero, she thought. After she left *The Times* to go to *You* magazine, she took him to lunch and told him that what he had said that day was the most incredible thing, and she would never forget it.

The divorce was so horrendous that she never married again. Instead, she found a long-term partner. They lived separately. She brought up her daughter on her own.

Valerie Grove had four children and the same nanny for eighteen years. 'She came from Maureen Cleave,' she said. 'I was in the *Standard* offices one day, while my mother was looking after my six-month-old baby. I said, "What am I going to do?"

'"Oh, you need my nanny's sister," said Maureen. "She's got very clean fingernails and won't run off with the postman."

'Eileen was brilliant. My age. Fell in love and bonded with Lucy straight away. I was totally dependent on her for eighteen years. When Oliver was eleven and we didn't need her any more we looked in the *Ham & High* for someone for Eileen to go to. She went to the columnist and broadcaster Jenni Russell, married to Stephen Lambert. One of their children, Jessica Lambert, is deputy editor of Londoner's Diary.'

Jennifer Selway went on working full-time, too. 'And running around doing all the chauffeuring, Scouts and Guides, sports this and that – it was a very 1980s life, wasn't it? It was Sloane Ranger time. You could be a bit posh and middle class and wear pearls and employ a nanny and it was fine. Nobody called you Tory scum.

'Tina was with me for nine years and was just wonderful and that made life so much easier. I'm still in touch with her. She came to Henry's wedding.' Jennifer said they spent their time at the kitchen table, talking about Rupert Campbell-Black, the fictional romantic hero of Jilly Cooper's Rutshire novel sequence. 'Then we had a cleaner who started to have an affair with her stepson, and she used to come in every week and tell us the latest details. Three of us round the kitchen table. Nobody got any work done. They were happy days.

'Mummy died in 1999. My father moved in with us around 2004. I seemed to be permanently on a tight schedule, nipping into the car, getting them all up and out in the mornings. We had a nanny who wasn't living in by that stage. I'd arrive home to a boot-faced girl who wanted to have left ages ago and I was like, "I work for a national newspaper and I'm afraid I can't guarantee what time I'll get home." So my father coming to us was quite handy. He was still fit and quite active, and could dish up supper and he wasn't too elderly, and he genuinely seemed happy to play with the kids. He would play hotels with Amelia endlessly. She'd be the angry client and he'd be the person explaining why her room wasn't up to scratch.'

In 1974 Mary Kenny married Richard West, the foreign correspondent and cousin of the actor Timothy West. 'I'd known Dick on and off over the years,' she said. 'I was pregnant. He felt that it was the right thing to do.'

Her *Evening Standard* colleague, the news reporter Anne Sharpley, warned her against it, telling Mary he was a wanderer, a loner, who would never settle to anything domestic.

'And he wasn't really suited to marriage,' Mary said, 'but he was a very nice man. He never did become domesticated. He was always nice to the kids, but he wasn't a nappy-changer. Not interested in taking out the bins. It was a bit of a learning curve for both of us. Times when I threw things. But he was fun, and we had friends in common.

'There wasn't any formal maternity leave at the *Standard*, but I was allowed to stay off work and be paid till the baby settled. Dick and I had a nice little flat in Lamb's Conduit Street. Another place with sloping floors. My mother-in-law lived in Holland Park. She wanted to go into a posh care home, and we took over her flat. The house had to be painted – £25,000 just to have the windows done. It's not the property, it's the maintenance. Curtains – John Lewis came and measured – £12,000. So I never did have any curtains.'

Within days of Patrick's birth, the Birmingham bombings happened. They took place in two pubs in the city centre. The pubs were crowded because people were calling in there after work. One pub had a forty-foot crater blown in the floor. Most of the dead and wounded were young. 'A soft target,' said Mary. 'A girl going to meet her boyfriend. Brothers going to meet each other. I burst into floods of tears. You go to all this trouble to make a human being and then blow them up.'

It changed everything. 'You just don't know what's going to hit you. Women are well able to compete with men but it's no easy thing to have a child, and there are no easy answers. Suzy Menkes, the *Standard*'s fashion editor, told me never to let on if the baby was sick. "That disadvantages you," she said. "Tell them you're waiting in for a call from Tokyo, or the car's broken down, anything. Being a mother is a disadvantage."

And it was, in a sense. You can't pretend your life's exactly the same. I was torn. I still had ambition, but I didn't realise what hit me.

'I had to find a way of pursuing journalism. So I struggled on. We had a series of Balkan au pairs, girls from what was then Yugoslavia, who were lovely. Some were more ditzy than others. They came from hard lives.

'I became much more of a freelance. I deputised as *Daily Mail* TV critic for Herbie Kretzmer when he went off to write *Les Misérables*. I wrote for the *Sunday Telegraph* and the *Sunday Independent*, and became more right-wing and, as the mother of sons, less of a feminist. And I took up the church again.

'I was at my most successful in the 1980s, during the rise of Margaret Thatcher. A lot of orthodox feminists said, "She's not a real woman, she's a man in drag," but I didn't think so. She was very charismatic. I admired her. She was a woman of conviction. She was a reader of the *Telegraph* and invited me to Downing Street several times: "My dear Miss Kenny, I read every word you write."'

Mary didn't know whether she believed that, but it was nice to hear, all the same.

'The difference came for me when I had children,' said Emma Lee-Potter. 'I know there are more women executives now but, in my time, though I hate to say it, once I had children no way could I keep on being a news reporter. It was to do with me, with what I wanted once my daughter was born. My mother coped, but she was in features. I went freelance just before my daughter was born, because I couldn't see a way of doing it. It was hard enough being a freelance, let alone going into the office in the middle of the night or setting out on a story at the drop of a hat. I've never read a news reporter writing about "having it all".'

'It actually makes me *rage*,' said Louise Court, 'when people pontificate about what working mothers should do! It's what works, what your family needs are, what your job is. Whenever I'm asked by girls about how they should balance jobs and motherhood, I say it all depends on you, your family, whether you've got childcare, whether your mum's there. Every situation is individual.'

Her partner, Warren, was working as a jeweller when she met him. His career has taken many different paths since then including going to university as a mature student, working as picture editor of *Ideal Home* magazine and then in the physio department of the local hospital. He has always been a hands-on dad alongside his work and they have shared parenting, but Louise has always been the main breadwinner.

'I feel I've been lucky because I've never had that guilt about working,' she said. 'As a family unit you work out what works for you. By the time we had children we could afford good childcare, and my parents – including my by-then retired dad – helped out. He had a chance to do all the school sports days etc. that he'd not been able to do when I was growing up. Men of that generation just didn't. But wanting to become a mother is why I went into magazines. My dad was a Fleet Street man and I'd seen what that entailed. He was doing long hours, part of that whole culture where you wouldn't rush home for bedtime/bath time. My mum was very much day to day the one who brought us up. I'd see Dad in the mornings and at weekends.

'During the end of my time in Fleet Street, I was a showbiz writer with a pop column on the *Daily Express*. You were permanently on call. It was the start of mobile phones. I'd get calls at night when the first editions dropped, saying, "The *Sun* has got this story, why haven't we? Can you write something now?" Followed by 7 a.m. calls – sending you off somewhere to cover a different story. Day to day you'd have to report to the news and features desks. I remember being sent to a concert at Wembley, and being given one of the first mobile phones. It was like something out of the First World War. Absolutely huge. I thought I was incredibly sophisticated and suave. But in reality I was standing filing copy from the middle of a car park in a bid to get reception, reviewing Michael Jackson and people were looking at me as though I was a madwoman. With pagers, too, there was nowhere I couldn't be got at.

'I'd seen women in the office stressing about getting to sports days or school assemblies. I saw one woman having a complete meltdown; her expenses hadn't been paid and she needed to pay her kids' school fees. It didn't seem to be men stressing about it. I thought, On a daily newspaper you have to file copy when it happens. As editor, if you're working for a weekly deadline for a magazine you might have to stay late but you could go to that school assembly in the morning. I knew that working in Fleet Street and having children wouldn't work for me.

'You do a job and then you wonder, what next? I thought, I don't want to be an executive on a newspaper, I don't want to tell people what to do.'

Louise left the *Express* in 1989 and went to work for *Woman's Own*.

At the start of the 1980s, Scarth Flett and John Pilger broke up. 'He was away a lot, which didn't help. We'd had fourteen years together, lots of travel and fun, a lovely, very much wanted son. But it wasn't meant to be.'

She sank her anguish about the break-up into work and Meeting People, her interview column. John Junor stepped down in 1986 – he moved to the *Mail on Sunday*. 'We always used to complain about him but he was pretty special and he protected us in a way,' she said. 'When he left, we had three editors in succession and the paper went downhill. It was awful, when you think of Junor's legacy. They messed about with Meeting People. It was a stressful time. I got moved to the magazine. It was a lifeline – I saved my bacon by doing a column called Going Shopping. Then, after another change of editor, I was brought back onto the main paper.'

Scarth took redundancy when it was offered and became a reluctant freelance. She wrote for *Saga* – 'I thought it was just an old person's magazine, but I got to do some wonderful interviews for them. They'd ring me up, I'd just send it through and they didn't touch anything.'

Her mother died in the early 1990s. By the end they had come to an understanding. 'In later life she was proud of me. A lot of my things were syndicated abroad, and her friends would see them.'

When Jack and I got married, I was twenty-one and he was twenty-two, and at that age you think it's going to last for ever, but of course each of us had a lot of growing up to do and mine was being done in Fleet Street. The split wasn't antagonistic. We didn't do much about it at first, except that I bought a house. Then he and his girlfriend Vicky wanted to get married, so we got around to a divorce. In our dotage, we still like each other enormously.

I took on the financial burden because I was the one who earned lots of money, a large chunk of which went on paying the fees of the boarding school I sent Fred to. I have never felt at all guilty about sending him away to be educated. I spent five years at boarding school myself and was aware of the pros and cons. I was a divorced single parent, the sole breadwinner, with a mortgage; I travelled and worked unsocial hours, and it was the only way I could do my job. Even then, it was hard work and I was often lonely.

Nevertheless, I managed to develop my scriptwriting career and, early in the 1980s, David Puttnam commissioned me to write a screenplay. It was called *Those Glory Glory Days* and was about a twelve-year-old girl uncannily similar to me who had a passion for the Tottenham Hotspur 1960–61 Double-winning side.

There's a symmetry about the beginning and end of my Fleet Street life, which started when I first saw the old *Observer* building in Tudor Street with the photo of Danny Blanchflower displayed outside, and made the decision that one day I would work there myself. When I did, it was to be a football reporter, and that was how I found myself covering Crystal Palace v Middlesbrough in September 1973. I've already said that it was the most important match I ever covered, because that was the afternoon I couldn't find a taxi, and Danny drew up in his Mercedes and gave me a lift back to Fleet Street. Ten years after that, he appeared in my film. *Those Glory Glory Days* opens with a scene in the press box, and a lot of my sportswriter friends were in it with Danny. They included Bob Houston, who gave me my first by-line, and Ron Atkin, the sports editor who sent me to cover my first football match. He was my Marvellous Chap, and in 1984 I married him. Our first son was born in 1985 and the following year I gave up being Girl In The Press Box to be a full-time writer.

One of my books is *The Biography of Tottenham Hotspur*, and a while back I was invited to read extracts at *The Spurs Show* Christmas party. Afterwards, despite the fact I now qualify for a Freedom Pass and need glasses for small print, I was approached by a man of considerably fewer years than mine.

'You are my ideal woman,' he told me sincerely, at which some long-buried indignation resurfaced and mentally I raised a finger. Spin on that, I thought, Man Who Said I Was Butch.

Epilogue

St Bride's Church, Fleet Street, May 2019

Fleet Street memorial services aren't like normal ones. There's a distinct lack of solemnity, an unconcealed rubbernecking: who's still got all their hair? Who looks as if they're about to go next? You hear muttered gossip and sense a current of anticipation at the thought of the post-obsequies booze-up. You try to be sombre but it's difficult.

I'm here with my Marvellous Chap, looking around for the other members of my tribe. This *is* something that makes me feel sad. Nearly all its original members, those wonderful mentors I learned from in my first couple of years at the *Observer*, are gone: Clifford Makins, Bob Houston, Arthur Hopcraft, Peter Corrigan, now Hugh McIlvanney, whose life we have come to celebrate. Marvellous Chap is the only one left. Even so, I feel the hairs at the back of my neck go up as someone squeezes themselves into the pew behind me, in case it's the ghost of that horrible man who sat in the press box telling the world I was rubbish.

But I'm soon over the temporary unease. It's a beautiful service: hymns you can sing out loud to, music that Hugh loved, a eulogy by Sir Tom Courtenay. There's a reception afterwards at the City Golf Club, one of our old watering holes, but while everyone is milling around outside the church,

I slip away for a while and linger on my own in the courtyard where I sat in summer 1973, waiting for my fate to be decided by the *Observer* NUJ chapel.

Curiosity prompts me to move on. What, these days, remains of my Fleet Street life? El Vino's is still there, but very smart these days; most of its original features have disappeared, including the whisky-drenched Gigantic Fleet Street Names. All I recognise is the painting of the Widow Clicquot in the back, over the table once commandeered by Philip Hope-Wallace. A brass plaque commemorates him. I can imagine him sitting there, telling his stories about *Guardian* misprints. He would have loved it that his name is misspelt Phillip. I leave the way I entered, by the *front* door.

The Printer's Pie is still in business, sort of. Now it's called Bar Fleet Street – ugh. That was where I told Peter Corrigan, then my sports editor, that I was packing it in. I'd decided to go quite a long time before that, in fact. The exact moment I realised I no longer wanted to be Girl In The Press Box was when I was sitting in the dugout at Wimbledon's stadium, Plough Lane, reporting on 'What It's Like to Sit in the Dugout at a Football Match'. It was a stunt. And I thought, For a few years now I've been older than most of the players I interview. A bit longer and I'll be older than the managers. What will I do then? The men can all carry on reporting football into their dotage. An old bag can't. It would feel . . . kind of indecent. And I'd achieved my greatest ambition in journalism almost as soon as I started – to be a sportswriter for the *Observer*.

I was lucky – I had the next steps already lined up: plays, books, a radio show. Not that I gave up journalism completely. When my two youngest boys started secondary school, I worked for the *Sunday Telegraph* and the *Independent on Sunday*. For a while, I was Middle-aged Matron In The Press Box. It wasn't so harrowing this time around, because there were more of us – Sue Mott, Cynthia Bateman, Louise Taylor, Amy Lawrence, Alyson Rudd, Vikki Orvice, the first to report the game for a tabloid, she really was a trailblazer. Of course, this influx didn't go down well with the dinosaurs. Wendy Holden wished she'd had a pound for every time she received a slap on the bum. I'd have liked the same for every time some scruffy lank-haired tosser with beer stains on his flying jacket joshed: 'It's all your fault.'

In *Selective Memory*, Katharine Whitehorn fulminates against the kind of people who claim they don't believe in luck, 'meaning: "I can claim credit for everything – clever me."' And yes, sometimes when I look back on my Fleet Street life it comes to me just how many random moments and 'what ifs' were responsible for my career there, how much was down to luck. What if I hadn't spotted that ad for the *Observer* sports department secretary that morning at secretarial college? Or if I hadn't mentioned Kingsley Amis when Clifford interviewed me for the job? Or if Arthur hadn't thrown that wobbler in the Black Friar and announced he was giving up football reporting? This little mosaic of reflection accompanies me as I head down towards Ludgate Circus, passing the Old Bell, where I once had such a furious row with Marvellous Chap I ripped his jacket in half. Though forty years have passed since then, Mary Kenny's words of self-reproach echo in my mind. What a plonker. What a silly billy.

And that split-second of mortification turns into actual pain as I cross New Bridge Street and round the corner into Queen Victoria Street where the *Observer* once stood. Bloody hell. Is that what happens to everything in the end? The enormity of it, the ugly, pavement-grabbing obscenity of the building that has replaced it, is so heart-wrenching I turn back and quicken to a half-run to get away from it. What had I been expecting? That New Printing House Square would still be there? That in some weird way I would tune in to the phantom racket of typewriters and rumble of presses, and smell the ink?

And for a moment I feel my shoulders drop. What, in the end, did we achieve? 'It was such fun,' Mary Kenny once remarked to me, 'but it *is* all writing on water.' She's right in a way, of course. Who except me remembers my greatest wise-crack of all time, about the Middlesbrough side of 1973–74: 'Middlesbrough are a steely bunch. Even speaking their names – Craggs, Spraggon, Foggon, Platt – feels like you're munching iron filings.' It was so good a *Times* reporter (male, of course) pinched it and didn't credit me. But it isn't only, or even mainly, that. I remember Sue Peart remarking, 'Getting into Fleet Street is bloody hard, isn't it?' And it's still harder for women than it is for men. You still have to climb the ladder by doing the unsocial hours; you get trolled on social media if you're deemed not to know your place; if you have children you still have to organise how they're looked after, you still have to make a choice between collecting them from school and being present for the night shift. And there were plenty of women at the top when the print industry was awash with money, but now everything's going digital and jobs are scarce the drawbridge is up. We'll keep the best for ourselves, say the blokes.

It's time to return to the wake. The City Golf Club – or the Humble Grape as it is now called – is just round the corner from St Bride's. That was the wonderful thing about Fleet Street. I remember how Valerie Grove described it, how everything was so contained and people-sized, how all the newspapers were together, how the drinkers drank together. Together – that was the important word. No one who hasn't worked in Fleet Street when it really was Fleet Street can possibly know what it was like. To understand, you need to have stretched your limits to meet a mad deadline, or been one of the last exhausted stragglers in the newsroom when all the lights were still burning at one in the morning. You need to have been part of the laughter and the jokes and the misbehaviour; to have walked into the pub as a young woman, satin-shirted, sexy, glowing, knowing that the men would turn to look, would make space for you to join them, because you were you. The point wasn't really the big story. It was the way you were as one, working for the same end, that fat bundle of paper that smelt slightly woody and blackened your fingers when you turned the pages and went out into the world with your name, *your name*, in it.

It was such a privilege to be allowed to work there, that unstoppable, life-consuming news factory. And to be allowed to play there, too. As I walk up the stone steps to the entrance to the club, a series of freeze-frames begins in my head. I'm going to see the Sites of Disgrace. Where's that little bar where I snogged various sportswriters after a six-hour lunch? And the alcove where we were gathered on the night my boob fell out. I thought everyone was transfixed by my conversation, then realised the strap of my skimpy Biba vest top had shifted to reveal a nipple.

And then, suddenly, it's like going from dead to alive. If we start thinking about all the good things that have changed, and the not-so-good things that haven't, it's just depressing. We should be celebrating what we have achieved. The straggling remnants of the army of old men in cardigans may grumble that the press has been feminised too much. The papers are full of menopause issues, they moan, there are whole sections devoted to love and sex instead of pages and pages of Important Opinions, and there is much more about breast implants than they want to know. Yes, but 50 per cent of the population are or have been in possession of breasts and actually do want to read about them. Plus, men, you can now read all about your prostate, which you couldn't in the past before women journalists ushered in a culture that made it possible. Men can write, now, about being fathers, about losing their libido and what bereavement is like. Men and women alike are unashamed to talk about their mental health. We broke the taboos. We didn't feminise the papers, we humanised them.

Inside the Golf Club, the decibel level is already rising. It's old, familiar Fleet Street noise, of laughter and jokes, of yarns being told. As I weave my way through the crowd to join my tribe, the men turn to look, then part to make space for me. And I feel a head-rush back into that time of being young and just going for it, determined to make my mark in that magical street, in that man's world.

Acknowledgements

I'm grateful to all my old friends in journalism (and some new ones) for helping me with research, contact details and queries both large and footling. A special mention goes to the wonderful James Mossop for telling me funny stories I'd forgotten and for reuniting me with Scarth Flett. Thanks also to my agent, Ariella Feiner, for keeping me going, and to Anna Valentine and Lucinda McNeile at Trapeze for their huge enthusiasm and encouragement. I'd also like to thank Reg Drury, John Moynihan, Brian James, Les Duxbury and Ken Montgomery for their kindness to me during my early years as a football reporter. They aren't around anymore, but I'd like their descendants to know what utter gents they were.

Credits

Trapeze would like to thank everyone at Orion who worked on the publication of *The Fleet Street Girls*.

Editor
Anna Valentine

Copy-editor
Lorraine Jerram

Proofreader
Simon Fox

Editorial Management
Lucinda McNeile
Jane Hughes
Claire Boyle

Audio
Paul Stark
Amber Bates

Contracts
Paul Bulos
Anne Goddard
Ellie Bowker

Production
Katie Horrocks
Fiona McIntosh

Design
Debbie Holmes
Joanna Ridley
Helen Ewing

Finance
Jennifer Muchan
Jasdip Nandra
Sue Baker

Marketing
Cait Davies

Publicity
Elizabeth Allen

Sales
Laura Fletcher
Jen Wilson
Victoria Laws
Esther Waters
Frances Doyle
Georgina Cutler
Jack Hallam
Barbara Ronan
Dominic Smith
Deborah Deyong
Lauren Buck
Maggy Park

Operations
Jo Jacobs
Sharon Willis
Lisa Pryde
Lucy Brem

Rights
Susan Howe
Richard King
Krystyna Kujawinska
Jessica Purdue
Louise Henderson